BALANCE IS MORE

平衡即是多

刘珩 著

同济大学出版社
TONGJI UNIVERSITY PRESS
·上海·

图书在版编目（C I P）数据

平衡即是多 / 刘珩著. -- 上海 : 同济大学出版社,
2023.9
ISBN 978-7-5765-0700-3

Ⅰ. ①平… Ⅱ. ①刘… Ⅲ. ①珠江三角洲 - 城市建设
- 研究 Ⅳ. ①F299.276.5

中国国家版本馆CIP数据核字(2023)第018355号

平衡即是多
刘　珩　著

责任编辑　由爱华　金　言　**责任校对**　徐春莲　**装帧设计**　鲁晓勇　林　芸

出版发行　同济大学出版社 www.tongjipress.com.cn
（地址: 上海市四平路1239号　邮编: 200092　电话: 021-65985622）
经　　销　全国各地新华书店
印　　刷　深圳市国际彩印有限公司
开　　本　889mm × 1194mm　1/16
印　　张　15.5　插页　36
字　　数　499 000
版　　次　2023年9月第1版
印　　次　2023年9月第1次印刷
书　　号　ISBN 978-7-5765-0700-3
审 图 号　GS(2023)1861号
定　　价　268.00元

前言

一晃十多年，这本迟到的记录，终于要出版了。

奥迪城市未来国际设计竞赛（AUFA）是2010年启动的项目，当时中国策展人由宓带着德国策展人克里斯蒂安·加特纳（Stylepark AG公司）来珠三角地区作调研。当时正值我们从南沙搬迁到深圳之际，策展团队选择了我和我的团队南沙原创建筑设计工作室作为中国的建筑师团队参与这个项目，其他的国际团队还包括了来自瑞士/巴西的Urban-Think Tank，美国的HY Architects，日本的石上纯也、土耳其伊斯坦布尔的SUPERPOOL，以及印度孟买的CRIT，这让我觉得非常荣幸。

我出生在广州，美国硕士毕业后回到香港和南沙工作和生活；在南沙参与了很多年的规划及建筑建设后又回到美国读博士，研究的课题是基于那几年在珠三角地区快速城市化大背景下的思考，包括新城、地方历史、生活方式，等等；接着我在香港中文大学兼职教授研究生的设计课，关注珠三角地区城市空间发展的课题。

本书项目研究的时间周期为2010—2012年，作为研究背景的几个城市来自地理概念上的珠江三角洲地区。这片于不同历史阶段形成的、有独特性及差异化的城市群，是目前全球发展最快、经济最发达的地区之一，也是人口及空间密度最高的地区之一。珠三角地区是个杂糅的地方，这里的城市虽然有共同的自然地理和气候条件，然而不同的地缘政治和经济发展背景，滋生了彼此差异的特质。正是这些特质给这个地区带来了独特的魅力和无穷的活力。

如果南沙是珠三角地区旋风式发展中安静的台风眼，那么深圳就是旋风地带，吹着人往前跑。深圳的一切与我之前在南沙的经验完全相反，所有人每时每刻都在忙于工作和事业。在这座严格规划、交通高效的城市中，我的生活也很快陷入两点一线中。唯有偶尔放松的周末，才开始思考是否要离开这“非人”的空间，过一种“正常”的生活。在我的眼里，深圳是没有什么慢生活的，也许是因为公共空间的缺失，但效率城市与公共生活是否真的不能共存？或者说，城市的高效与基础设施的建设相关，而中国式的公共生活，多多少少与“灰色地带”相关，如果刻意去设计这些公共空间，那么它们的使用真的能如人所愿吗？或者说公共空间如工程性的基础设施一样，是可以被精准设计出来的吗？

十多年前，我们考虑的问题是，一座城市及一个集体的“人”都在追求高速地发展，人服务于经济；大量的基础设施投入建设和使用，占用了大量的土地，以保证经济的迅猛发展和城市的高效运营。但当土地越来越有限的时候，这些经济空间似乎挤掉了人的空间或者说生命体的空间，同时面临的问题还有环境的恶化、自然的丧失……这种失衡的状态令人反思发展的目标究竟是什么，这是否是一个得不偿失的选择？我选择了交通基础设施作为这个项目研究及设计的对象，尝试在有限的空间里，尽量给人及生命体留多些“闲”的余地。总而言之，在经济、社会及环境的三者关系中重新寻找一种新的平衡——或者说，平衡才能可持续，平衡才能获得更多。

十多年后，高速经济依然在路上。虽然调研数据已成为过去时，但当年的想法和设计也没褪色，反而更加适时，例如物流及手机等智能设备的运用等，似乎已成为现实；与此同时，“不平衡”的方方面面也依然在变本加厉地持续。这是一个史无前例的时代，在多重复杂性、不确定性和不安定感交织在一起的当下，人类和地球经历着气候变化带来的恶果；虚拟信息和互联网改变了我们对物质存在的认识和生活的意义，只有瞬间而就的朋友圈、碎片化的知识和局部地方性的解决手段。城市和建筑的未来将何去何从是个需要重新思辨的问题，但无论准备好与否，未来已经到来。未来是多向、相对、灵活而自由的，它隐藏在当下，甚至没有固有和清晰的模样。但讨论它，接受它，并从中寻找在城市和建筑中物质属性的、新的可能性是必要而急迫的。

这些林林总总，依然把我们带回对基础设施研究性设计的初心和愿望，借十多年前的研究来说，还是那句话，平衡就是多。不过时、正合适。2019年2月18日，《粤港澳大湾区发展规划纲要》（以下简称《纲要》）印发，粤港澳大湾区包括香港特别行政区、澳门特别行政区和广东省广州市、深圳市、珠海市、佛山市、惠州市、东莞市、中山市、江门市、肇庆市。《纲要》明确了粤港澳大湾区五大战略定位，即充满活力的世界级城市群、具有全球影响力的国际科技创新中心、“一带一路”建设的重要支撑、内地与港澳深度合作示范区、宜居宜业宜游的优质生活圈。面对存量时代城市发展的多元性和复杂性问题，城市基础设施成为破题的重要空间类型。这几年来，南沙原创建筑设计工作室把对基础设施的研究和理念付诸于建筑本体的设计实践，将在日常生活中缺位的基础设施重新解读为富有体验感的城市公共空间；在依然高速发展的城市化进程中，基础设施作为空间类型从外在到内涵，都需要重新成为一种真正的公共资源——一种重塑日常生活方式、建立公共价值和美学意义的空间资源。

十多年，是个不长不短的时间，当年参与研究和设计的同事和研究生们一起进行的高强度、高密度的平等讨论及良好的工作气氛，给之后多年的实践埋下健康的种子。今天重启此书的出版，也是我们反思这些年来实践的开始，书中所及问题和内容依然鲜活，也借此机会与同行们分享，并希望得到批评和指正。我们始终保有当年那种对城市的即时观察和敏锐的思辨力，也始终在研究和设计交叉实践的路上，不忘初心，与时俱进。

刘珩

2022年12月4日

FOREWORD

How time flies and ten years later, this belated brochure finally gets published.

The Audi Urban Future Award (AUFA) was launched in 2010 when Chinese curator Mi You brought her German counterparts Christian Gärtner and Stylepark AG to the Pearl River Delta (PRD) region on a research trip. At that time, NODE just relocated its office from Nansha to Shenzhen, and it was a great honor that me and my team NODE were selected by the curatorial team to submit proposal for AUFA as Chinese architect. Other participating international teams included Urban-Think Tank from Switzerland/Brazil, HY Architects from the US, Junya Ishigami + Associates from Japan, SUPERPOOL from Istanbul, Turkey, and CRIT from Mumbai, India.

As a native of Guangzhou, I got an offer to work in Hong Kong and Nansha after earning my master degree in the US. Then with many years of planning and architecture practice in Nansha, I returned to the States for my doctoral study which was based on the thoughts about the new city, local history, lifestyle, etc. in those years of rapid urbanization in the PRD. Later on when I worked as an adjunct professor to teach the postgraduate architecture course at the Chinese University of Hong Kong, I continued my research interest in urban space development in the PRD.

The research period of this book lasted from 2010 to 2012, and the researched cities were all from the PRD region in a geographical sense. This unique, internally differentiated PRD urban agglomeration formed at different historical stages is one of the world's fastest growing and most developed economies, and one of the regions with the highest population and spatial density around the globe. The PRD is a region of hybridity, where PRD cities, while sharing similar geographical and climatic conditions, show distinctively different traits due to the difference in geopolitics and economies. It is exactly those traits that add unique charm to and inject infinite vitality into the region.

If I could describe Nansha as the quiet eye of typhoon in the drastic development of the PRD, Shenzhen was undoubtedly the whirlwind zone where people were all pushed forward by intense storms. Everything in Shenzhen was totally opposite of my previous experience in Nansha, and everyone was busy with work all the time. In this strictly planned and efficiently transported city, I soon surrendered myself to the hectic daily life of running between work and home. Only occasionally I could relax on weekends and began to think about leaving the "inhuman" space for a "normal" life. As far as I could see, there was no place for slow life in Shenzhen, perhaps due to the lack of public spaces. But did that really mean efficient city and public life cannot coexist? Or in other words, as the efficiency of a city is related to infrastructure development and the Chinese-style public life is more or less associated with "gray areas", would the deliberately designed public spaces get used exactly as we desire or, to say the least, can public spaces be precisely designed like engineering infrastructure?

More than ten years ago, our consideration was that, both cities and people in a collective sense were pursuing high-speed development and people had to serve the economy; meanwhile, massive construction of infrastructure were launched to ensure rapid economic growth and efficient city operation, which occupied a great deal of land. Yet as land resources became increasingly rare, these spaces for economic development seemed to have squeezed out the spaces for people or life, let alone the deterioration of the environment and the loss of nature... Such imbalanced status already made us rethink what exactly the goal of development was, Was this a choice of more loss and less gain? On that account, I took transportation infrastructure as the object of my research and design project, trying to leave more possibilities of "leisure" for people and life within limited spaces. In short, I tried to redefine a new balance between economy, society and environment. Or we can say, only balance sustains and balance is more.

Over ten years later, the rapid economic development is still underway. Though the research data collected in those years might have become outdated, the ideas and designs remain inspiring, and even better fit the current situation, where the assumptions about logistics and use of smart equipment like mobile phones seem to have become reality, while the problem of "imbalance" continues to worsen. This is an unprecedented era. Nowadays when multifold complexity, uncertainty and instability intertwine, human beings and our planet are experiencing the terrible consequences of climate change; and virtual information and the Internet have changed our understanding of material existence and meaning of life, leaving us only instantaneous social media posts, fragmented knowledge and local solutions. Rethinking on the future of cities and architecture is necessary. The future will come whether the preparation is in place or not. The multi-directional, relative, flexible and free future hides in the present, without even an inherent or clear appearance. Be that as it may, discussing, accepting the future and searching new possibilities of material attribute in cities and architecture is still necessary and pressing.

All these things can bring us back to our original aspiration for research-based design of infrastructure. Still, we believe that balance is more, as elaborated in our research ten years ago. The concept is not outdated, and instead, well fits the world today. On February 18, 2019, the *Outline Development Plan for the Guangdong-Hong Kong-Macao Greater Bay Area* was issued, where the Greater Bay Area (GBA) covers Hong Kong SAR, Macao SAR, and nine cities of Guangdong province including Guangzhou, Shenzhen, Zhuhai, Foshan, Huizhou, Dongguan, Zhongshan, Jiangmen and Zhaoqing. The Outline set up five strategic positioning for the GBA, namely, a vibrant world-class urban agglomeration, a globally influential international sci-tech innovation hub, an important support pillar for the the Belt and Road Initiative, a showcase of in-depth cooperation between the Mainland and Hong Kong and Macao, and a quality living circle for living, working and travelling. The multiplicity and complexity of urban development in the stock era has made urban infrastructure an important spatial typology for working out some solution. In recent years, NODE has been employing its infrastructure research findings and concept to the architecture practice, re-interpreting the infrastructure that is absent from our daily life as highly experiential urban public spaces. In the rapid urbanization process same as before, infrastructure, as a spatial typology, needs to be reconsidered as a public resource in its true sense, from both appearance and connotation, to reshape the way of daily life, establish public value and define aesthetic significance.

Ten years is not over-long. The intense, heated and equal discussions between my colleagues and graduate students working on the project research and design back then laid a solid foundation for their professional practice afterwards. The restarted efforts to publish this book today also marks the beginning of our reflections on our practice in the past decade. We'd like to take this opportunity to share with our peers the topics and content discussed in the book, which remain fresh and alive, and welcome any comments from them. We will, as always, keep an instant observation and strong insight on cities as we did in the past, and remain committed to our original aspiration while progressing with the times in our practice across research and design.

Doreen Heng LIU
Dec. 4, 2022

目录

CONTENTS

PROLOGUE

序篇

GUE

IDENTITY × INFRASTRUCTURE

PEARL RIVER DELTA

DOCUMENTARY AND INTERVIEW ABOUT FOUR CITIES

身份×基础设施

珠三角地区
四个城市的采访与记录

13714416770
13554865033

SHENZHEN

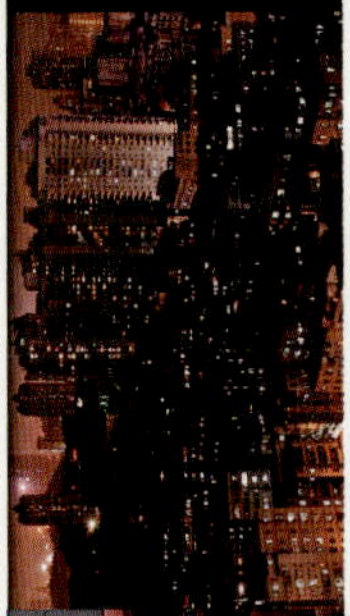

此路段
禁止停车

GUANGZHOU

DONGGUAN

HONG KONG

COME BUY

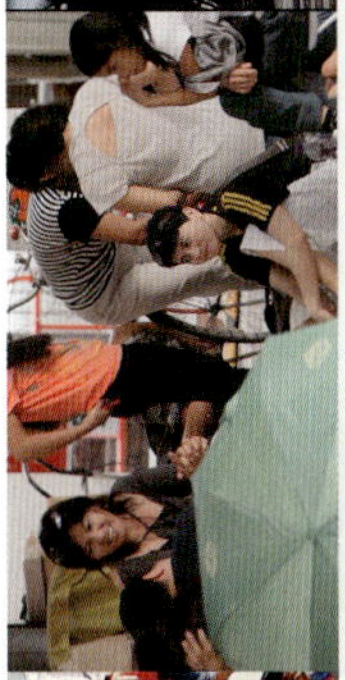

RESEARCH

研究篇

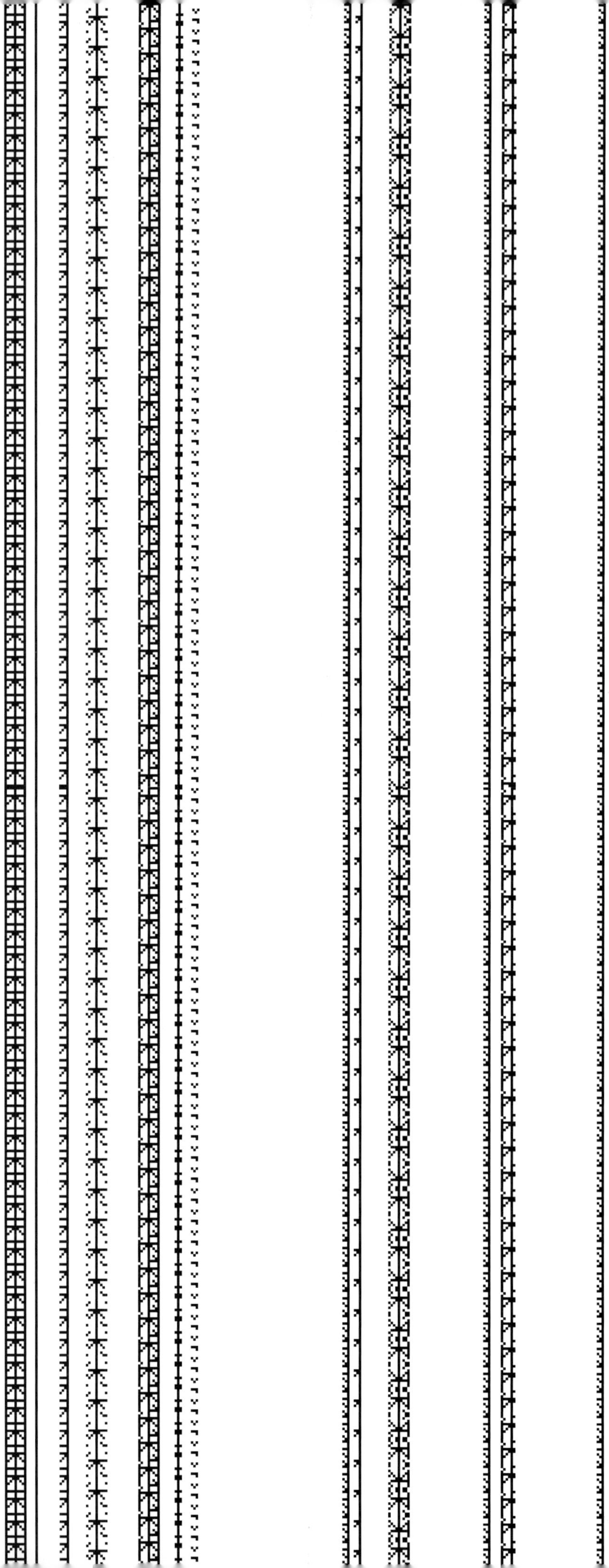

WHAT IS THE PEARL RIVER DELTA?
什么是珠三角地区?

WHO IS NODE?
我们是谁?

WHERE ARE WE?
我们在哪里?

WHAT IS THE ROLE OF THE INFRASTRUCTURE?
基础设施的角色是什么?

WHAT ARE THE ISSUES OF NOW?
现在的问题是什么?

WHAT ARE OUR VISIONS FOR THE IMMEDIATE FUTURE?
我们的愿景是什么?

南沙原创建筑设计工作室——奥迪城市未来大奖宣言，2012年

从困到闲
深圳2030：平衡即是多

刘珩

困境

这是一个关于一个中国城市未来的故事，也是一个关于城市中的生命、空间、边界与流动性在发展中不断冲突与平衡的故事。它很熟悉，也很陌生。

在世界日趋多元化和复杂化，以及城市化进程不断加快的今天，土地缺失、能源短缺、气候变化、人口膨胀和环境持续恶化等很快成为全球共同关注的问题。中国沉睡百年后终于搭上了加速城市化的末班车，却很快遭遇发展的瓶颈，继续加快还是开始放缓是个问题。其中，作为中国这30年快速城市化的试验室和急先锋的深圳，在今天的确已经站在了发展的十字路口。

聚集着众多城市和4230万人口、总面积41 698平方公里的珠三角地区，是中国增长速度最快的大都会区之一。被誉为"世界工厂"的珠三角地区有无数的工厂，它们被密集的交通基础设施所连接。水路、高速公路、国道、铁路系统为物流的高效和畅通服务。然而工业转型、可持续发展、社会和空间的变化，以及向信息和知识的转变，作为新的"产品"的需求，正迫使该地区重新想象其未来。

地处珠三角地区，毗邻香港，地缘政治的先天条件使深圳成为中国重要时代转型的缩影。深圳的30年，从一座边陲小镇一跃成为人口超过千万的大都市，浓缩了西方工业革命150年的历程。在扫荡式的全球化浪潮、自上而下的中国特色管理模式和西方现代主义规划的三重体系推动下，在短短的时间里深圳已经奇迹般地成为象征效率城市的代言人；然而现实的深圳在繁荣的外表之下，也存在种种危机。对快速和高效的追求必然伴随城市功能分区的高度明确和单一，以及城市生活"机动性"的高度强化，而这种大规模的功能性和机动性也必然导致了今天城市空间的切裂、社区的孤立、生活的简易、土地的快速流失以及对外部资源的过分依赖等问题。目前，深圳的社会生活以及生态环境处于与经济强势发展严重不匹配的失衡状态。这种深圳式的快速高效发展所造成的"困"境具有普遍性和典型性，因而也具有全球性。

解困

未来的深圳是继续复制西方城市的发展模式，还是另辟路径，原创一条前所未有的新型城市发展模式？我们的选择是后者。旧有城市以资本运营为核心和唯一的发展逻辑已经陷入了困境。理解"困"字帮助我们重新回到困境的原点，重新思考边界和流动性与城市中个体群体的生命和空间之间的基本关系。流动带来生命，生命在于体验；城市作为生命、流动以及体验的重要空间载体，是解"困"的起点与终点。是的，我们的任务是解"困"，实现由"困"向"闲"、资本效率向生命体验的转化。通过对影响生活和体验空间的边界和流动性的多向（多维度）解读和重新设计，从而达到"平衡即是多"的理想城市目标，而不是重走"多，再多"的单向发展的困境之路。

未来的模式以“物尽其用，各得其所”为原则，对城市空间作为整体的空间资源进行系统性的拆解和重构，借助新的信息及材料技术的发展，以期激发这些空间的容量和可能性。一方面，对现有基础设施，特别是道路基础设施的单一机动性进行重新建构，并与城市的物流系统相整合，共同形成一个全新的物品空间界面（道路+物流混合层），这个新的隐性的物品空间界面“将错就错”地与现有技术条件及城市建设的程序相结合，因而具有了未来的可实施性；另一方面，将现有城市建筑空间（地面与建筑）和信息系统相整合，共同形成一个全新的显性的生活空间界面（建筑+信息混合层）。这个“显性”生活空间界面和“隐形”物品空间界面同时组合在一起，共同形成未来城市的基础设施支撑系统。通过这套新型支撑系统的建立，可以将城市的流动性进行分离，从而使可见的城市生活空间真正转化为“体验和休闲”的生活空间，而非被机动性和物流系统所控制、分隔、异化的空间。这个转变过程同时也会释放出大量的空间资源，提供给未来城市农业、果园、游戏、生态、淡水等与人和自然相关的要素。从而给生活界面带来更多的空间和时间，更多的内容和体验，让社会和自然有了全新的视野和环境，使得经济、社会与生态这三者最终得以在动态的界面上平衡发展。

闲境

未来就是需求更多，平衡就是多，多向流动的平衡就能更多。2030年的深圳依然是个高效密集的城市，但更是个休闲自由的城市、心想事成的城市、自给自足的城市，以及充满无限可能性的城市。通过从“困”到“闲”，这座城市正在实现和接近中国哲学里天人合一的理想生活境界。

NODE Architecture & Urbanism – AUDI Urban Future Award Vision Statement, 2012

FROM KUN TO XIAN SHENZHEN 2030: BALANCE IS MORE

Doreen Heng Liu

Trapped

This is a story about the future of a Chinese city. It is also a story of constant conflict and balance among lives, spaces, boundaries, and mobilities in the city as it has developed; it is familiar yet unfamiliar.

Today, the world is becoming more diverse and complex, and urbanization is accelerating; crises such as the lack of land, energy shortages, climate change, increasing populations, and environmental degradation have become common concerns worldwide. After a century of slumber, China has woken up and taken advantage of the last opportunity for rapid urbanization, but it has also confronted development bottlenecks and the dilemma of whether to slow down or continue to accelerate. The Pearl River Delta, a pilot region for China's rapid urbanization over the past three decades, now stands at a crossroads.

Located in southern China, the Pearl River Delta is a cluster of cities over a total area of 41 698 km^2 that supports 42.3 million people, making it one of the country's largest and fastest-growing megalopolis. Known as the "world's factory", the Pearl River Delta is home to countless factories connected by a dense infrastructure network of waterways, highways, roads, and train systems designed to efficiently transport manufactured goods. However, new demands for industrial transformation, sustainable development, social and spatial changes, and a shift toward information and knowledge as the new "products" are forcing the region to re-imagine its future.

Thanks to its inherent geo-political location in the Pearl River Delta and immediate proximity to Hong Kong, Shenzhen is an epitome that has witnessed the rapid economic growth of the region and significant transformation of China urbanism. In just three decades, Shenzhen experienced the explosive growth from a small frontier town to a metropolis of over 10 million residents, a process that might have taken 150 years in the industrial revolution of the Western countries. Driven by the trinity of sweeping globalization, the powerful top-down rule of the Chinese government and Western modern planning, Shenzhen has rapidly and miraculously become the representative of the high efficiency city. However, as a matter of fact, the city's prosperous mien hides all sorts of crises. The pursuit of fast growth and efficiency inevitably lead to clear and singular urban functional zoning as well as emphasized mobility infrastructure of urban life. Today, we see that such massive constructions have resulted in numerous urban problems, such as divided urban spaces, isolated communities, unsophisticated life, rapid land drain and excessive reliance on imported resources. Presently, the development of Shenzhen is out of balance and when compared to its robust economic growth, both the city's social and ecological environments have significantly fallen behind. The stranded situation that was produced through Shenzhen-style rapid and efficient development is both universal and typical, as well as global.

Solutions

Should the future Shenzhen repeat the pattern of Western development, or try another way and pioneer an unprecedented urban paradigm? We would choose the latter. The city's current focus on profit maximization and one mode of development has laid a trap. An analysis of the Chinese character kun (trapped) enables us to return to the starting point of this predicament and reconsider the basic relationship between boundaries and mobility, as well as individual and collective lives and spaces in the city. Mobility creates life, and life lies in experience. As the important spatial vessel for life and experience, the city is the first and last place to find a solution and release the trap. Yes, our mission is to find a way out of this trap, to move from trapped to free, and from the efficiency of capital to the experience of life. With the multi-dimensional reading and re-design of the boundaries and mobility that affect life and experience, the goal of an ideal city, where balance is more, can be achieved while avoiding the trap of one-dimensional development that demands more and more resources.

The future urban paradigm, which is based on making the best of things and putting them in the right places, systematically deconstructs and reconstructs urban spaces and, based on the development of new information or material technologies, it generates capacities and possibilities for these spaces. On one hand, this paradigm means to reconstruct the manoeuvrability of infrastructure, in particular the roads, and integrate it with the city's logistical system to create a brand-new object-space interface (a road + logistics layer). This new yet invisible object-space interface can be incorporated into existing technical conditions and planning procedures, however they currently stand, so its implementation could be feasible in the future. On the other hand, existing built spaces (ground + architecture) can be integrated with information systems to form a brand-new, visible life-space interface (a building + information layer). The visible life-space interface and the invisible object-space interface together shape the supporting infrastructure for a future city. With this new system, we could easily separate different modes of mobility, truly transforming visible urban life-spaces into places of experience and leisure, rather than spaces controlled, divided, or alienated by manoeuvrability and logistics. Moreover, during the transformation, numerous spaces could be released to provide the future city with things that would connect human beings with nature, such as agriculture, orchards, play, animals, and fresh water. This would offer more space and time, more content and experiences to the life interface, provide a brand-new vision and environment for both society and nature, and allow for highly dynamic yet balanced economic, social, and ecological development.

Free

The future demands more. Balance offers more, and the balance of multi-dimensional mobility could offer even more. Shenzhen in 2030 can still be envisioned as a highly efficient and densely populated city, but it is more likely to be a leisurely, free-minded city, a true dream city, a self-contained city, and a city full of infinite possibilities. Shenzhen's shift from trapped to free will be the true realization of the city, which approaches the ideal way of life advocated in Chinese philosophy: the great harmony of nature and men.

THE PEARL RIVER DELTA REGION IN SOUTHERN CHINA

CLOSE TO THE SEA, ACCESS TO ALL DIRECTIONS

位于中国南方的珠三角地区

临近海洋，四通八达

PEARL RIVER DELTA

LOCATION OF MAJOR CITIES

珠三角地区 *主要城市区位*

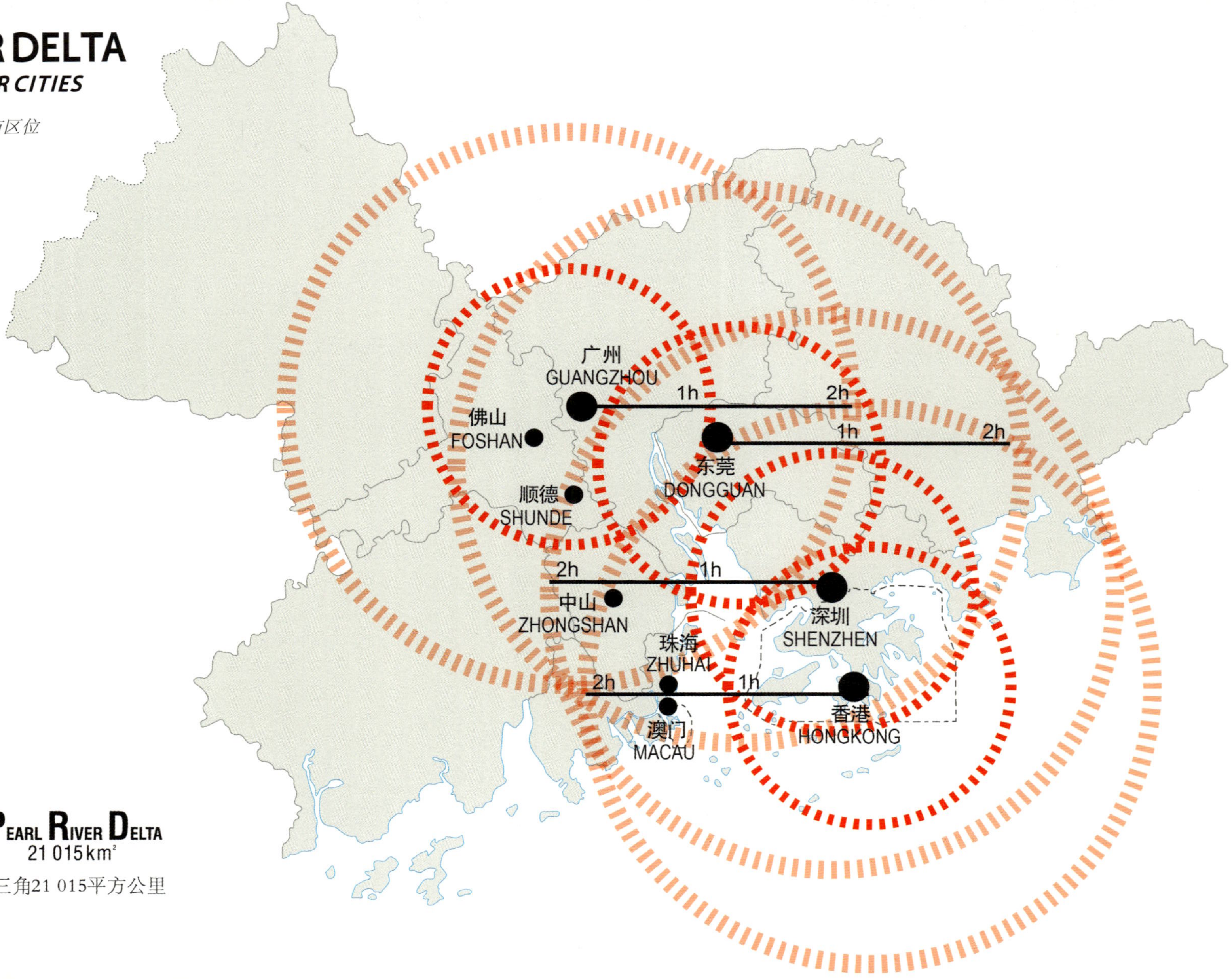

PEARL RIVER DELTA
21 015 km²
珠三角21 015平方公里

奥迪城市未来大奖展览后记，2012年

创新的都市性

由宓

事实上，我们对未来交通的研究源自人类的一个破灭之梦。让我们回溯历史，了解一下未来学家阿尔文·托夫勒20世纪80年代早期在其著作《第三次浪潮》中提出的具有家庭办公混合功能的“电子小屋”概念。为了克服“第二次浪潮”工业革命带来的巨大影响，“第三次浪潮”应带来更环保的生活方式，形成更稳定的社区，甚至在志愿组织中发动一场复兴运动（Morozov）。这一切都基于这样的构想：信息流能支撑新的组织秩序，以及重点推进新秩序下的地方复兴。

这种预测得到了部分证实：工作和家庭确实结合起来了，但二者结合的方式却让工作侵蚀了由认知资本主义所构筑的生活。而预测的其他部分则是彻底的错误：事实上，信息交流越频繁，交通活动的密度越高（Kluitenberg）。这就引发了一系列生态问题，而其中更出现了另一个值得警惕的因素。

我们面临着资源枯竭的危机，以及信息过载和数字垃圾的问题，而不仅仅是《资源消耗性设计》的编辑卡罗琳·维德曼和索恩克·泽勒在卷首语中所指出的那样：“我们没有时间或被告知没有时间制定应对紧急情况的、新的政治系统，因为接踵而至的危机耗尽了代表制政治的作用。这种代表制政治面对突发情况时反应过慢，过度忽视政治机构的分配，过于注重金融架构的管理能力。然而，当我们面对未来的资源枯竭，学会生活、关爱和工作，以及探索自我扶持和相互扶持的意义时，新型的个人和集体机构再次出现。”

这构成了未来城市设计的背景。我们依然需要交通，但更重要的是，要形成新的交通概念。同时，我们需要应对自然资源的发展涸竭问题，还需要建立机构网络，整体应对各种事务。

2010年举办的第一届“奥迪城市未来大奖”重点描绘了概念性的未来，而在本届大奖赛中，建筑师则重点关注各自的地方和区域问题。南沙原创建筑设计工作室（以下简称南沙原创）提交了有关深圳未来城市发展的设计作品，该案例同时体现了高度的复杂性和直观性。正是因为这一原因，深圳得以在世界城市之林中崭露头角，展现了独特魅力。深圳的城市发展历程仅有30年，这座城市的发展基石就是高效。深圳是中国改革开放的试验田，这座城市从零开始，迅速崛起，为制造产业的发展提供了广阔的空间。“时间就是生命，效率就是金钱”正是那段时期的口号。

通过深入研究深圳的城市发展逻辑，南沙原创准确地找出了初步的问题，如城市中的物理屏障、社会隔阂和身份认同感、后工业化，以及上述各因素交织的种种方式，对相当庞杂混乱的城市现象进行了精准的剖析。以此为基础，南沙原创着手编制了珠三角地区未来城市发展的蓝图。

城市未来设计是一个复杂的过程。这一过程最多只能称为“尝试”；但在能否反馈“错误”这一点上，却又并非如此，因为我们无法超越自身的规划能力，去预测一个系统的效果。实际上，这种系统在不同的特定环境、特定时间和特定空间下有多种表现性，我们甚至不能说这是个城市系统。此外，还有一些“未知的可知因素”，通常在处理重大生态问题时被提出，是阻止人们真正相信灾难可能发生的“被否定的信仰和推测”。这些“未知的可知因素”往往又与“未知的不可知因素”相互交织。

南沙原创对于塑造深圳的各种因素进行了扎实的研究，审视了因后工业化问题的出现而导致的废弃空间，因为这一问题会极大地阻碍目前深圳的城市管理方式，包括交通管理方式。的确，当旧产业被迫迁出城市时，会出现怎样的情况呢？随着时间推移，如何才能激活大片的厂房空间呢？（在提出这些问题时，我们也意识到，即使是像“新工厂工人的未来将会如何”这样宽泛的问题，我们也无法回答；因为这些工人在城市去留不定。我们也无法预测后工业时代哪些产业会兴盛崛起。）

南沙原创锁定这一问题，仔细研究可用废弃空间的分配方式，但在制定新的组织规划时遇到难题。谁来负责这项规划？在很多情况下和众多的历史节点上，集中管理在土地和资源调配方面发挥了良好的作用。然而，在资源匮乏的时代，这种做法只是无用的应对方式，并且在调动个人或集体机构积极性方面缺乏想象力。因此，相对于“如何为不同群体分配供其使用的空间和时空资源”这一问题，真正的挑战会更加深刻，并提出了解资源这一关键问题。对于资源的属性或状态，可以从不同于“静态的所有权”的方面进行重新思考，也可以结合个人和集体机构的权力进行理解。要应对最紧急的需求，哪种空间和资源管理形式是可行的？这个问题反过来，也能回应对于其他方面（都市人以及作为城市生态组成部分的空间）的新道德需求，还能在城市的实体、机构和城市环境间建立新的关系；而对这些新型关系的讨论必是一个创意迸发的过程。

在研究的后期，南沙原创审视了城市中事物的新组织原理。这是参考框架的一次巨大改变，创造性地将目光转向了事物的“行动性”。跟人类一样，事物也共同参与了城市的交通活动，并争夺其在城市环境中的空间。负责将事物运送到目的地的货运占用了约20%的交通资源。这种对事物和货物的思维方式在城市发展的讨论中获得了认可，因此也成为规划和塑造城市的因素。因此，事物对城市有一定影响；从城市规划者的角度来看，这反过来也让事物具有行动性。

当然，事物以多种方式融入城市的生态系统。举一个简单的例子，事物在其生命周期内会以不同方式参与能量流动的活动。南沙原创最关心的问题就是产品或服务等事物的分配和布置过程。就交通负荷而言，这一过程会占用与时间性相关的物质化的城市基础设施，并以人类应对生命中的事物的方式，融入用户端的时空网络。南沙原创因此大胆地提出了一种思维方式，即：精准提升物联网络，并将其嵌入城市景观中的隐形基础设施中，从而将城市与事物分开考虑。因此，设计师建议设置地下交通路线，以及区域性的建筑间传送带和局部性的建筑内部传送带等。用户（事物的所有者或接受者）与事物系统互动的方式借鉴了从云端服务器检索数字文件的方式，且与之极为类似。在这一点上面，管理事物的规章和条例几乎与管理人、空间和资源的规章和条例相一致。

就像处理空间分配问题时一样，我们不禁自问，是谁决定了这些规章和条例？“时间就是生命，效率就是金钱”的口号回荡在深圳的历史发展道路上，深深印刻在人们的脑海和相关事物中，展示了深圳令人敬畏的“超级工厂”的城市形象。因此，南沙原创当时面临的设计难题是：对于一个处于全盛期、聚集了组织高效的大型工厂的城市，建筑师和城市规划师有哪些用武之地？南沙原创提出一些构想方案，使人们可以主动利用那些因交通系统的再规划而释放出来的公共空间，如：进行园艺活动和体育活动，甚至将动物引入钢筋混凝土森林中。自发而创新地利用城市空间的例子有很多，不胜枚举，处处体现着人类的智慧。然而，作为建筑师，南沙原创意识到了过分美化这种自发性干预行为的负面作用，因此为这些行为设定了界限，使其能对系统性的问题发挥作用。归根结底，自发性是无法设计的，因为这属于 “未知的不可知因素”。

然而，无法设计城市的未来并不意味着不能对此提出建议。“奥迪城市未来大奖”使我们有机会跨区域增长见识，并从跨环境视角审视自己的研究和设计实践。对珠三角地区而言，孟买的案例似乎很有借鉴意义。CRIT是一家总部位于孟买的研究集团，它提出了“交往能力”的概念，来替代单纯的量化交通数据，以此来确定街道、临时商店或其他地方发生聚集性活动的可能性。CRIT以此为基础，借助多种类型的空间干预工具包，如在老旧的空中天桥加装钢筋结构，并沿着这些天桥设置互动空间等，提出了多种关于城市未来的蓝图，以促进实现或提升其在研究中发现的各种城市发展潜力。

CRIT的研究和设计与土壤研究大致相符。建筑设计师莉莉・詹克斯、梅根・伯恩和海琳・弗珍表示，土壤是设计而成的。它们构成独特，具有在地性和天然的智能性。土壤是一种设计工具。汇集和组合土壤物质为创造空间、人工制品和环境提供了丰富的基础。土壤研究包括直接的研究方法，而这种方法涉及的调查模型又受研究结果的属性或质量的影响，因此需要不断进行调整。

这种理念可能有助于城市未来发展的构想。想要克服政治不确定性或保守主义，以及创造力的财务工具化，就需要不断出现各种声音。各种声音碰撞产生一些完全随机的方案，如在社区内配送日用品的小型商业理念或自发组织的年轻母亲日托服务，CRIT据此为孟买建立了一个创意汇集档案。让这些讨论的声音形成看法观念不是设计师的工作，也绝不是市场分析师、政治家或其他人的工作。事实上，正如媒体理论家奈德·罗斯特所说，土壤研究以图表展示了公众讨论生态系统中的力量和改革的关系，而这个生态系统充满了难控的主题、不变的目标和算法文化。因此，土壤研究最大的用处就是为未来发展提供多种场景。变革的能力超越了物体和准则，并具备一种在主体更倾向于无意识的惯例时偶尔展现的明确作用。由此看来，南沙原创指出“深圳未来的发展之路不仅取决于政府和人民的意愿，还取决于各种突变，也就是城市系统中的各种偶发事件”，是正确的。这正是城市设计研究的潜力所在，研究的尺度大到足以涵盖各种各样的运动和力量、偶发事件和干扰因素，以及改革和改良活动。如前所述，这种介于（自然和人力）资源、（个人和集体）机构，以及其复杂关系的讨论活动是一项创意性工作。我相信城市设计有机会解决这些问题。

南沙原创展现了进行此类城市研究的广阔潜力，并以坚实的基础开创了城市未来构想的新领域，以促进未来项目（研究项目以及其他开放式项目）的开展。

由宓，独立作家兼策展人，曾任奥迪城市未来大奖珠三角地区的本地策展人。

A Postscript to AUDI Urban Future Award Exhibition, 2012

CREATIVE URBANISM

Mi You

One premise of working on future mobility is, in fact, a broken dream of mankind. Let us take an excursion and look back on the "electronic cottage" home office idea proposed by futurologist Alvin Toffler in *The Third Wave* in the early 1980s. Overcoming the brutal effects of "second wave" industrialization, the "third wave" should bring a more ecological lifestyle, as well as provide greater community stability, and even trigger a renaissance among voluntary organisations (Morozov). All are based on the assertion that information flows afford new organizational principles and the focus on the local reemerges out of this.

Part of the prognosis proved true: work and family are brought together in such a way work erodes life configured by cognitive capitalism. The other part went hopelessly wrong: it is proved the more information is exchanged, the denser mobility activities grow (Kluitenberg). This leads then to a series of ecological questions, among which another alarming factor emerges.

We are facing a depletion of resources, and along with it, an overload of information and digital waste. And not just that Carolin Wiedemann and Soenke Zehle, editors of *Depletion Design* addressed in the opening words:

We, or so we are told, are running out of time, of time to develop alternatives to a new politics of emergency, as the constant crisis has exhausted the means of a politics of representation too slow for the state of exception, too ignorant of the distribution of political agency, too focused on the governability of financial architectures. But new forms of individual and collective agency already emerge, as we learn to live, love, work within the horizon of depletion, to ask what it means to sustain ourselves, and each other, again.

This laid the context of the urban future design. We still need mobility, but more than that, a new conceptualization of mobility. At the same time we need to address the depletion in development in terms of natural resources, but more than that, we need to create agential networks that deal with matters.

Unlike the first edition of the Audi Urban Future Award in 2010 which highlighted a conceptual future, this time the architects were to focus on their respective local and regional issues. For the work of NODE Architecture & Urbanism (NODE) on the urban future of Shenzhen, the case presents heightened complication and straightforwardness at the same time. It is all because of the one fact that makes the city distinctive from most of the cities in the world. Shenzhen is a city built in 30 years. And above all, the city is built on efficiency. Having been designated as the experiment lab of China's reform and opening-up scheme, Shenzhen was quickly built up from scratch to accommodate industrial production at a large scale. "Time is Life, Efficiency is Gold" was the motto of this period.

In close examinations of the urban logic of Shenzhen, NODE rightly posed the initial questions of physical barriers in the city, social segregation and identity problem, post-industrialization, and the many ways through which they are all intermingled, a sharp cut through an considerably chaotic myriad of an urban phenomenon. Based on this, NODE set out to draw a blueprint of the urban future of the Pearl River Delta.

Design for a urban future is complex process. At the best it could be called "trials" but not being at the position of knowing if it would return with "errors", for we cannot project the response of a system beyond our programming capability. In fact, the system appears as multiplicity in different given contexts, given times and given spatialities, we cannot even speak of The urban system. Moreover, there are "unknown knowns", which Žižek asserted when addressing the big ecological question, are "the disavowed beliefs and suppositions...that prevents us from really believing in the possibility of the catastrophe, and they combine with the unknown unknowns."

After a sounded research on the forces that shaped Shenzhen, NODE looked into the particular of issue of obsolete space relative to emerging problems of post-industrialization, as this will most eminently thwart the current logic by which the city is ruled mobility included. Indeed, what will happen when the old industries are forced out, what could enact the vast factory spaces, over time? (Being aware when posing this question, that the even larger question of the future of the new factory workers cannot be answered, as they might leave the city, or they might stay. Nor could we predict what industries will prevail in the post-industrial era.)

NODE pinpointed this problem and researched into ways of distributing available leftover spaces, yet met problems when devising a new organizational program. Who should be responsible for the program? Centralized systems, which, in many cases and time points in history, did do a good job in mobilizing land and resources, yet in the age of depletion is rendered hopelessly reactive, and lacking imagination in activating individual or collective agencies. Thus the challenge is more profound than how to allocate spaces or time-spaces for different parties to make use of, it rather poses the critical question of understanding resources. The properties or status of resources could be reconsidered in a term different than the now static ownership, and they could be understood in conjunction with individual or collective agential powers. What forms of managing spaces and resources for the most urgent needs are possible? This, in turn, will answer to new ethical demands towards the other (urbanites as well as space as part of urban ecology) and establishes new relations among entities, institutions and urban environment in the city. Negotiating these new relations will necessarily be a creative process.

At a later point in the research, NODE examined new organizing principles of things. This was a dramatic shift of reference frame and a creative turn to look at the "performativity" of things. Things co-participate in the urban mobility just as humans do, and compete for their space in the urban environment as well an estimated 20% of traffic is taken by cargo that brings things to their destinations. These thinking awards things and cargos with recognition in the urban discussion to the extent that they, too, program the city and determine its shape. Thus, things perform something in the city; this, in turn, renders this regard from an urbanist point of view performative.

Of course, things integrate into the ecology (ecologies) of the city in many ways, to give a simple example, in the life span of things they participate in the energy flow in different forms. NODE is most concerned with the process through which things such as products or services are allocated and distributed. This process takes up the physical infrastructure of the city intertwined with temporalities in terms of traffic load, and is also interwoven into the temporal-spatial matrix on the ends of the client in the form of, how we deal with things in our lives. NODE thus boldly proposed a way of thinking the urban away, or separate from, things by precisely uplifting the matrix of things and embedding them in invisible infrastructures in the city scape in this case the designer suggested underground transportation ways and regional inter-building as well as local inner-building conveyor belts, and so forth. Clients (people to whom the things belong or are headed) interact with the system of things to borrow an example pretty much the same way we retrieve digital files from cloud servers. Here, we almost arrive at the point where the protocols and rules that regulate things are identical to the ones governing the people, space and resources.

We find ourselves asking, as we did with the spatial allocation question,who decides for the protocols and rules. The motto Time is Life, Efficiency is Gold resounds through the history of Shenzhen, and grasps on the human mind and things alike, illuminating a daunting image of the city being one mega factory. In light of this, the challenge to NODE's proposal then becomes, what could architects and urbanists do to a city that is at its best, a very efficiently organized assemblage of a massive factory? NODE provided scenarios in which people take the initiative to use public spaces that are released from the reprogramming of transportation system, such as doing gardening, sports, and even reintroducing animals in the midst of concrete jungles. Certainly, this is not an exhaustive list as the genius of the people has demonstrated in many cases of creative spontaneous uses of urban space. As architects, however, NODE is aware of the pitfalls of over-romanticizing such spontaneous interventions, and draws a line for it to work on systematic problems. The aspect of the spontaneous, after all, cannot be designed, as it factors in the "unknown unknowns".

That the urban future cannot be designed doesn't mean, however, that it cannot be suggested. The Audi Urban Future Award afforded us an opportunity to develop trans-local knowledge and to view our research and design practices inter-contextually. The Mumbai case appeared very interesting for the Pearl River Delta. CRIT, the Mumbai based research collective, devised the concept of transaction capacity instead of mere quantitative mobility data to locate potentials of accumulated activities that happen on the street, in a makeshift shop or elsewhere. Based on this, they proposed multiple futures aided by multiple toolkits of spatial interventions, such as reinforcement structures and at the same time interaction spaces along old sky walkways, which would enable or strengthen each of the potentialities that they identified.

CRIT research and design loosely corresponds to new studies on Dirt research. Architect-designers Lily Jencks, Megan Born, Helene Furjn suggest, Dirt is designed. It is uniquely composed, site-specific, and innately intelligent. Dirt is a design tool. Collecting and composing dirty matter is a fruitful foundation for the creation of spaces, artifacts, and atmospheres. Dirt research, then, entails a direct research method that involves a model of investigation that is itself informed by the properties or qualities of the result and therefore constantly readjusted.

This thinking may prove useful for thinking about urban future(s).What overcomes political indeterminacy or conservatism, and financial instrumentalization of creativity, is constant acts of noises, articulated as to name some completely random examples a small business concept of delivering daily essentials in a neighborhood, or a self-organized young mothers' daycare service, CRIT created a dossier of ideas for Mumbai. It is not the designer's task to give these noises a form of consciousness nor is it, for that matter, the task of market analysts, politicians or anybody at all. Indeed, as suggested by media theorist Ned Rossiter, Dirt research diagrams the relations of force and transformation operative within ecologies of noise populated by unruly subjects, persistent objects and algorithmic cultures. As such, the best it can do is to give multiple scenarios of future. The faculty for change is beyond the reckoning of objects and code and assumes an articulated agency only occasionally displayed in the case of subjects more inclined toward the unconscious routines of habit (Rossiter). In this regard, NODE was correct in pointing out that the future course of Shenzhen will be determined by wills of the government and people but also mutations, understood as contingencies in the urban system. Exactly this is what makes up the potential of the studies of urbanism, itself set on a scale big enough to contain heterogeneous movements and forces, contingencies and ruptures, transformations and modifications. As said earlier, such negotiations between (natural and human) resources, (individual and collective) agencies and their complex relations are creative works, and I believe urbanism has a chance to address these issues.

NODE has demonstrated the vast potential of such urban studies, and on solid foundations, opened up new avenues of thinking urban futures for the next (research as well as other open-ended) projects to come.

Mi You, an independent writer/curator. She served as local curator for the PRD region at AUFA.

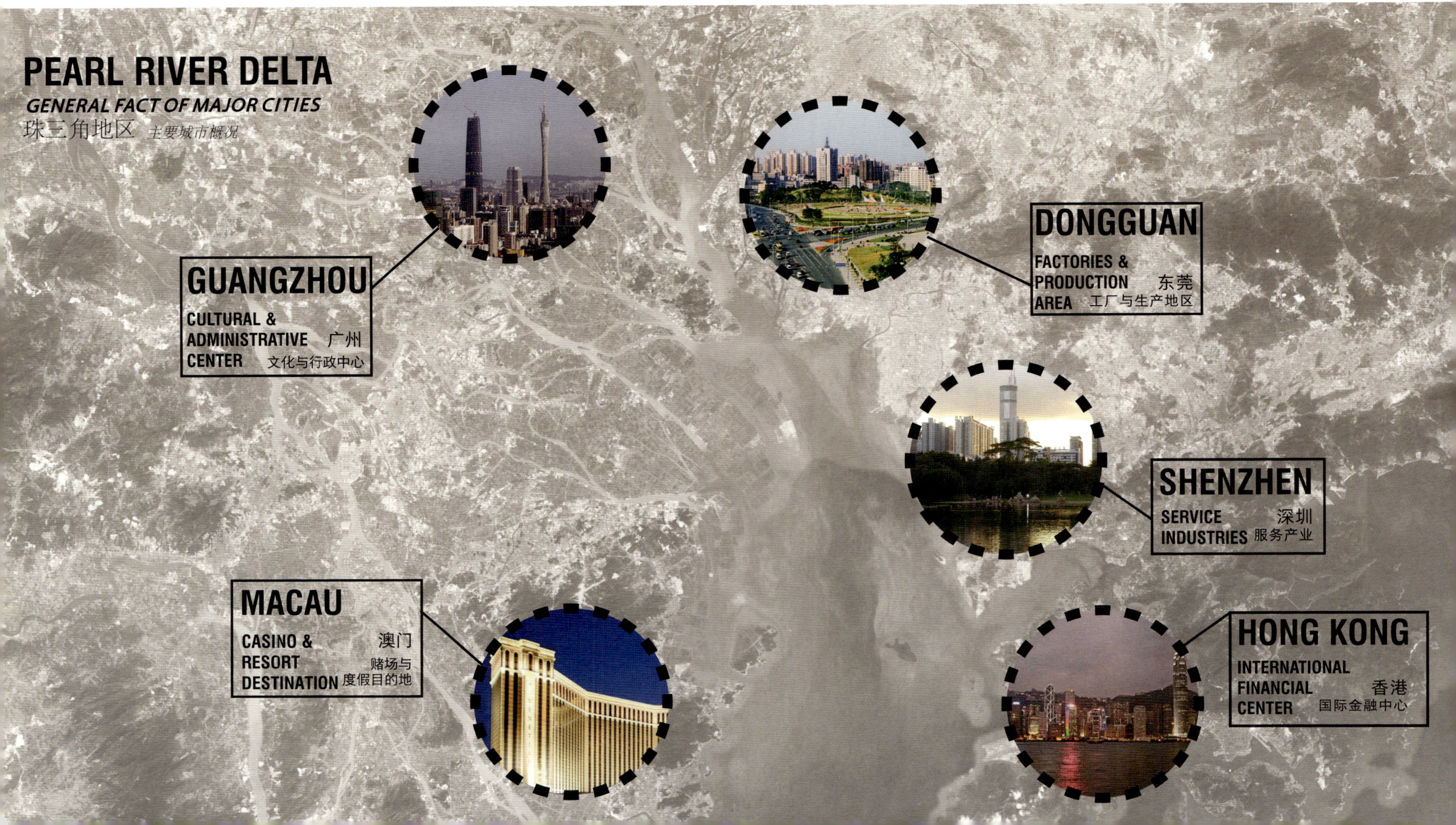
PEARL RIVER DELTA
GENERAL FACT OF MAJOR CITIES
珠三角地区 主要城市概况
GUANGZHOU
CULTURAL & ADMINISTRATIVE CENTER
广州
文化与行政中心
DONGGUAN
FACTORIES & PRODUCTION AREA
东莞
工厂与生产地区
SHENZHEN
SERVICE INDUSTRIES
深圳
服务产业
MACAU
CASINO & RESORT DESTINATION
澳门
赌场与度假目的地
HONG KONG
INTERNATIONAL FINANCIAL CENTER
香港
国际金融中心

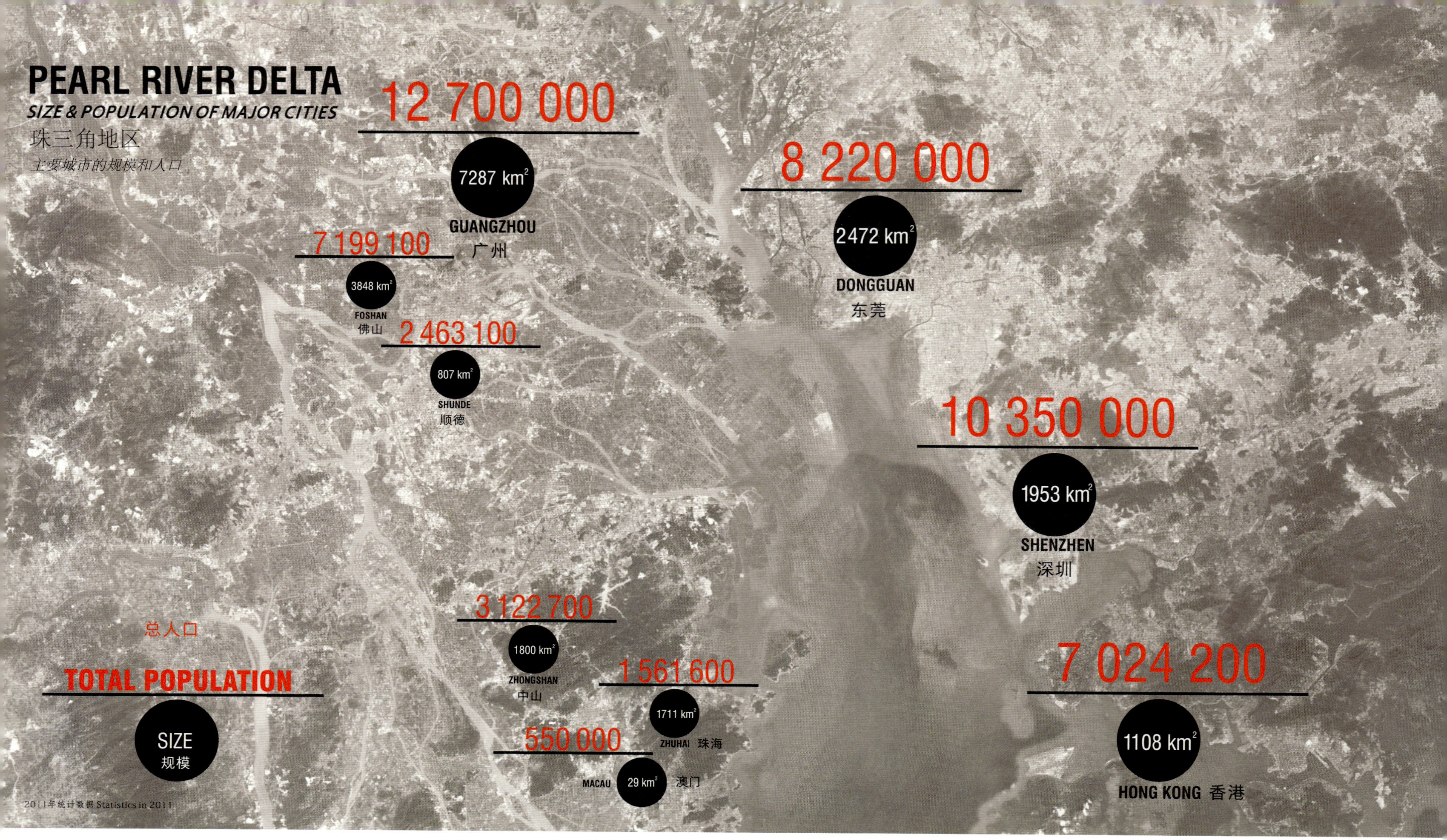
PEARL RIVER DELTA
SIZE & POPULATION OF MAJOR CITIES
珠三角地区
主要城市的规模和人口
12 700 000
7287 km²
GUANGZHOU
广州
7 199 100
3848 km²
FOSHAN
佛山
2 463 100
807 km²
SHUNDE
顺德
8 220 000
2472 km²
DONGGUAN
东莞
10 350 000
1953 km²
SHENZHEN
深圳
3 122 700
1800 km²
ZHONGSHAN
中山
1 561 600
1711 km²
ZHUHAI 珠海
550 000
29 km²
MACAU 澳门
7 024 200
1108 km²
HONG KONG 香港
总人口
TOTAL POPULATION
SIZE
规模
2011年统计数据 Statistics in 2011

"深圳2030：平衡即是多"学术评论，2013年

糊状城市

张宇星

深圳的快速发展和独特城市状态

近30年来深圳从一座边陲小镇，发展成为人口超过千万、全年生产总值（GDP）约为2000亿美元的大都市。伴随城市的高速发展，深圳城市形态一方面表现出西方大都市近一百年来的集中、分散、再集中的波浪式发展过程中所呈现出来的典型的"碎片化"特征；另一方面，深圳的城市形态也表现出一些非常有趣的独特性，诸如：模糊不清的空间状态、有黏性的空间组合机制、弹性生长、高度城市活力、自适应的形态变化、复合的流动性，市场化和非市场化机制的混合等，可称之为"糊状化"特征，类似于淀粉的"糊化作用"。

西方大都市空间的碎片化

西方传统城市受郊区化的巨大影响，形成了所谓"后城市"或"后郊区"状态，表现为间断的、不连续的城市景观；这种断裂的后城市景观不再是由相邻的自然物体构成，而逐渐变成无形网络系统，从全球范围来看，这种网络系统正逐渐超越城市之间的相邻空间联系，将城市连接起来，城市的物质性变得相对虚拟化，这种演化过程，可称之为"碎片化"过程，表现出两个特征，即：流动性的碎片化和空间的碎片化。

以汽车交通为核心的均质分布的流动性，彻底改变了传统大都市的空间发展，加速了城市空间的碎片化进程。网络结构逐渐成为城市基础设施的主导模式，后城市环境支离破碎的碎片不仅是被城市空地所分割，而且也被不受空间逻辑支配的无形网络所控制。时间已经取代距离成为决定城市空间关系的决定性因素，时间和速度削弱和解体了城市空间的整体性，最新的交通运输方式使得城市流动性越来越趋于碎片化。另一方面，交通流动性和资本与信息的流动性结合起来，彻底消除了空间的局域性，不断增强的流动性和信息技术缩短了人类交往的距离，在全球一体化过程中，后福特经济没有转向以商业—工业城市为中心的当地市场，而是受到操纵资本流动的跨国财政集团的驱使而发展。货币经济的"虚化过程"与城市空间的"虚化过程"紧密相连，跨国性的全球网络和通信技术加速了上述分裂的进程。

伴随流动性的碎片化，西方大都市空间碎片化的过程主要经历了四个阶段，即：住宅空间的碎片化、商业空间的碎片化、工业空间的碎片化和生产服务业空间的碎片化。在上述碎片化和离心化的过程中，也伴随着城市中心的复兴，特别是20世纪80年代城市中心办公楼的发展以及绅士化的商业文化区等，促成了旧的城市中心区的复兴，这种城市在中心与边缘之间的彷徨，形成了独特的"中间景观"或"外城市"状态。城市、边缘以及郊区的区别逐渐消失，由此带来了很难定义的特定环境，这是一种无定式的连绵结构，如同"城市星云"。后城市（后郊区）空间的结构非常松散，总体上由道路基础设施组合而成，高速公路网以及沿高速公路网分布的商业、工业带构成了空间架构，形成一种新型的城市生活和城市形态"碎片集合体"。

专栏3-2

深圳糊状城市的特征分析

流动性和空间的碎片化

深圳30年交通体系的发展，几乎重演了西方大都市的交通系统演进过程，从早期沿广深铁路沿线的“城市走廊”式的向心发展，到中期均质化的高速路网系统，再到近期以轨道（地铁和轻轨）系统为核心的网络系统，交通系统的流动性加速了城市空间的碎片化过程，整个城市基本形成典型的“网络化的多中心组团”格局。深圳城市形态的“城市星云”特征非常明显，在十几个城市组团之间，已经不能分辨出明晰的组团边界，整个城市成为一个巨大的连绵区，在这个高度密集的“中间景观”里，散布着各种类型的典型的“碎片化空间单元”，其中，最为典型的是“孤岛化的产业园”。这些产业园相对独立于城市其他功能，自成体系，犹如小的“产业王国”，犹如城市肌理中的“孤岛”，将城市结构撕成碎片。

超高速度的空间增长

深圳近30年来，城市空间的增长速度极其惊人，建成区面积从1980年的约10平方公里，扩张到2012年的约900平方公里。城市总建筑规模，也从约500万平方米，增长到约15亿平方米。极高速度的城市空间增长，如同淀粉糊化的临界温度一样，在最短时间内激破了所有城市空间的固有边界和生长惯性，使得工厂、豪华住宅、商场、员工宿舍、文化馆等多种多样的城市空间，在极小的空间范围内相互叠加、镶嵌，相互冲破空间边界，形成含糊不清的“混沌的空间汤”。

独具特色的能量单元

国有企业化的社区：深圳在建立特区之初，全国各地为了支援特区建设，有很多大型国有企业从内地来深组建专门的开发建设公司，其中以所谓“八大金刚”为代表，即8家大型国有企业（主要是央企），每一家企业均由政府以协定方式进行土地出让，为其提供了独立范围的城市空间，最终形成了很多独具特色的国有企业社区，如华侨城、华强北、蛇口工业区等（每一个社区的占地范围均为2～3平方公里）。在2000年之前，这些社区的绝大部分社会管理职能（如规划土地管理、人口管理、治安管理等）均由企业独立承担，也就是说，企业成为了一个社区管理的角色。正是由于这些企业的双重角色，这些企业化社区以一种非常“模糊”和多元的角色参与深圳的快速增长过程中。这些大型社区的功能随着城市的发展，已经发生了巨大改变，成为高度混合和交融的活力区域，它们如同一个个“能量单元”，将城市乃至区域范围内的人流、经济流、技术流、信息流等吸引进来。如华强北，从一个电子产品加工园区，转变为中国最大的电子产品交易市场；华侨城则转变成为一个集合旅游、居住、高新技术、文化产业等多种生产、生活和消费休闲功能的混合区。

集体产权的城中村：城中村是城市快速发展过程中，原有集体产权的村落，被相邻的城市空间快速包裹的独特现象。深圳现状全市共有原行政村320个，其中原特区内91个，原特区外229个，总用地面积

108.7平方公里，其中新村82.9平方公里、旧村25.8平方公里，全市共有私宅建筑29万栋，总建筑面积约1.5亿平方米。城中村的最重要特征，是其集体产权属性。由于城中村是中国特色社会主义市场体制的最直观和现实运营的“细胞”，城中村虽然已经完全采用市场化的经营方式，但其产权结构仍然是集体产权（非市场化产权结构），即由村民自主形成“村股份公司”和村民委员会，村长即董事长。城中村按照公司化模式发展，村民共享发展红利。城中村的经济，具有正规经济和非正规经济的双重属性。深圳的城中村规模大、分布广、自成体系，承担着巨大的城市服务功能（如廉租房、低收入人群就业等），与城市相邻空间犬牙交错，有很大的社会包容性和巨大的空间密度。城中村的内核封闭，边界渗透，非常像一个“活的细胞”和“能量单元”，其生长呼吸带动着相邻城市空间一起处于一种亢奋、模糊、黏稠、混沌的状态，是深圳“糊状城市”的主要载体和基质。

活性包容的缺位控制

在城市快速发展的过程中，刚性的严格管理有助于规范城市的经济社会行为，但也由于缺乏弹性而难以适应变化。深圳作为“糊状城市”的一个重要特征，就是在城市控制中，既存在完全按照市场规则和法制环境要求的标准化的程序和准则，也存在大量的“空间运行潜规则”，这样的潜规则客观上反而成为包容城市活力生长的基础，因此，这种“缺位控制”是一种模糊和有效的“城市增长活性剂”。缺位控制包括两种：一是被动的缺位控制，如原特区外大量的违法用地和违法建筑，以及伴随城市快速发展过程中产生的“土地历史遗留问题”；二是主动的缺位控制，即政府为了扶持或培育某个特定地区的发展和转型，适当放松空间管制，在诸如功能改变、临时建筑管理等方面，给予原产权业主以巨大发展的弹性以及较低的发展成本条件，有利于整个地区的孵化和膨胀式增长。

从糊状城市到未来城市

糊状城市的本质，在于探讨城市与生俱来的“黏性”，而这种黏性在现代主义功能分区的城市模型中已经消失殆尽。碎片化的城市空间被各种各样的流动性切割得支离破碎，如何恢复城市的黏性，也许是未来城市的重要研究课题。未来城市的“黏性”主要体现在以下两个方面：一是“流动性的黏性”，即以现有道路基础设施为架构，黏合各种流动性，包括物的流动性、人的流动性、信息流动性；二是“空间的黏性”，即以现有城市空间为基础，通过高度压缩的功能混合和建筑交融，将城市空间黏合成镶嵌的拼图，而非割裂的碎片，这种空间复合体与新的城市流动性结合起来，最终形成未来城市的雏形。

张宇星，建筑学博士，城市学者，“深圳2030：平衡即是多”竞赛方案学术顾问。

Academic review for Shenzhen 2030: Balance is More, 2013

PASTE CITY

Yuxing Zhang

Shenzhen's Rapid Growth and Unique Circumstances

Over the course of 30 years, Shenzhen has developed from a border town into a metropolis with a population of over 10 million people, and a GDP of about US$ 200 billion. With the rapid growth of the city, Shenzhen has experienced the fragmentation typical of Western metropolises, which have developed in waves of centralization, de-centralization, and re-centralization over the past century. While on the other hand, it also reveals some very interesting uniqueness, such as the blurred space state, sticky space combination mechanism, elasticity growth, a high degree of urban vitality, adaptive morphological changes, composite liquidity, and a mix of marketization and non-marketization mechanism, etc. Such uniqueness may be called the "paste" characteristics, which is similar to the "pasting".

The Fragmentation of Western Metropolitan Space

Under the tremendous influence of suburbanization, traditional Western cities form a so-called "post-urban" or "post-suburb" state, showing continuous and discontinuous urban landscape. The fracture post-urban landscape is no longer constituted by adjacent natural objects, but gradually becomes an invisible network system. From a global perspective, this network system is gradually beyond the neighbouring spatial contact between cities, connects the cities and the city materiality has become relatively virtualized. This evolution process can be called the process of fragmentation, showing two characteristics, namely, the current fragmentation and space fragmentation.

The mobility of homogeneous distribution centered on motor traffic has completely changed the spatial development of traditional metropolis and accelerated the fragmentation of urban space. Network structure gradually becomes the dominate mode of urban infrastructure, and the post-urban environment fragments are not only segmented by urban open space, but are also under the control of intangible networks not subject to space logic. Time has become the decisive factor of determining urban space relationship instead of distance. Time and speed has weakened and disintegrated the integrity of urban space; likewise, the latest traffic and transport way has make the urban mobility increasingly tend to fragmentation. On the other hand, the combination of traffic mobility and the mobility of capital and information has completely eliminated the space locality. The growing mobility and information technology has shortened the distance of human interaction. In the process of global integration, the post-Ford economy has not turned to the local market centered by commercial-industrial cities, but moved forward driven by the cross-border financial group in the manipulation of capital flow. The "virtual process" of money economy is closely associated with the "virtual process" of urban space. Multinational global networking and communication technology has accelerated the aforementioned process of split.

Following the fragmentation of mobility, there have been four main stages to the fragmentation of Western metropolitan space: the fragmentation of residential spaces, commercial spaces, industrial spaces, and producer services spaces. This fragmentation and centrifugation followed the revival of the city centre, particularly the development of city-centre office buildings and gentrified commercial and cultural areas in the 1980s, which promoted the revival of older city centres. This indecision between centre and periphery created unique intermediate landscapes or outer cities. The disappearing differences between the city, the periphery, and the suburbs have resulted in a specific environment that is difficult to define. This is an unfixed, continuous structure, like an urban nebula. The structures of post-urban (or post-suburban) spaces are very loose, generally consisting of road infrastructure. Highway networks and commercial-industrial belts make up a spatial framework, thereby shaping a new kind of urban life and an urban way of joining these fragments.

Analyzing Shenzhen as a Paste City

Mobility and spatial fragmentation

The 30 years' development of transport system in Shenzhen almost repeated the evolution of the transport system of Western metropolis, from the centripetal development of "urban corridor" along the Guangzhou-Shenzhen railway in the early stage, to the homogenized high-speed road system in the medium-term and the recent rail-centered (subway and light rail) network system. The mobility of the transportation system has accelerated the process of urban space, and the entire city basically formed the pattern of "networking multi-center group". Shenzhen has obvious characteristics of "city nebula", because it is impossible to distinguish clear boundaries between a dozen of urban clusters. The entire city has become a huge interlocking region. A variety of typical "fragmented space units" are distributed in this highly intensive "intermediary landscape", of which the most typical one is the "island industrial parks". These industrial parks are relatively independent from other urban functions and establish their own systems to tear urban structure into shreds like small "industrial kingdom" and "islands" in the urban texture.

Rapid Spatial Growth

Shenzhen enjoyed extremely fast growth rate in the past 3 decades, with the built-up area expanded from about 10 km^2 in 1980 to approximately 900 km^2 in 2012. The city's total construction scale also increased from about 5 million m^2 to around 1.5 billion m^2. Like the critical temperature (53℃) of starch pasting, high-speed growth of urban space broke the inherent boundaries and growth within the shortest time and form diversified urban space including plants, luxury residences, shopping malls, staff quarters and cultural centers. These layouts were mutually superimposed, inlaid, broke the space boundaries and formed a vague "chaotic space soup".

Unique Energy Cells

State-owned enterprise community: in the beginning of the establishment of Shenzhen special economic zone, to support the building of the special zone, many large inland state-owned enterprises went to set up a special development and construction company. Among them, the most renowned were the so-called "eight giants", 8 large state-owned enterprises (mainly central enterprises). The government made land transfer by agreement to each of them, providing them with the independent range of urban space, and ultimately formed a number of characteristic communities of state-owned enterprises, such as OCT, Huaqiangbei, and Shekou Industrial Zone (the coverage of each community is about 2 to 3 km^2). Before 2000, the major social of these communities (such as planning land management, population management and security management, etc) were independently borne by enterprises. That is to say, the enterprises played the role of community management. Because of the dual role of merchants and officials, these entrepreneurial communities participated in the fast growth of Shenzhen via the "fuzzy" and multiple roles. Consequently, the functions of these large communities had tremendous changes along with the urban development, and has turned into highly mixing and blending areas with great vitality. Like "energy units", they have attracted the flow of people, economic flow, technology flow and information flow in the city and even the local scope. Among them, Huaqiangbei has become China's largest electronics market from an electronic product processing park; OCT has transformed into a mixing zone with a variety of production, life and consumption and leisure functions integrating tourism, residence, high-tech and cultural industries.

Village-in-city with collective property: village-in-city is a unique phenomenon in the process of rapid development, which refers to the original villages with collective property being fast wrapped by the adjacent urban space. Currently, Shenzhen has 320 original administrative villages, including 91 in the original special zone and 229 out of the original special zone, covering an area of 108.7 km^2, including 82.9 km^2 of new village and 25.8 km^2 of old village. The city has 290 000 private buildings, with a total construction area of approximately 150 million m^2. The most important feature of village-in-city is the characteristics of collective property. The phenomenon of village-in-city is the most intuitive and realistic operational cell in China's socialist market system. Although it has been in complete market-oriented mode of operation, the property structure is still the collective property rights (non-market property rights structure); that is, villagers autonomously set up "village joint-stick company" and villagers' committee, and the village head serves as the president. Village-in-city develops in accordance with the mode of companization and villagers share the development dividend together. The economy of village-in-city has the dual attributes of formal economy and informal economy. Featured by large-scale, wide distribution and unique system, the village-in-city of Shenzhen bears huge urban service functions (such as low-cost housing, low-income population and employment), interlocking with the adjacent urban spaces, with great social inclusion and huge spatial density. The closed kernel and penetrated boundary makes village-in-city in high resemblance of a "living cell" and "energy unit". Its growth and respiration mobilizes the adjacent urban spaces to enter the exciting, fuzzy, viscous and chaotic state, serving as the main carrier and matrix of Shenzhen as a "paste city".

The Absent Control of Active Inclusion

In the process of rapid urban growth, rigid management helps to regulate the city's economic and social behavior it is difficult to adapt to changes. An important feature of Shenzhen as a "pasting city" is in control of city, there are the standard procedures and norms in full compliance with the requirements of market rules and legal environment, and also a lot of "hidden rules of space running". These hidden rules have dramatically become the basis for the inclusive growth of urban vitality. Therefore, the "absent control" is a kind of vague and effective "urban growth activator". There are two kinds of absent control. First, the passive absent control: such as the widely illegal use of land and illegal construction out of the original special zone, as well as "the land problems left over by history"; second, the positive absent control: it is a kind of government practice which consciously relaxes the space control to support or foster the development and transformation of a particular region. For example, in terms of functional changes, temporary construction management, the original property owners were granted with the great flexibility of development and relatively low development cost, which was conductive to the incubation of the entire region and expansion growth.

From a Paste City to a Future City

The essence of paste city consists in the innate "viscosity" of the city, but this viscosity has disappeared in the city model of modernist functional zoning. Fragmented urban space is cut by a variety of mobilities, so how to restore the viscosity of the city may be an important research topic of future city. The viscosity of the future city is mainly reflected in the following two aspects: the first is the "mobility viscosity": with the existing road infrastructure as the architecture, bond all kinds of mobilities, including material mobility, people mobility and information mobility; the second is the "space viscosity": based on the existing urban space, bond the urban spaces into mosaic puzzle via highly compressed urban space, rather than fragmented pieces. Then the prototype of the future city will be ultimately. This space complex of the future city is ultimately formed by combining this space complex with the new urban mobility.

Yuxing Zhang, Ph.D. in architecture, urban scholar, academic consultant of Shenzhen 2030: Balance is More project.

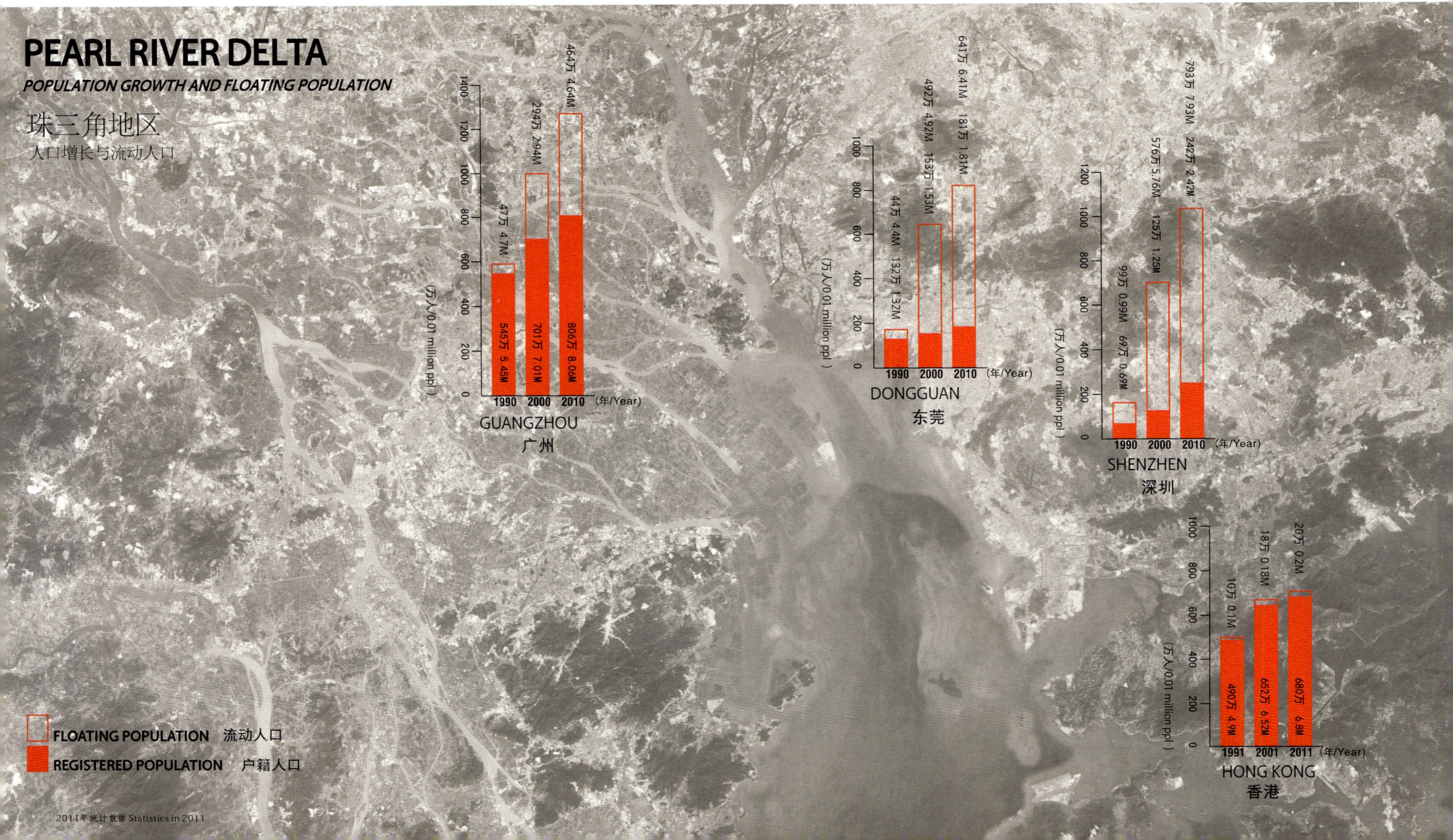
PEARL RIVER DELTA
POPULATION GROWTH AND FLOATING POPULATION
珠三角地区
人口增长与流动人口
GUANGZHOU
广州
1990 545万 5.45M 47万 4.7M
2000 701万 7.01M 294万 2.94M
2010 806万 8.06M 464万 4.64M
(年/Year)
(万人/0.01 million ppl)
DONGGUAN
东莞
1990 132万 1.32M 44万 4.4M
2000 153万 1.53M 492万 4.92M
2010 181万 1.81M 641万 6.41M
SHENZHEN
深圳
1990 69万 0.69M 99万 0.99M
2000 125万 1.25M 576万 5.76M
2010 242万 2.42M 793万 7.93M
HONG KONG
香港
1991 490万 4.9M 10万 0.1M
2001 652万 6.52M 18万 0.18M
2011 680万 6.8M 20万 0.2M
FLOATING POPULATION 流动人口
REGISTERED POPULATION 户籍人口
2011年统计数据 Statistics in 2011

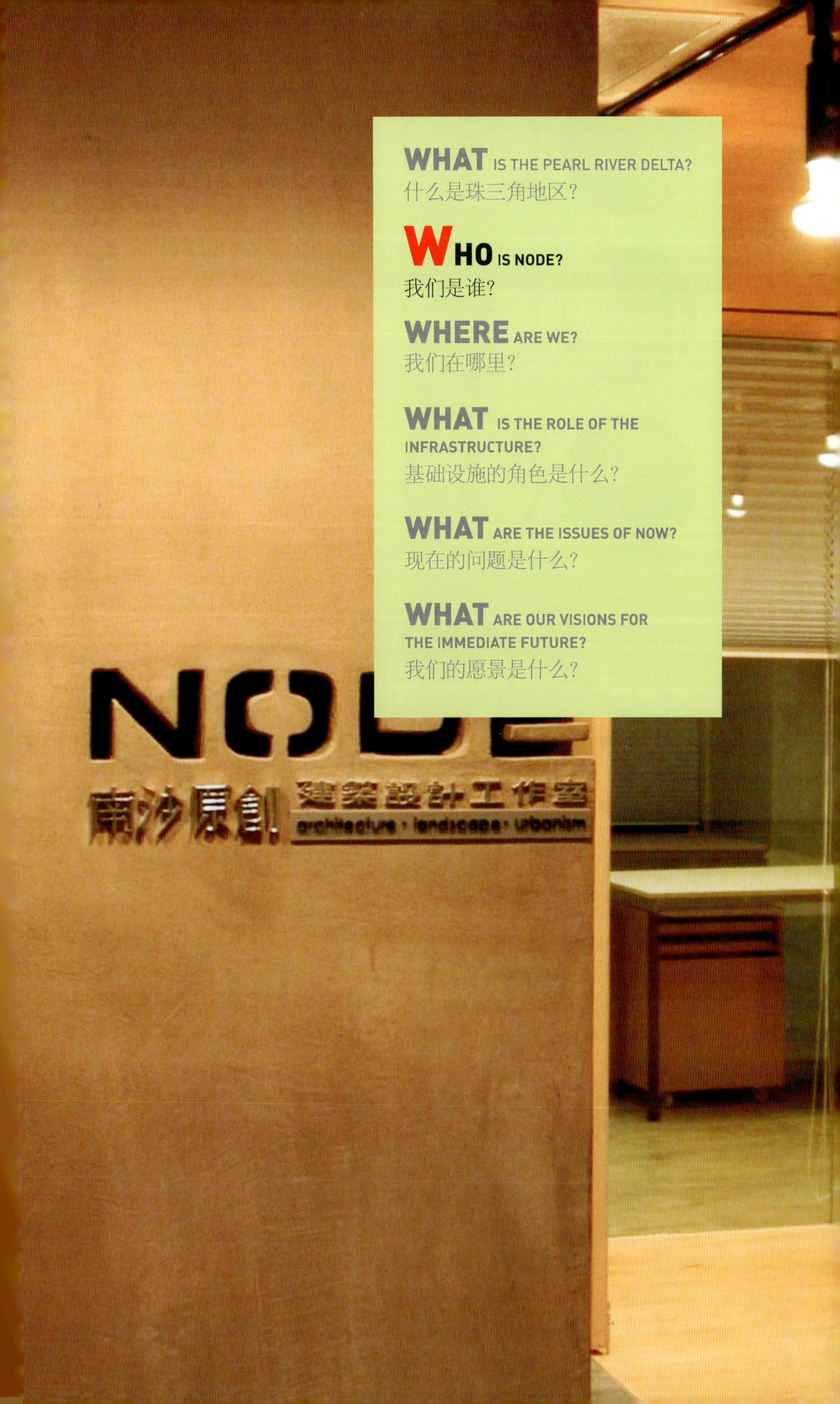

WHAT IS THE PEARL RIVER DELTA?
什么是珠三角地区?

WHO IS NODE?
我们是谁?

WHERE ARE WE?
我们在哪里?

WHAT IS THE ROLE OF THE INFRASTRUCTURE?
基础设施的角色是什么?

WHAT ARE THE ISSUES OF NOW?
现在的问题是什么?

WHAT ARE OUR VISIONS FOR THE IMMEDIATE FUTURE?
我们的愿景是什么?

NODE ARCHITECTURE & URBANISM

NANSHA, HONG KONG & SHENZHEN

南沙原创建筑设计工作室

南沙、香港&深圳

NANSHA
南沙

HONG KONG
香港

SHENZHEN
深圳

NODE PROJECTS

ARCHITECTURE, URBANISM & LANDSCAPE

南沙原创项目介绍

建筑设计、城市规划及景观设计

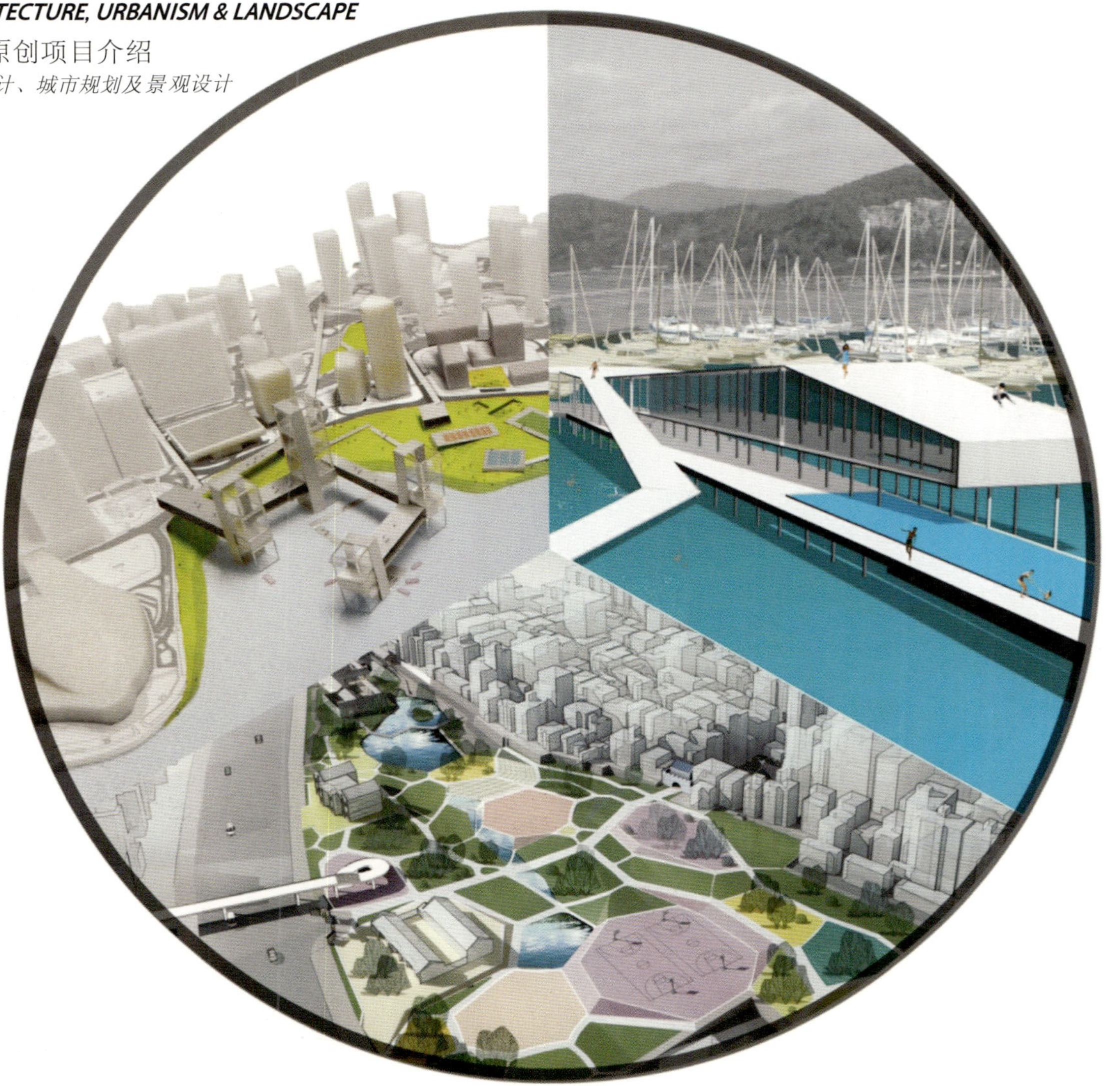

WHAT IS THE PEARL RIVER DELTA?
什么是珠三角地区?

WHO IS NODE?
我们是谁?

WHERE ARE WE?
我们在哪里?

WHAT IS THE ROLE OF THE INFRASTRUCTURE?
基础设施的角色是什么?

WHAT ARE THE ISSUES OF NOW?
现在的问题是什么?

WHAT ARE OUR VISIONS FOR THE IMMEDIATE FUTURE?
我们的愿景是什么?

EAST VS. WEST 东方vs.西方

CONFUCISM *儒家文化*

宗教，文艺复兴 ***RELIGION, RENAISSANCE***

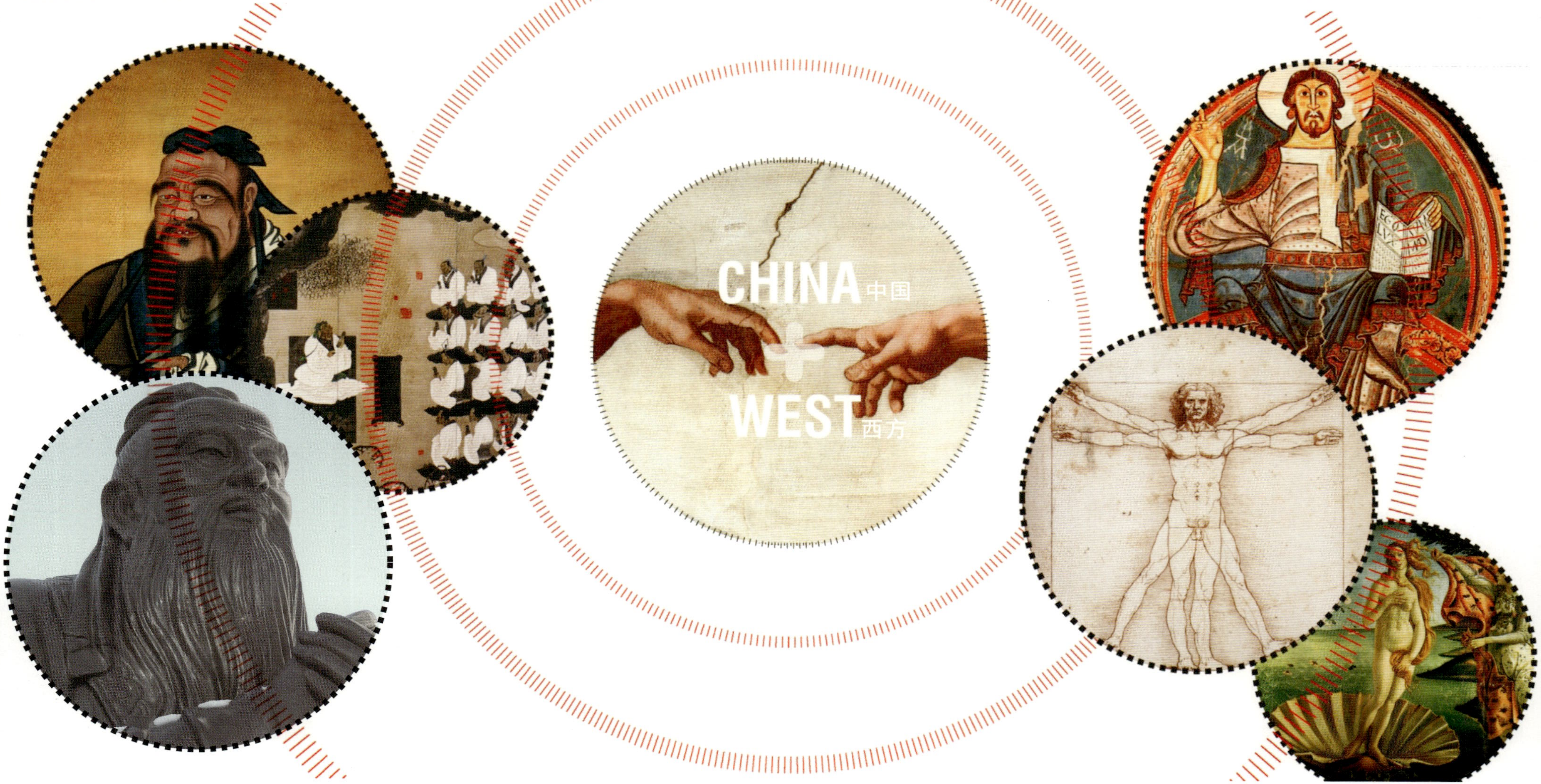

《Domus国际中文版》，2011年9月，第57期

三角四方：后“普通城市”的珠三角

刘珩

历史总让人纠结，尤其是没了束缚，面对全新未来的时候。

2008年我博士毕业后回归珠三角地区，除了延续以往的建筑实践外，也开始了我在珠三角地区的城市空间研究。第一个研究课题是顺德容桂沿江厂房的保护改造，接着是深圳华强北街区的升级改造，然后是广州大塘历史街区的保护与发展。这几个课题都有着一个共同的问题：我们拿历史怎么办?

由于地缘和政治的边缘化，珠三角地区在历史上有着更多向外寻求发展以及交换的机会。密集的河网、临海的地理条件和宽松的社会政治环境，在20世纪初近代工业化发展进程中，让珠三角地区毫无悬念地成了世界列强必争的资源和通商宝地。随着历史的演进，汇通中西文化的地缘分别催生了香港和澳门这两座独特的城市，也深刻影响了广州这座有着两千年历史的中国南方大城的发展；更不用说，在同样的地缘逻辑框架下，深圳作为新一轮的试验田在短短三十年里所创造的中国特区奇迹。分布于珠江口的这四个城市，在不同的历史阶段作为不同文化的“孵化器”，均扮演着贸易交流、体制冲突、经济竞争和全球化背景下的中国视窗等特殊角色，而这些独特的基因也层层烙在了这些城市的空间和肌理当中。

然而这些层次鲜明的独特性在过去30年的快速城市化进程中陷入了被“普通”的困境。无论是经过两千年发展历史的广州，还是经过30年发展的深圳，都同样具有当下中国快速城市化中典型的规划意识形态，就是几乎无一例外地权宜选择历史归零为起点，以方便创造崭新的“身份”。容桂沿江老厂房展示的是20世纪初中期典型珠三角地区工业化历史，而今让位于快速交通，是保留还是有如所有规划所示的一样建设一片公共绿地？深圳华强北展现的是开放改革前沿快速城市化下“普通城市”所能达到的繁荣巅峰，为维持这个繁荣，拆了重建还是保留加建？2008年之前我在广州南沙这块处女地的十年建筑实践，加剧了我对珠三角地区这30年城市发展的困惑。雷姆·库哈斯早在20世纪90年代中就敏锐地观察到珠三角的未来会成为一座巨大的“普通城市”：“它什么都不是，它是座没有历史的城市……它也很随意，不需要维护。如果它太小，它只需要扩大；如果它太旧，它只需要自我毁灭和更新……每个周一早上，它都能制造出一个新的身份。”过去的三十年，中国城市不停地在停—拆—建这几个简单机械的运动中似乎快速地完成“变脸”，然而获得的是“千城一面”的新面目。我们求“变”，但这“脸”是我们想要的未来吗?

所幸这只是珠三角故事的一部分。香港及澳门，依然故我地遵循自己的步伐，它们今天超然的身份和独特的城市空间源于对历史传统的尊重。对比今天的“普通城市”，这两个谨慎前行的城市带给珠三角地区的是一道不可复制、层次鲜明的人文风景。

显然上述的广州、深圳、香港和澳门在不同历史阶段中所呈现的浮躁或淡定、快速或缓慢、普通或独特，以及颠覆或保护，构成了一个非常有趣也令人深思的立体动态画面。出于对快速城市化过程中丧失独特性而走向趋同化的“普通城市”的对抗和批判，并尝试建立一种动态接纳历史的观念，我在今年三月与哥伦比亚大学的杰弗里·约翰逊共同主持了“三角四方”行进中的历史博物馆——广州/深圳/香港/澳门”城市设计论坛。

如何看待自己的历史直接影响了今天这些城市对历史空间再生历程的决策和塑造：是无序的简单或是清晰的复杂；平面匀质化或是立体层次化等都是值得讨论的问题。“三角四方”专题的研究是希望借学术讨论和设计实践两个层面，对珠三角独特的历史进行重新梳理和比较，更重要的是关注这些独特性共同的“未来”，为它们在未来的城市空间塑造中所能扮演的角色提供更多有益和有效的线索。专题以著名人文学者李欧梵教授关于这四个城市的故事与记忆开始，随后规划学者与建筑师从各自的角度和实践去诠释和阐述他们心目中对这些城市规则和冲突的想象，最后以库哈斯先生和我的一场关于珠三角未来的对话回应后“普通城市”时代的珠三角地区想象。如同“行进中的历史博物馆”，珠江三角洲这四座城市一衣带水，过去、现在以及未来都不会是静态和简单割裂的历史，之间维系着各自宝贵的经验和教训，又一如既往地充当着中国世界化的前沿基地，走向相对独立而又共同承担的未来。

尽管如此，我对珠三角地区的未来还是持有怀疑态度和充满矛盾的。在“三角四方”研究专题中我有意屏蔽了官方对珠三角地区的未来想象，是因为我并不认同这些想象的意义和建设性；但是我没有回避对全球共同面临的一些问题，例如资源与能量等方面的思考。作为建筑师和学者，我们相信独立的声音和自主的实践能为珠三角的未来和我们的城市提供更多富有启迪性和创造性的线索和思维，呈现出的就是我们在这方面所做的一点努力。

Domus China, Sept 2011, Vol. 57

DELTA FOUR: POST-GENERIC PRD

Doreen Heng Liu

History is always haunting you, especially when you face a brand-new future, unrestrained.

After obtaining my doctoral degree and returning to the PRD in 2008, I began the researches into the PRD urban spaces in addition to continuing my architectural practices. My first research subject was the preservation and redevelopment of the riverside factory premises of Ronggui, Shunde District, followed by upgrading of the Huaqiangbei neighborhood, Shenzhen and preservation and development of the historic block of Datang, Guangzhou. These subjects share one common issue: how should we deal with history?

Throught the history, the geographical and political marginalization brought the PRD more opportunities to open up to the outside for two-way trade and development. Thanks to the crisscrossed rivers, seaside location and relatively loose social and political environment, the PRD was undoubtedly turned into a resource and business destination for which great powers must vie during the industrialization in the early 20th century. As the wheel of history rolled forward, the geographical location integrating the Chinese and Western cultures has acted as a catalyst for the birth of two unique cities, Hong Kong and Macau, and also exerted a profound impact on the development of Guangzhou, a metropolis in South China with a history of more than two thousand years. Moreover, under the same framework of geological logic, Shenzhen has made a miracle as a new round of experimental field for the special administrative region in China within a short period of thirty years. As the incubator for different cultures on different historical stages, the four cities at the estuary of the Pear River all played the role of the Window of China against the background of trade exchange, system conflict, and economic competition and globalization. These unique genes have been interwoven layer upon layer into the spaces and fabrics of the four cities.

However, such uniqueness of distinct hierarchies has got into the predicament of being forced to become generic over the past thirty years of rapid urbanization. Whether Guangzhou with a history of more than two thousand years or Shenzhen with a soaring development of thirty years, they are both characterized by the typical planning ideology during the rapid urbanization of China, namely to unexceptionally start with eliminating the history as an expedient to facilitate the creation of a brand-new identity. The riverside old factory buildings of Ronggui displays a typical history of the PRD industrialization in the mid-20th century, but now have to give way to rapid transit infrastructure. Do we choose to preserve them or build a green land there as all plans require? The Huaqiangbei neighborhood, Shenzhen represents the peak of prosperity a generic city can reach under rapid urbanization at the forefront of China's opening up and reform. In order to maintain such prosperity, do we choose to demolish and rebuild it or preserve and expand it? In addition, my architectural practices for one decade on the virgin land of Nansha District, Guangzhou until 2008 only ended up making me more perplexed at the thirty years' urban development of the PRD. As early as in the 1990s, Rem Koolhaas had a sharp insight that the PRD would become a huge generic city in the future: "it is nothing but a city without history...it develops randomly and requires no maintenance. If it is too small, it only needs to be expanded; if it is too old, it only needs self-destruction and renewal...in the morning of each Monday, it can produce a new identity." In the past thirty years, it seems that China has critically changed its face in the ceaselessly simple and mechanical motions of suspension, demolition and construction, yet the result is a new identity of identical appearances of all towns. We do pursue change, but is this face the future we desire?

Fortunately, this is only part of the PRD story. The other part – Hong Kong and Macau – the ties are always marching in their usual manner. Their aloof identity and unique urban space are attributed to their respect for history and tradition. Compared with the generic city today, the two cities in cautious advancement bring an unreplicable and clear-cut cultural feature and attraction to the PRD.

Obviously, the above hustle or ease, rapidness or slowness, genericness or uniqueness, and subversion or preservation that Guangzhou, Shenzhen, Hong Kong and Macau showed at different historical stages presents an interesting and thought-provoking 3-dimensional and dynamic picture. Out of challenge and criticism against generic cities which lost its uniqueness and became convergent during rapid urbanization and as an attempt to establish a concept of dynamically accepting history, I co-hosted an urban design forum in March this year with Jeffery Johnson from the Columbia University, which was entitled "Delta Four": A Living Museum of Urban History – the Four Cities in the PRD Guangzhou/Shenzhen/ Hong Kong/Macau.

How to see the direct impact of their own history on the decision-making and shaping of historical space regeneration of these cities: unordered simplicity or clear complexity; planar homogeneousness or dimensional layering, etc. is an issue worth discussing. The research of Delta Four aims to, via both academic discussion and design practices, review and compare the unique history of the PRD; and more importantly, to pay more attention to the common future of such uniqueness, thus offering more helpful and effective clues for possible roles of the unique history of the PRD in urban space shaping. This paper collection begins with the memory and story of Prof. Leo Ou-fan Lee, a famous humanistic scholar, about the four cities; then presents the observations several planning scholars and architects made regarding the rules and conflicts of these cities from their own perspectives and practices; and concludes with a dialogue between Mr. Koolhaas (representing global) and me (representing local) in response to what is envisaged about the PRD in the era of post-generic cities. The four cities in the PRD, just like the said A Living Museum of Urban History, are connected by a strip of water and their histories were not, are not or will not be static or simply isolated whether in the past, at present or in the future, tying each other by their own experiences and lessons. They will persistently serve as the forefront in China's advance towards globalization, seeking relevant independence while sharing a common future.

Yet I am still skeptical and harbor contradictory ideas about the future of the PRD. In this research, I deliberately block out the "official" imagination about the future of the PRD for I don't identify myself with the significance and constructiveness of such imagination. Nevertheless, I do not evade some problems we are all confronted with, such as resources and energy. As architects and scholars, we are convinced that independent voice and practice could offer more enlightening and creative clues and thoughts to the future of the PRD and our cities. This is just what we contribute in this research.

"三角四方"行进中的历史博物馆——广州/深圳/香港/澳门城市设计论坛

Urban Design Forum "Delta Four": A Living Museum of Urban History
The Four Cities in the PRD Guangzhou / Shenzhen / Hong Kong / Macau

EAST VS. WEST 东方vs.西方

TEA vs COFFEE 茶vs.咖啡

GLOBALIZATION

WEST DESIGN, CHINESE MANUFACTURATION

全球化 *西方设计，中国制造*

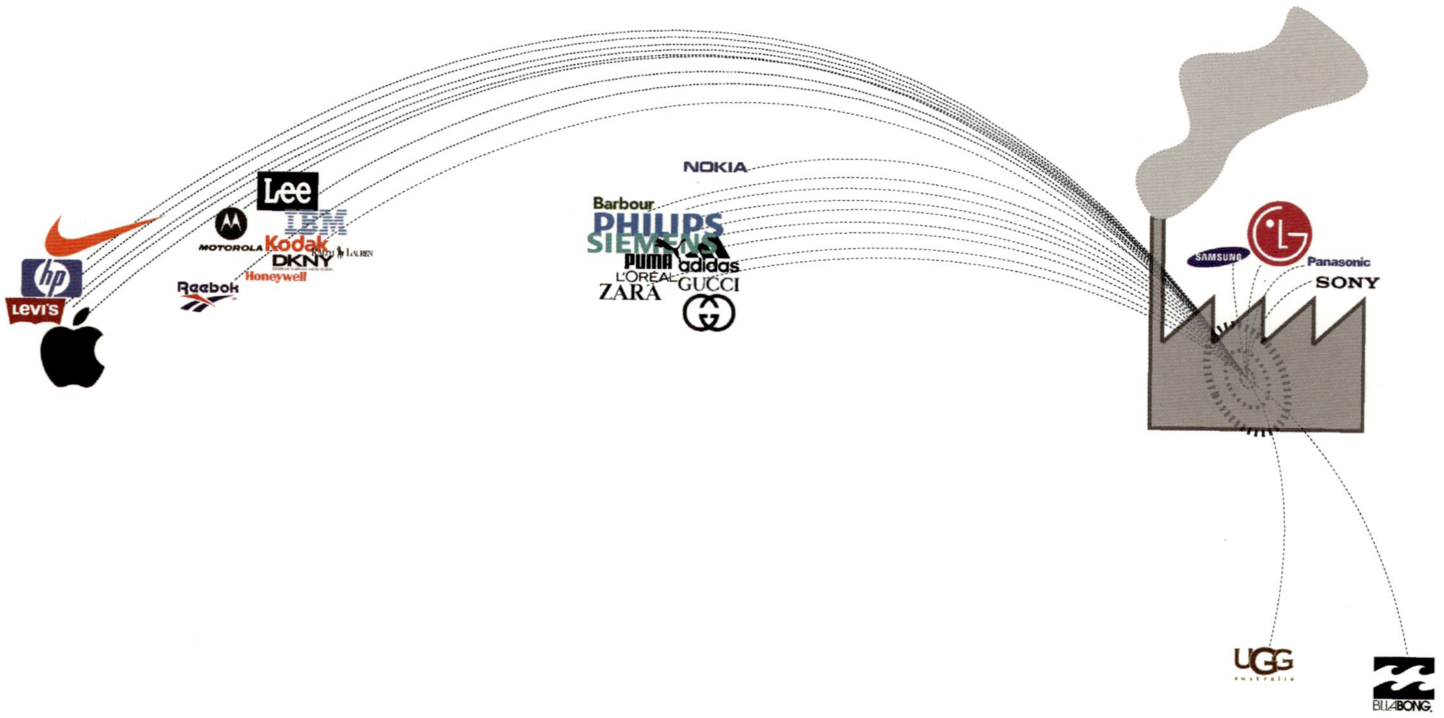

INDUSTRIALIZATION

HYBRID CULTURE & UNEVEN DEVELOPMENT

工业化 *杂糅文化&发展不均衡（飞利浦）*

PHILIPS

- 1891 Foundation in Eindhoven(NL) 成立于埃因霍温(荷兰)
- 1910 2000 employees in Netherlands 在荷兰拥有2000名员工
- 1994 First manufacturation factory in Hubei(CN) 在湖北开设第一家制造厂
- 2010 Second manufacturation factory in Shanghai(CN) 在上海开设第二家制造厂

珠三角飞利浦工厂分布

PHILIPS PLANTS IN THE PEARL RIVER DELTA

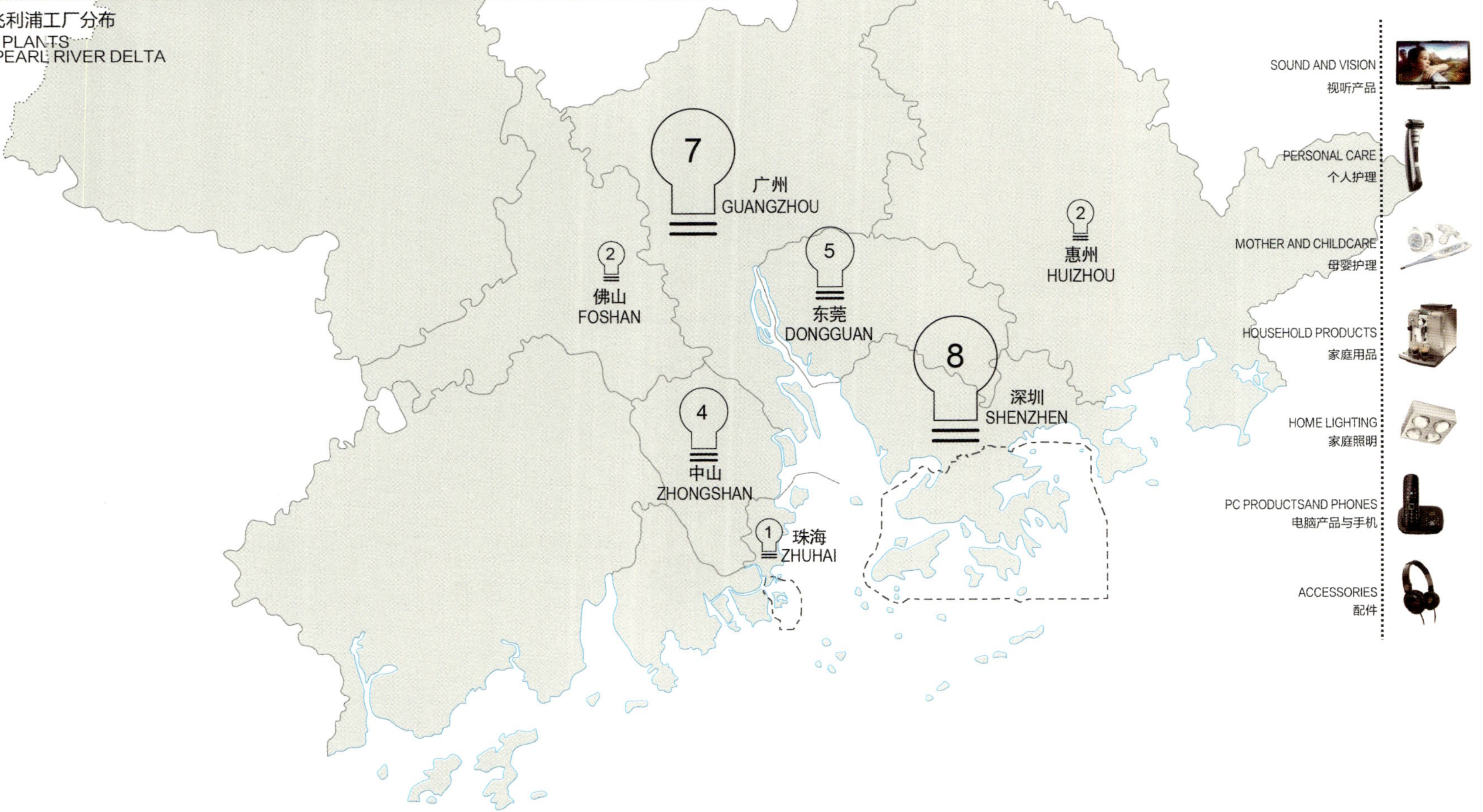

INDUSTRIALIZATION

HYBRID CULTURE & UNEVEN DEVELOPMENT

工业化 *杂糅文化&发展不均衡（耐克）*

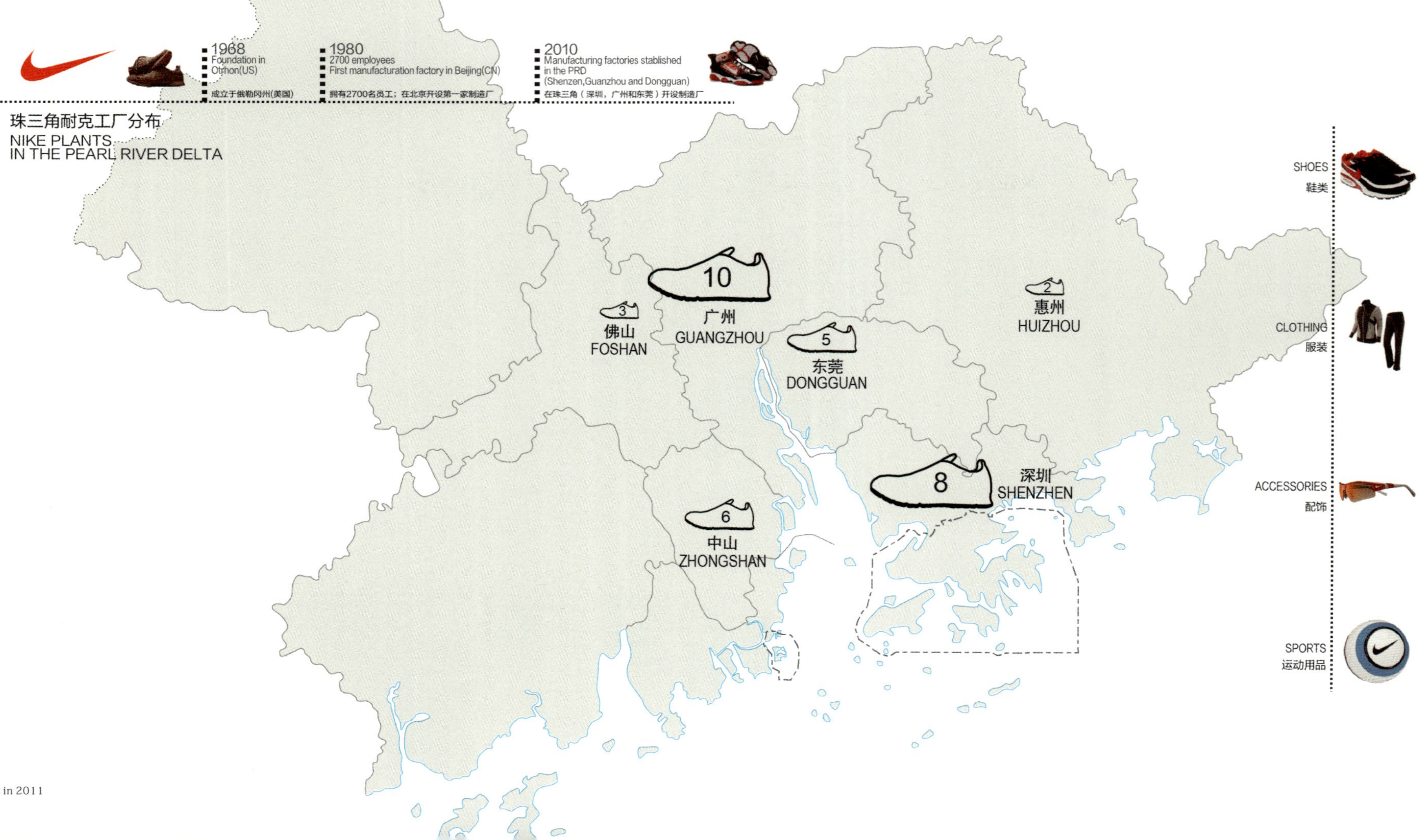

INDUSTRIALIZATION

HYBRID CULTURE & UNEVEN DEVELOPMENT

工业化 *杂糅文化&发展不均衡（西门子）*

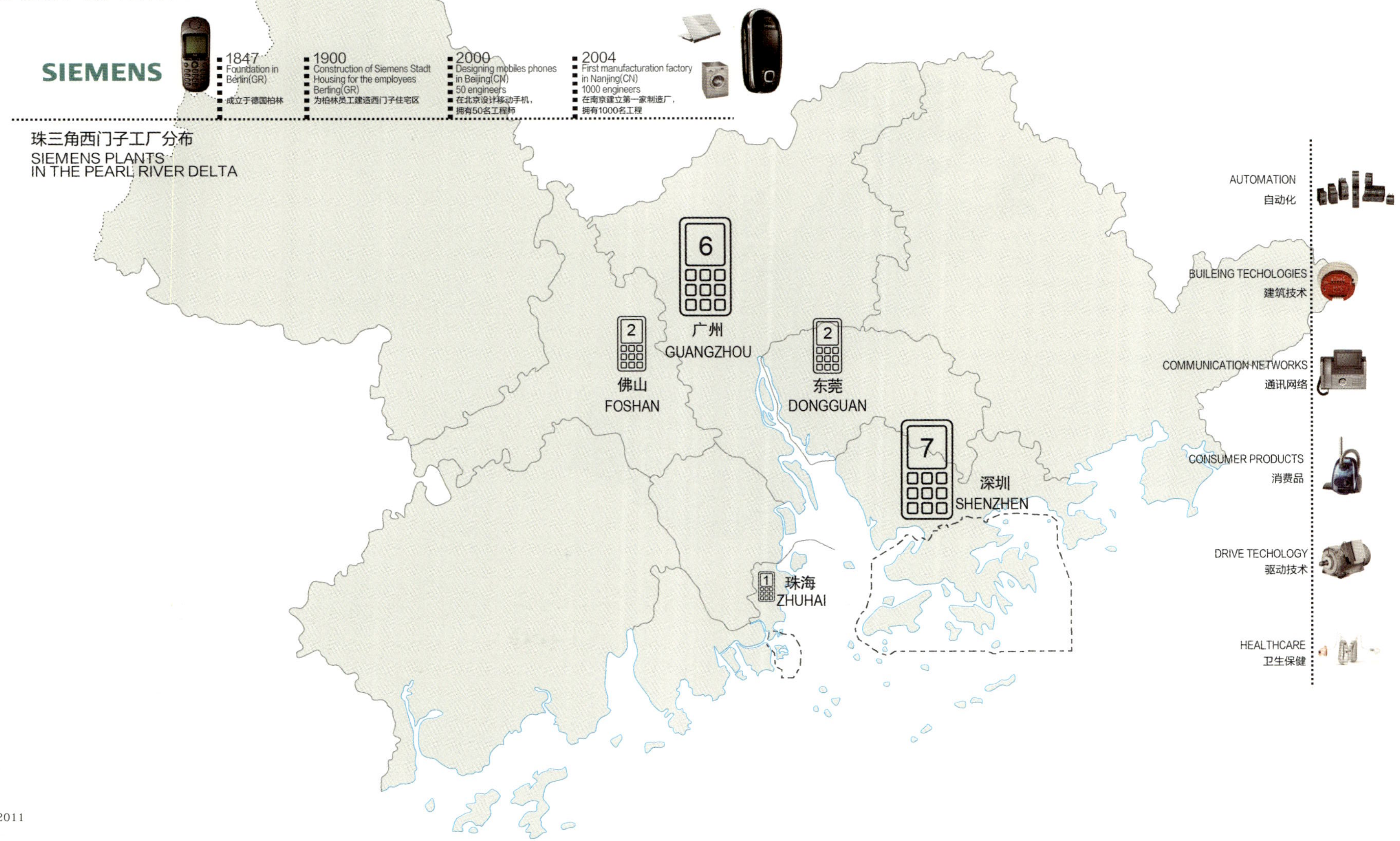

FOUR REPRESENTATIVE PRD CITIES

GUANGZHOU, DONGGUAN, SHENZHEN AND HONG KONG

四座具有代表性的珠三角城市

广州、东莞、深圳、香港

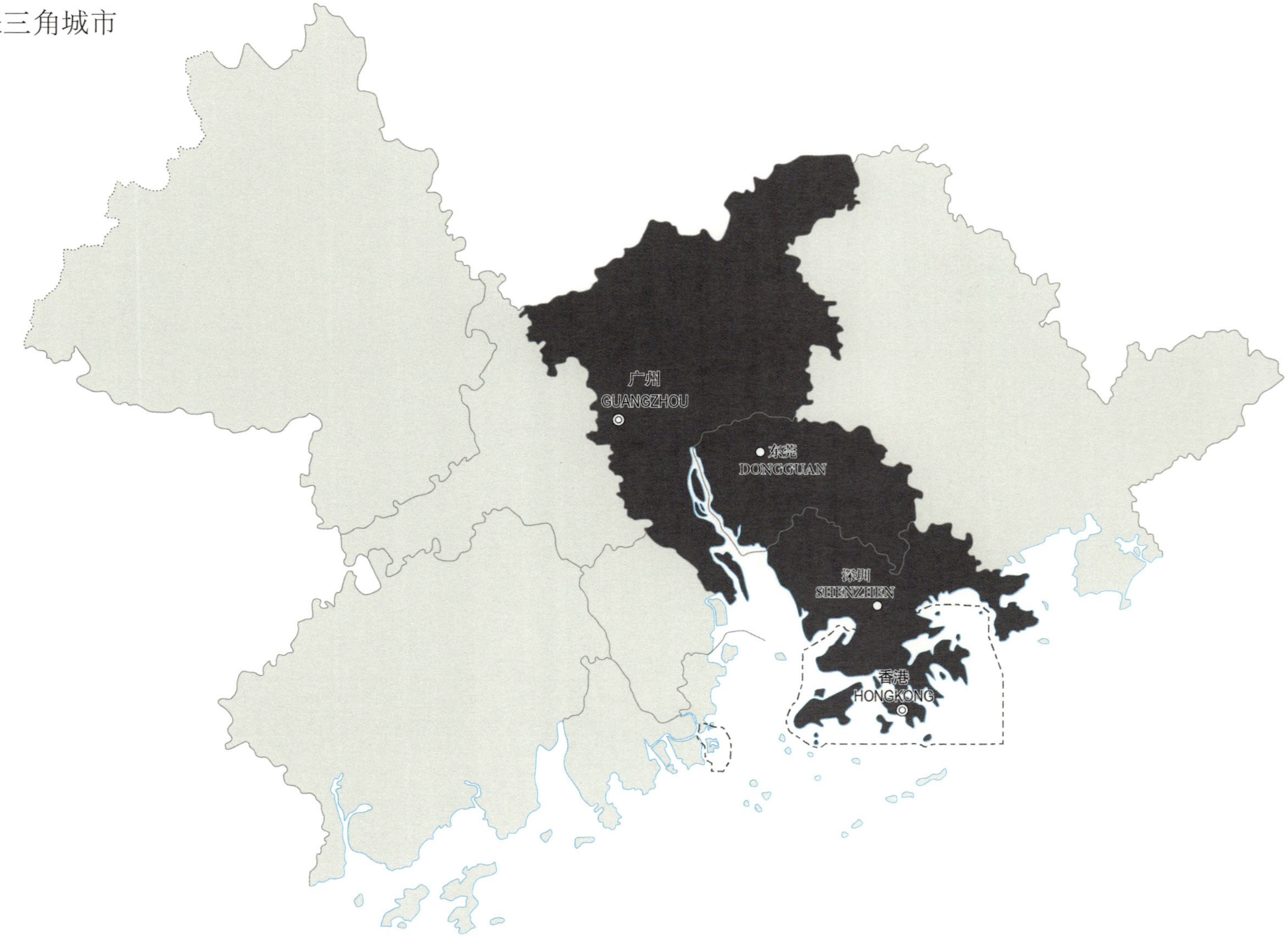

GUANGZHOU

URBANIZATION OF GUANGZHOU

广州 | 城市化

GUANGZHOU

URBANIZATION OF GUANGZHOU

广州 *城市化*

7287平方公里

7287km²

AREA

面积

2011年统计数据 Statistics in 2011

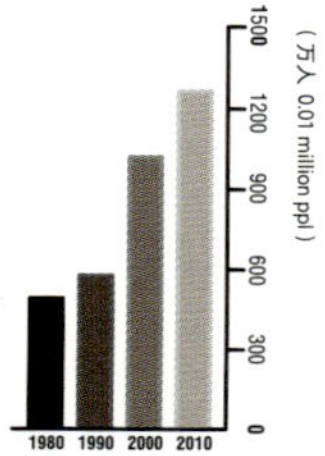

POPULATION

人口

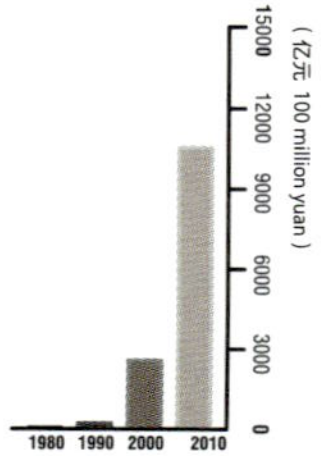

Regional GDP

地区生产总值

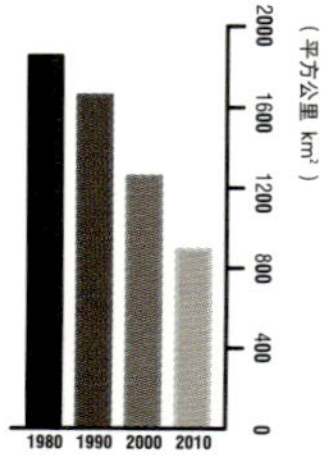

ARABLE land

耕地

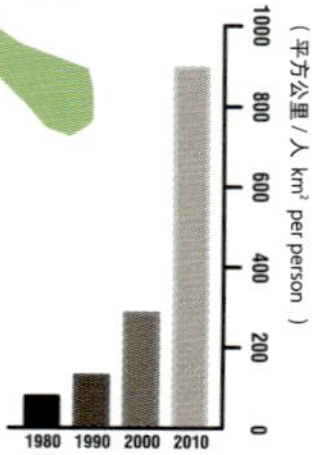

BUILT UP / person

人均建设用地

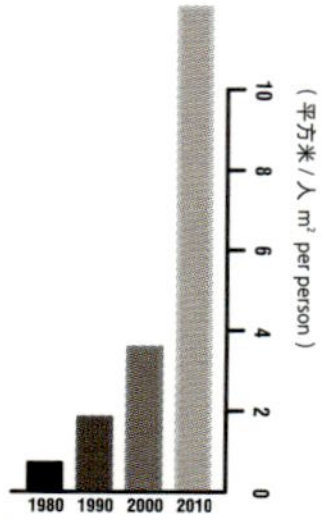

ROAD AREA / person

人均道路面积

DONGGUAN

URBANIZATION OF DONGGUAN

东莞 *城市化*

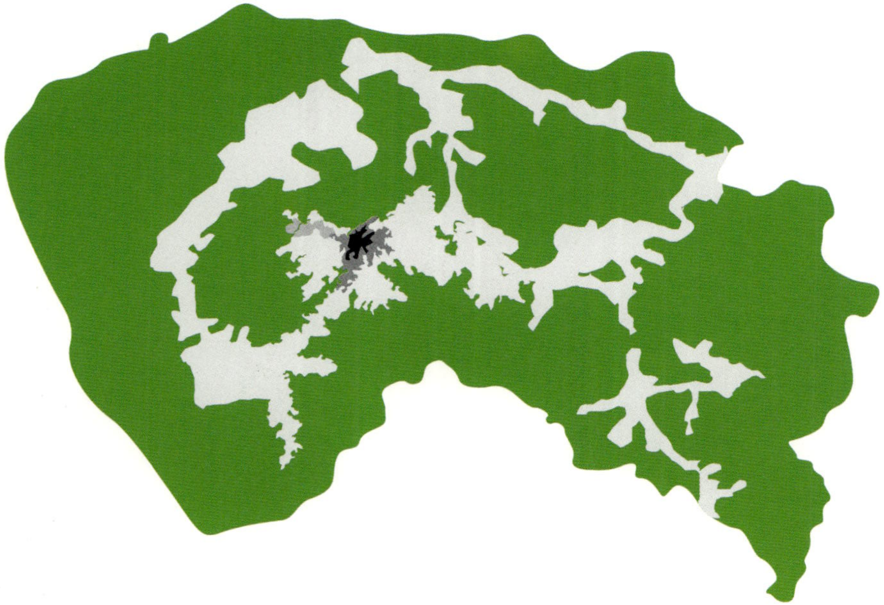

DONGGUAN

URBANIZATION OF DONGGUAN

东莞 *城市化*

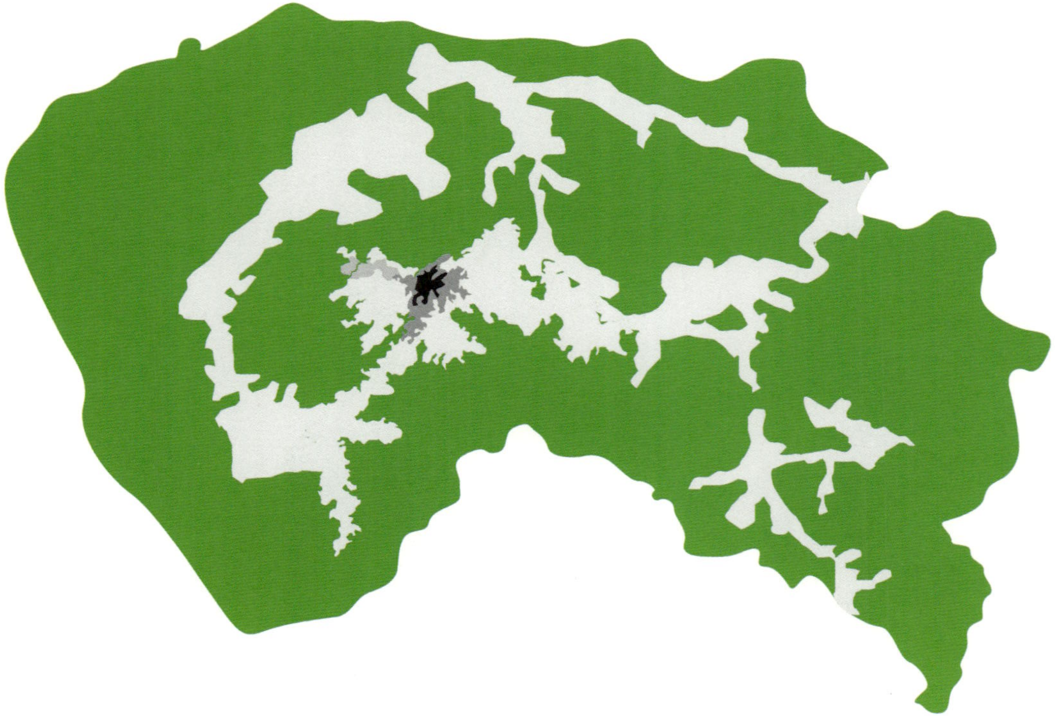

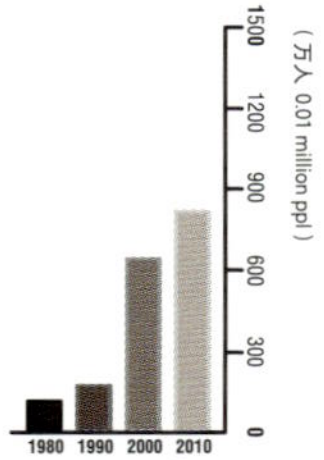

POPULATION
人口

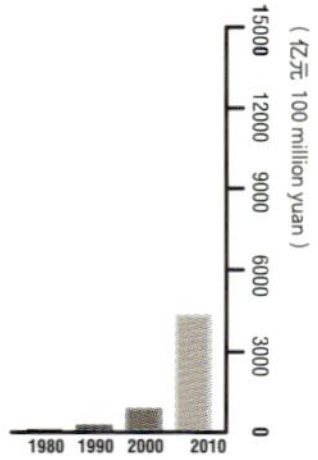

Regional GDP
地区生产总值

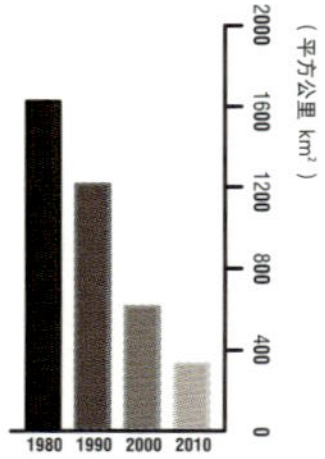

ARABLE land
耕地

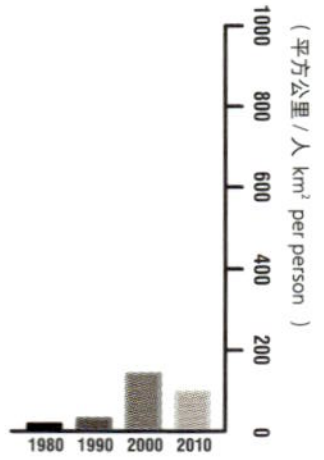

BUILT UP / person
人均建设用地

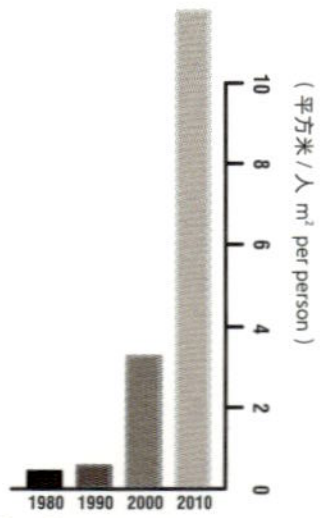

ROAD AREA / person
人均道路面积

2472平方公里

2472km²

AREA

面积

2011年统计数据 Statistics in 2011

SHENZHEN

URBANIZATION OF SHENZHEN

深圳 城市化

SHENZHEN

URBANIZATION OF SHENZHEN

深圳 *城市化*

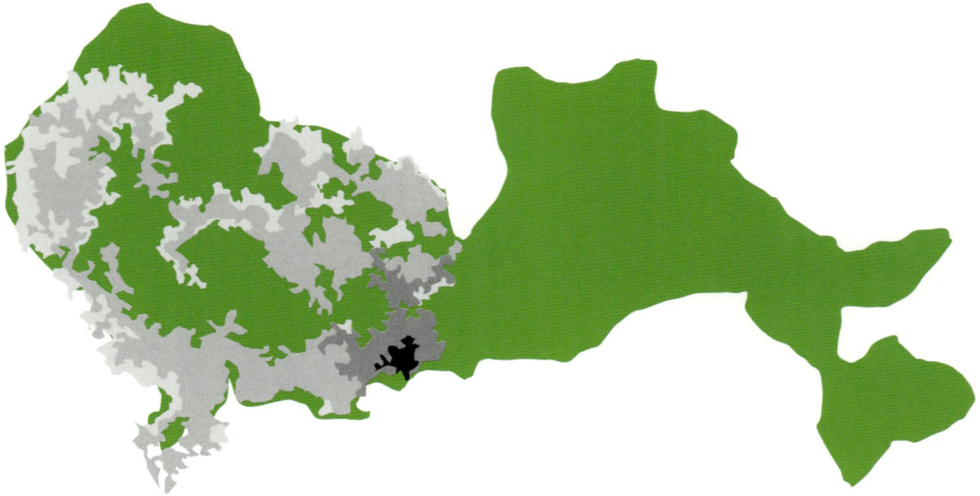

1953平方公里

1953km²

AREA

面积

2011年统计数据 Statistics in 2011

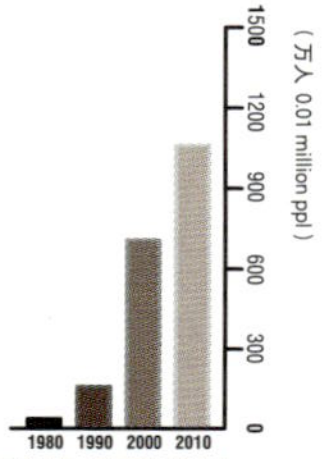

POPULATION

人口

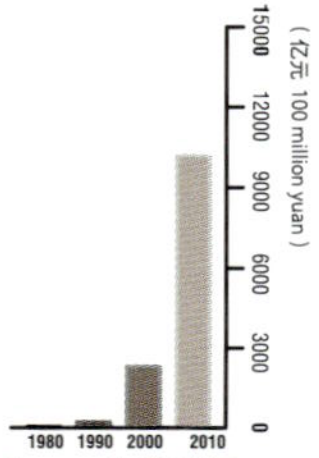

Regional GDP

地区生产总值

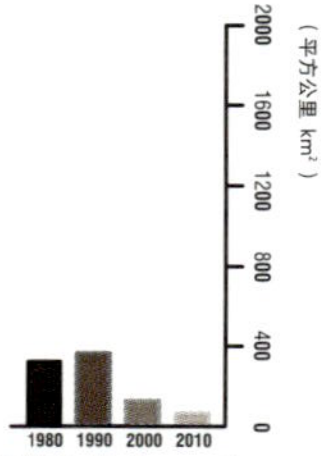

ARABLE land

耕地

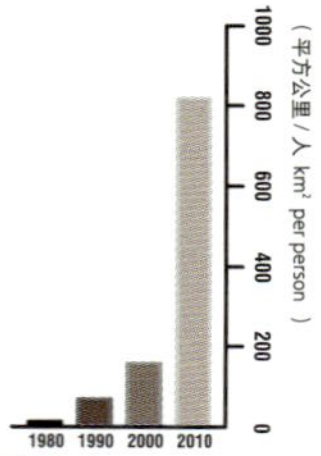

BUILT UP / person

人均建设用地

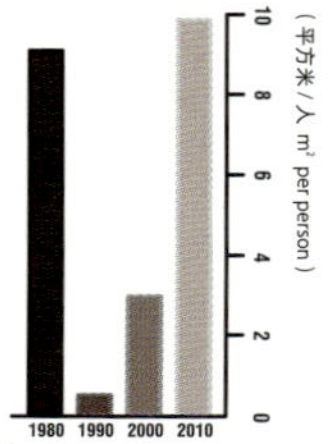

ROAD AREA / person

人均道路面积

HONG KONG

URBANIZATION OF HONG KONG

香港 *城市化*

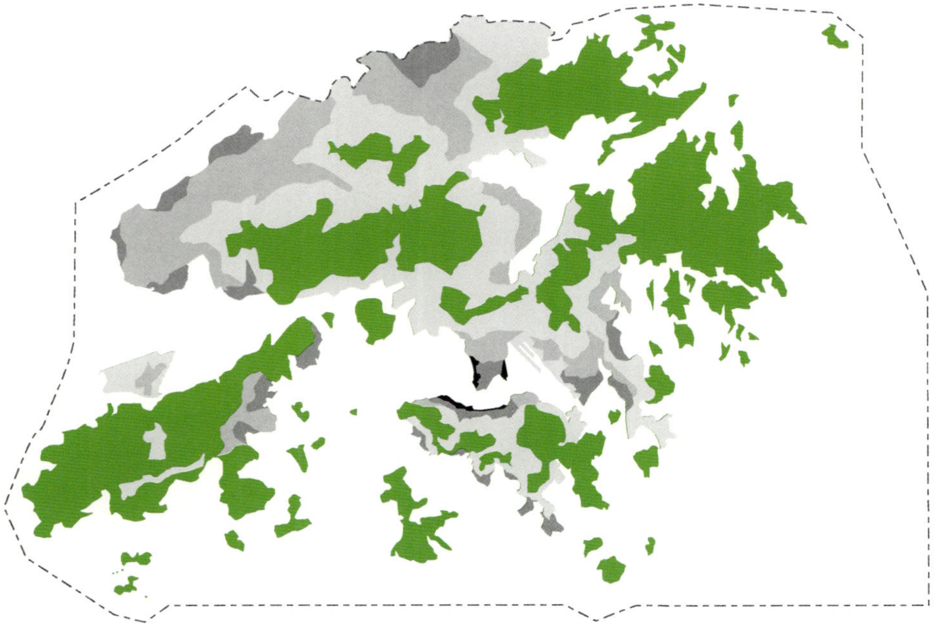

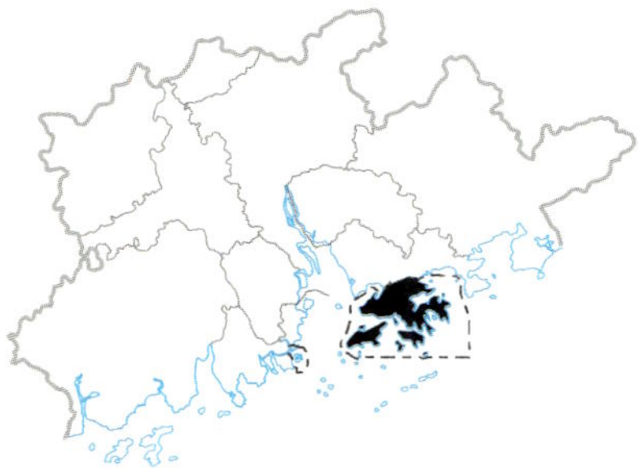

HONG KONG

URBANIZATION OF HONG KONG

香港 *城市化*

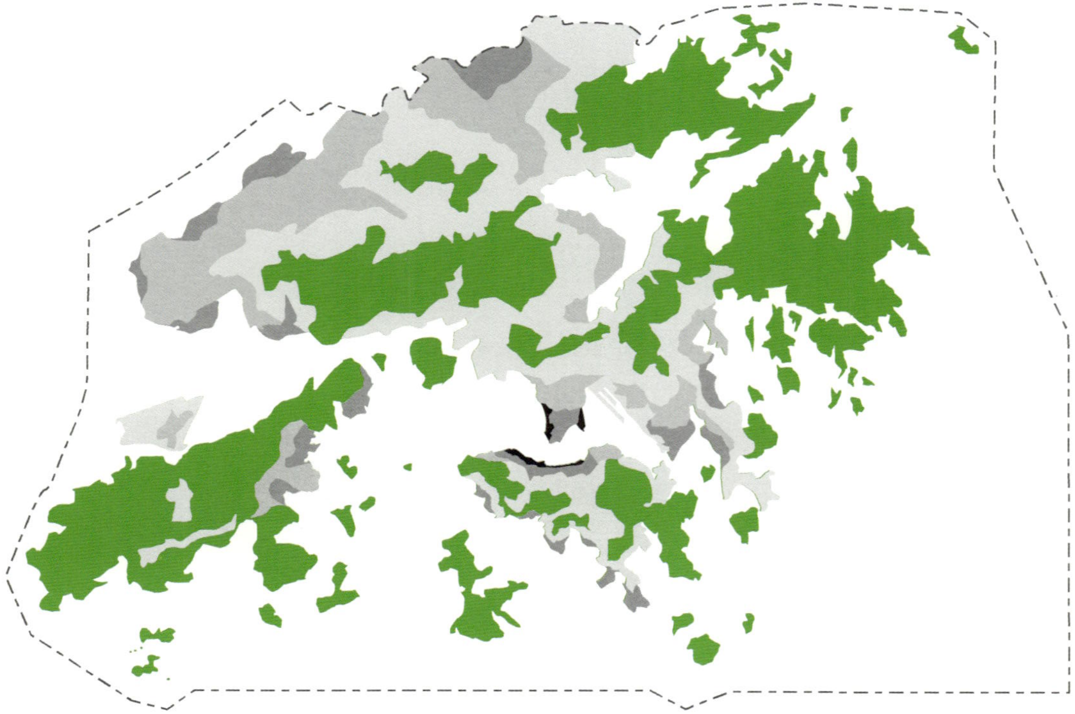

1108平方公里

1108km²

AREA

面积

2011年统计数据 Statistics in 2011

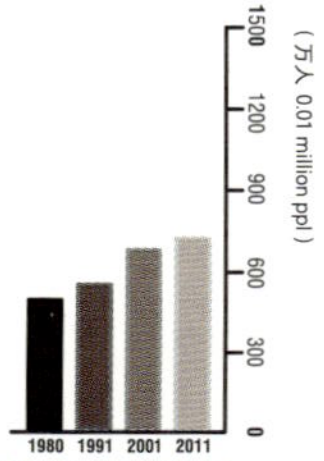

POPULATION
人口

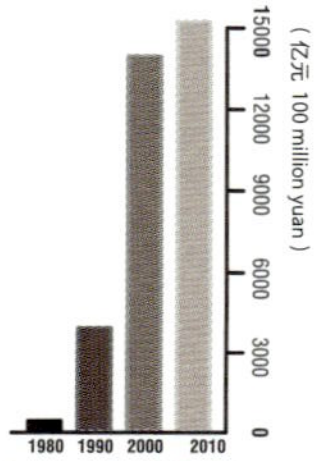

Regional GDP
地区生产总值

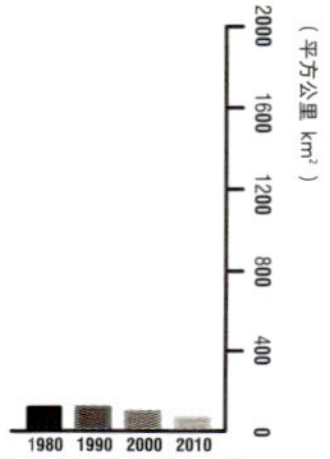

ARABLE land
耕地

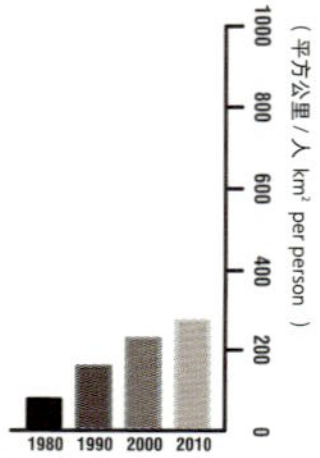

BUILT UP / person
人均建设用地

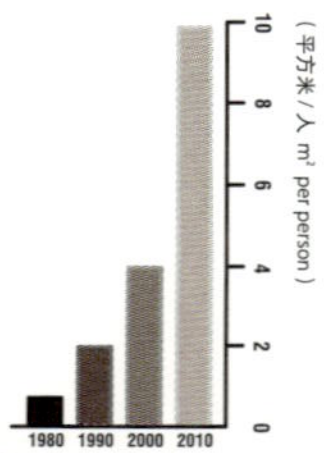

ROAD AREA / person
人均道路面积

GDP

UNBALANCED GROWTH

国内生产总值

增长不均衡

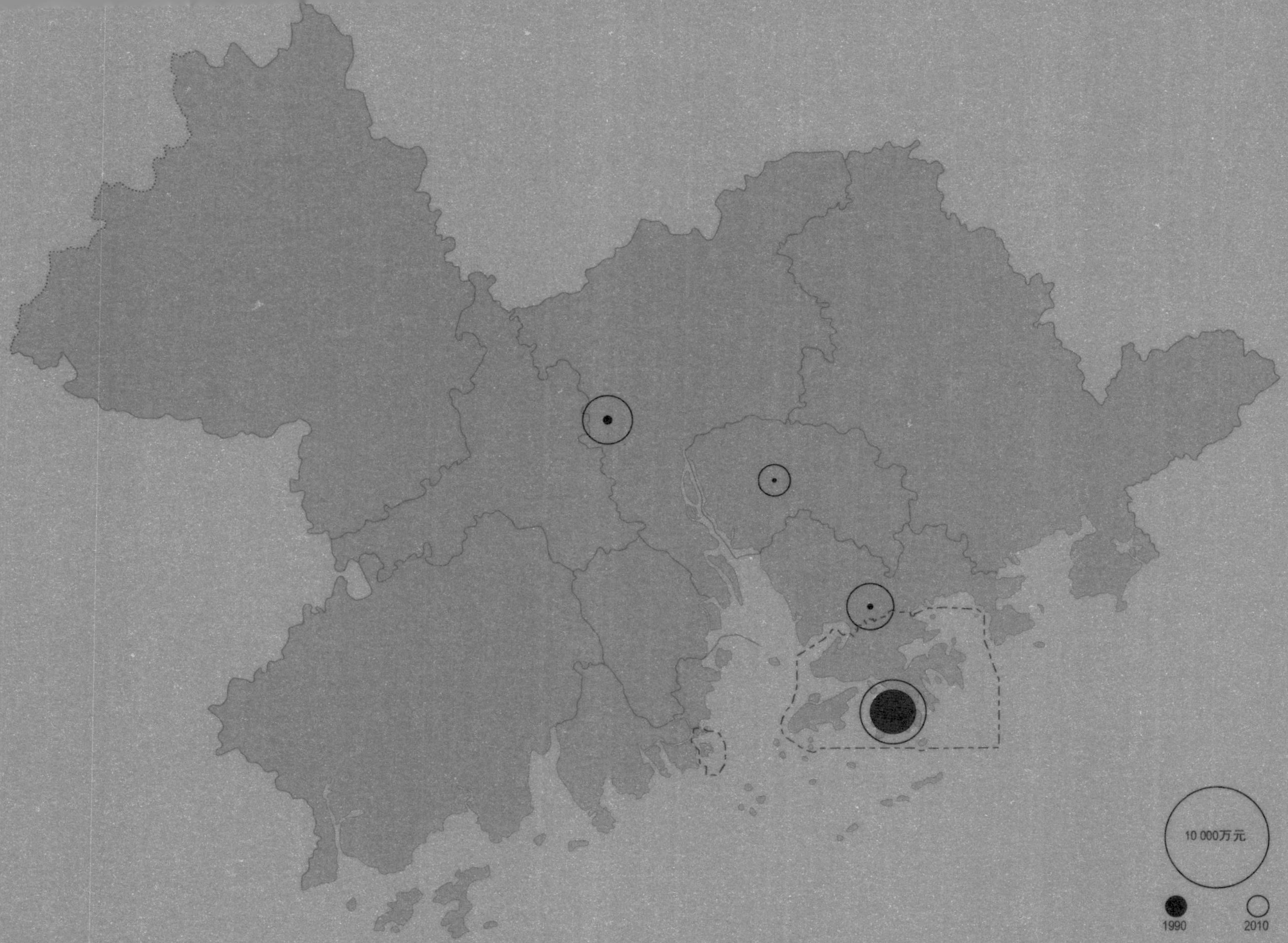

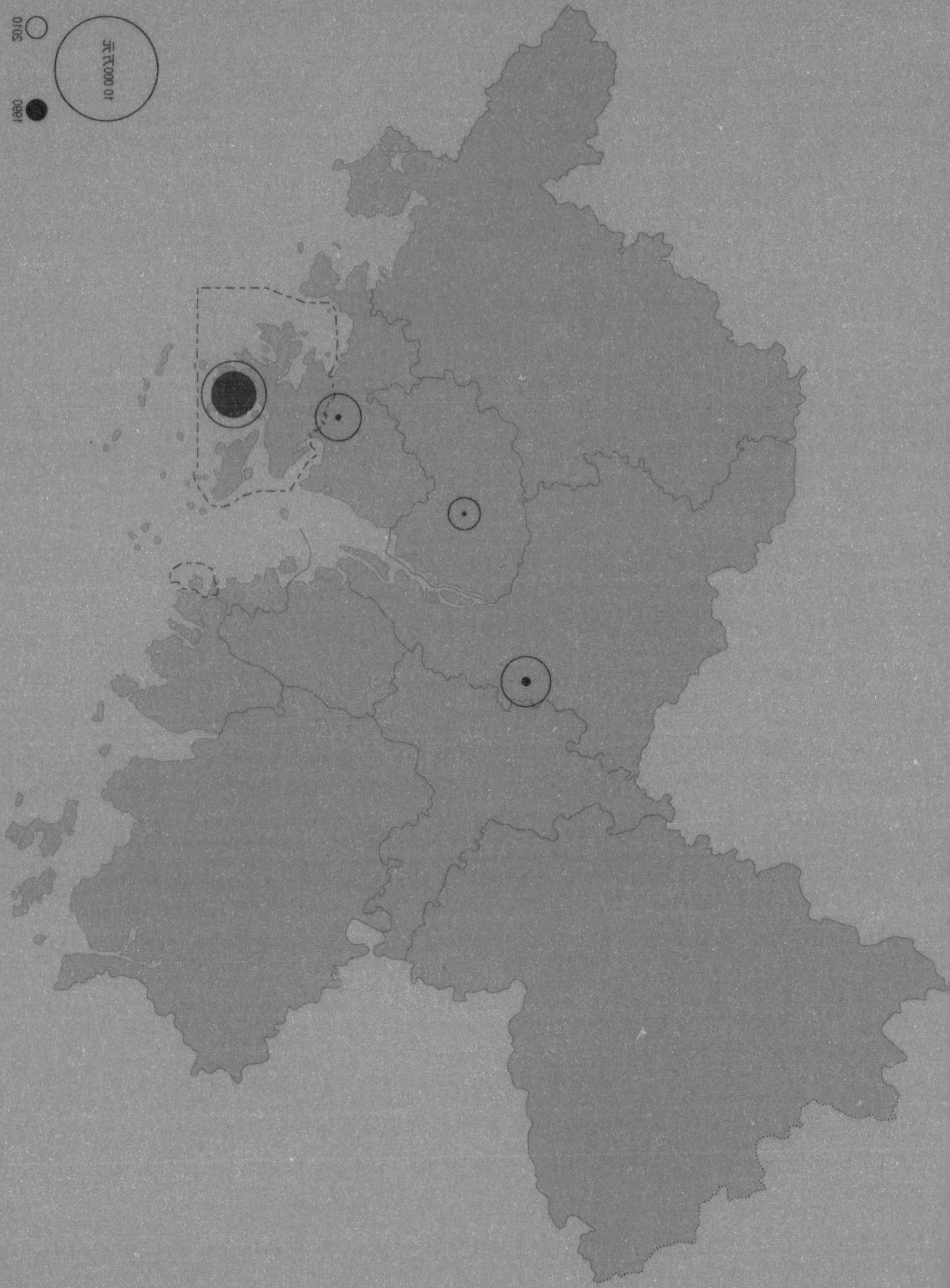

GDP

国内生产总值

增长不均衡

UNBALANCED GROWTH

POPULATION

UNBALANCED GROWTH

人口

增长不均衡

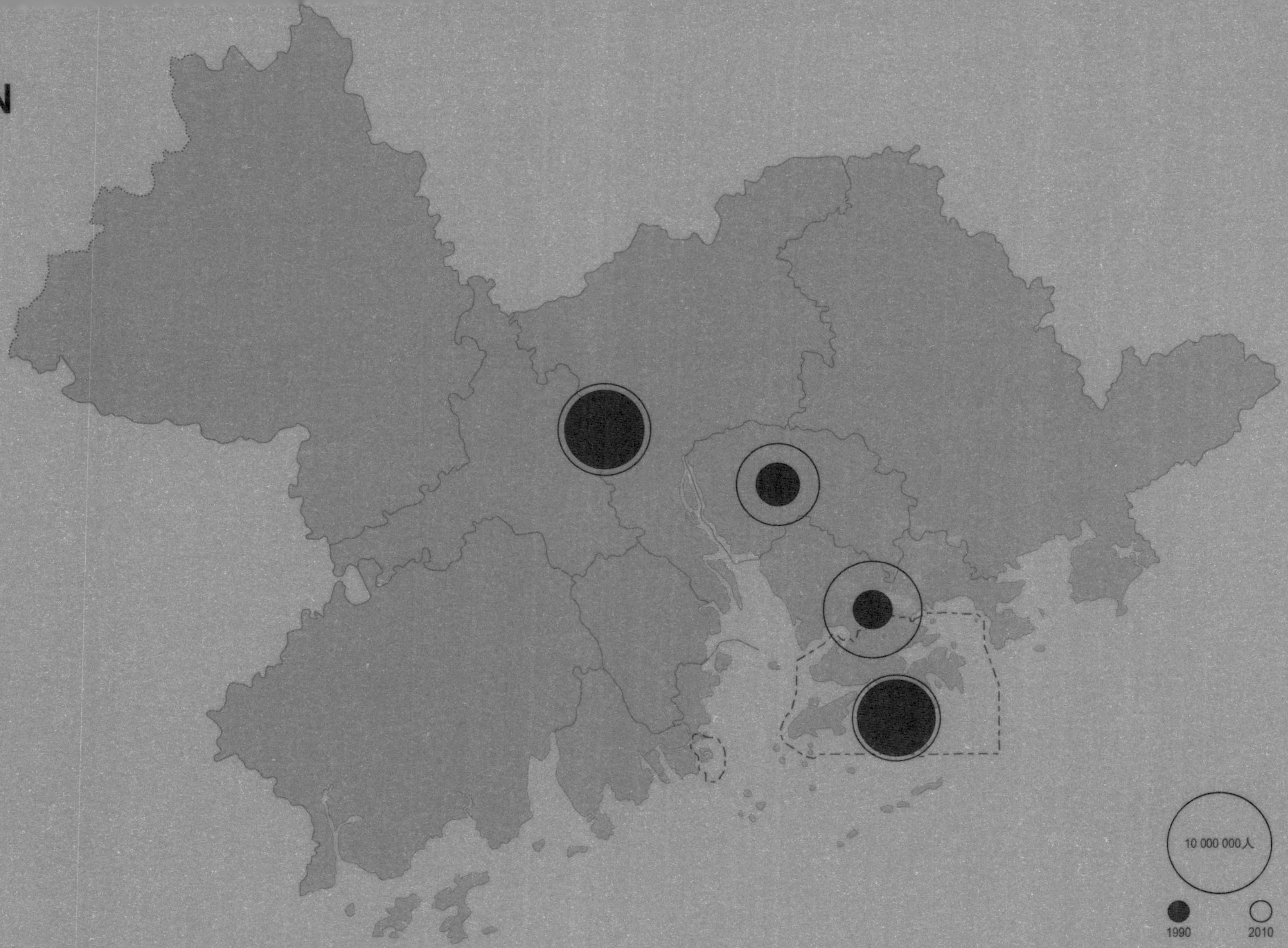

POPULATION
UNBALANCED GROWTH

人口
增长不均衡

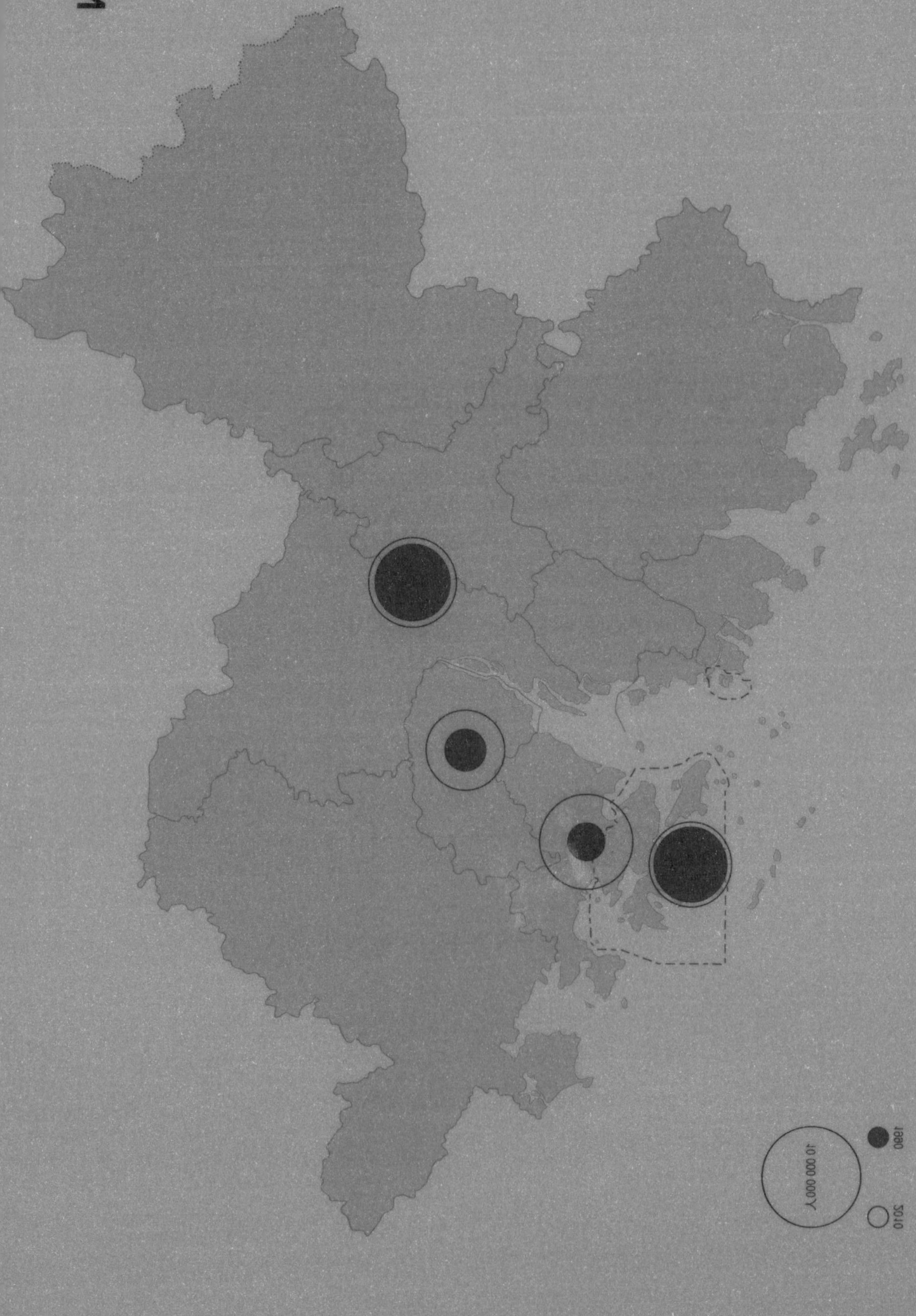

BUILD UP LAND

UNBALANCED GROWTH

建设用地

增长不均衡

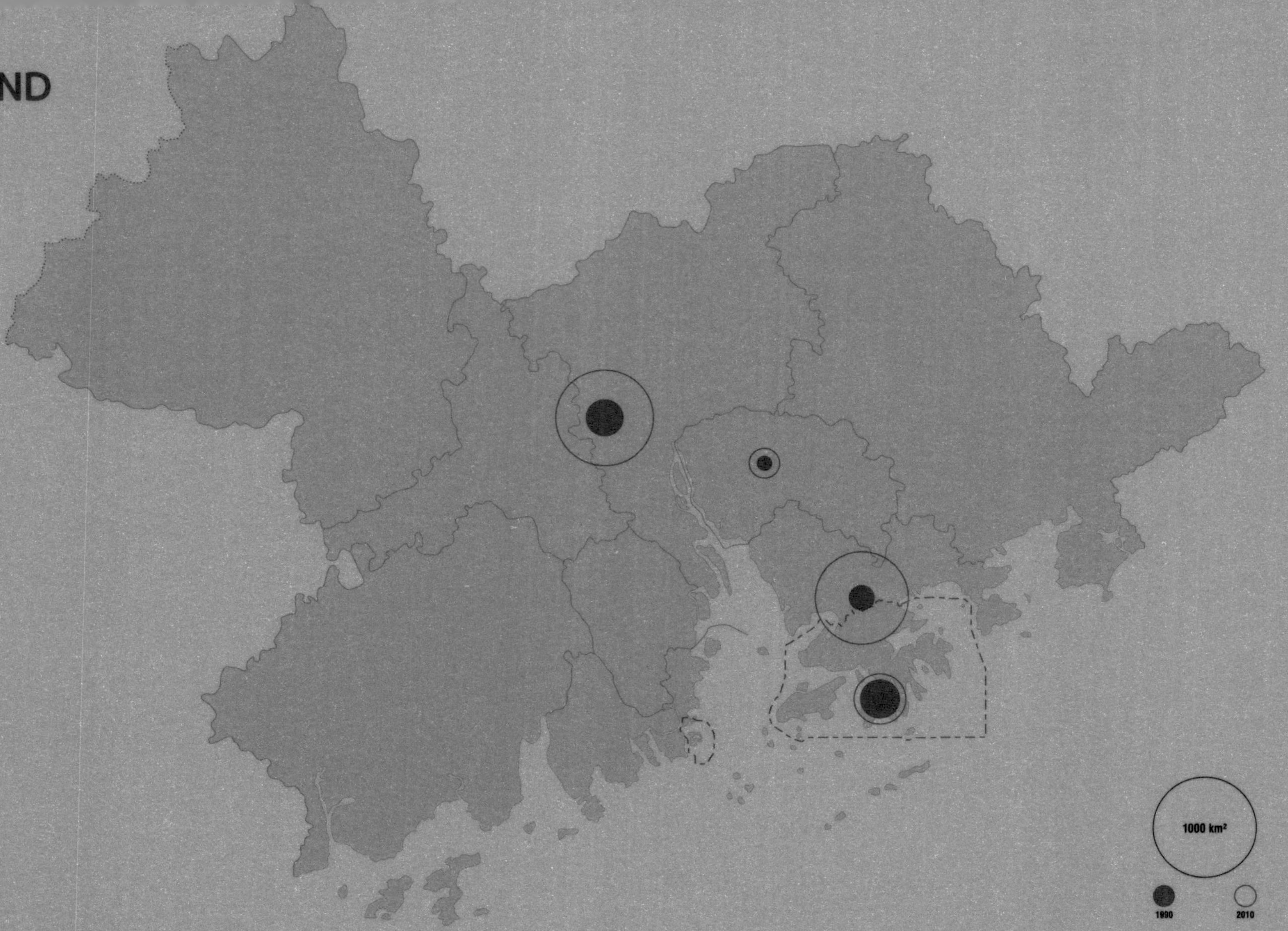

BUILD UP LAND

UNBALANCED GROWTH

建设用地

增长不均衡

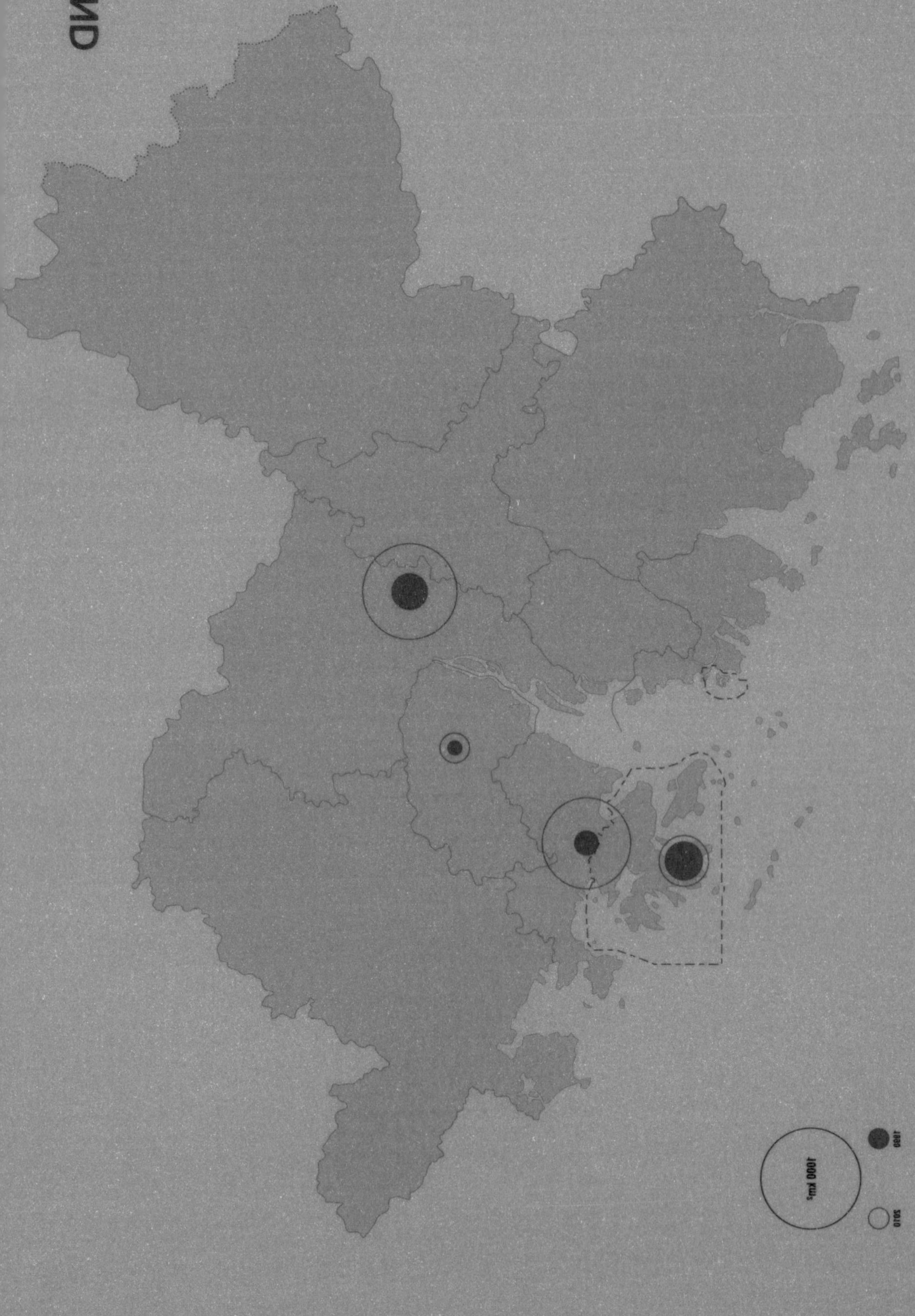

ARABLE LAND

UNBALANCED GROWTH

耕地

增长不均衡

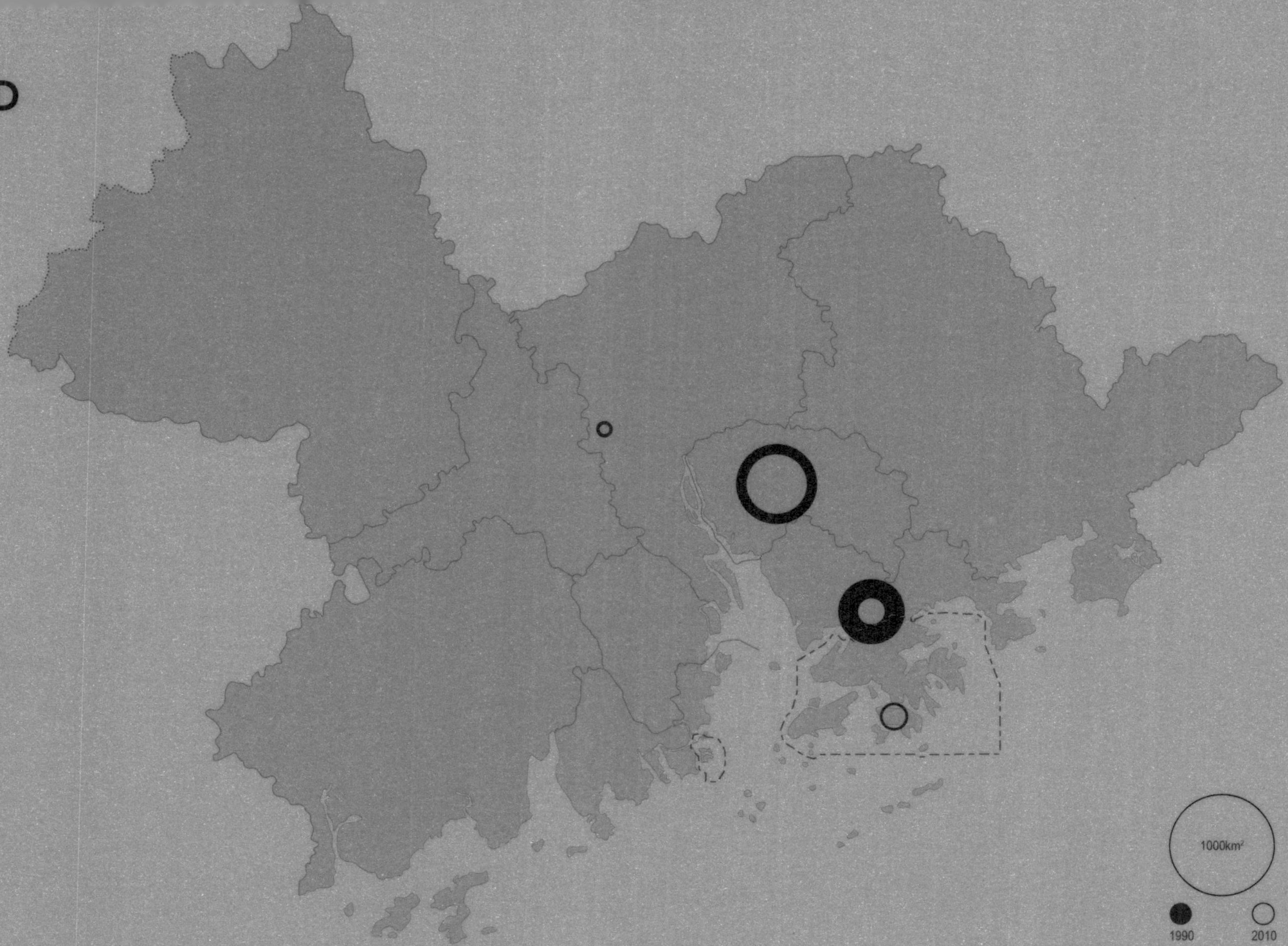

ARABLE LAND

UNBALANCED GROWTH

耕地

增长不均衡

ROAD AREA per person

UNBALANCED GROWTH

人均道路面积

增长不均衡

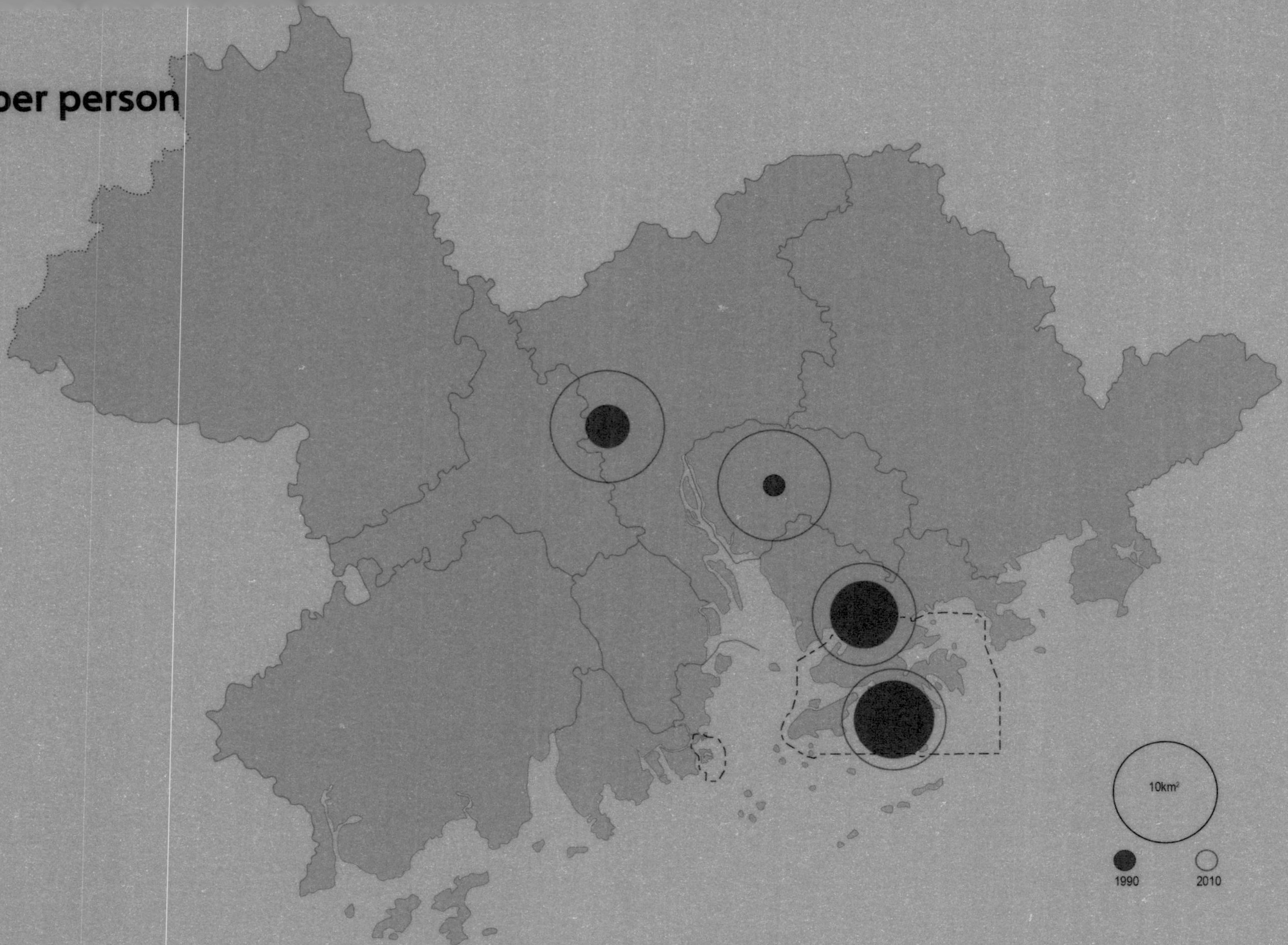

ROAD AREA per person

UNBALANCED GROWTH

人均道路面积

增长不均衡

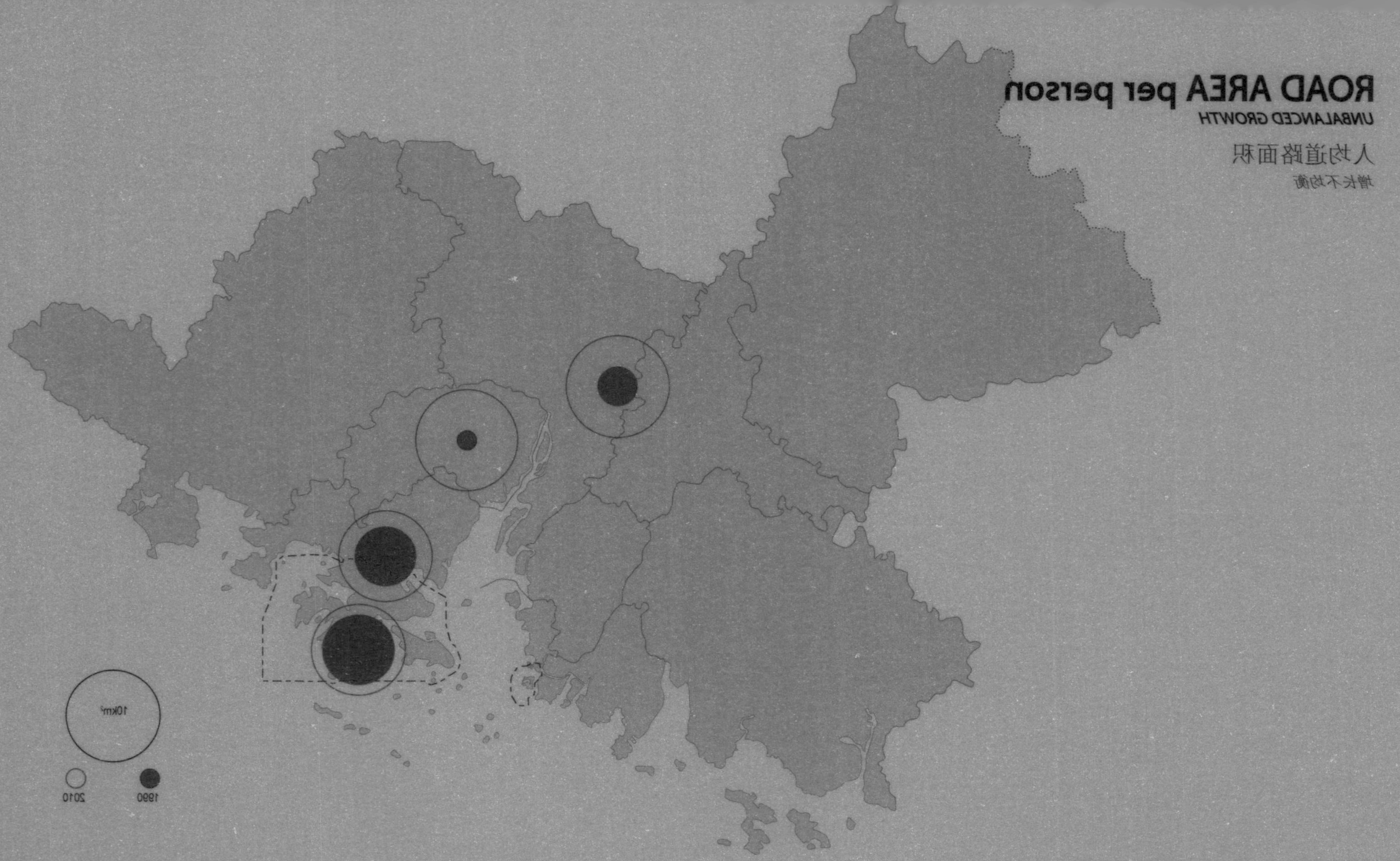

INFRASTRUCTURE 1.0

WATER WAY INFRASTRUCTURE

基础设施1.0

水路基础设施

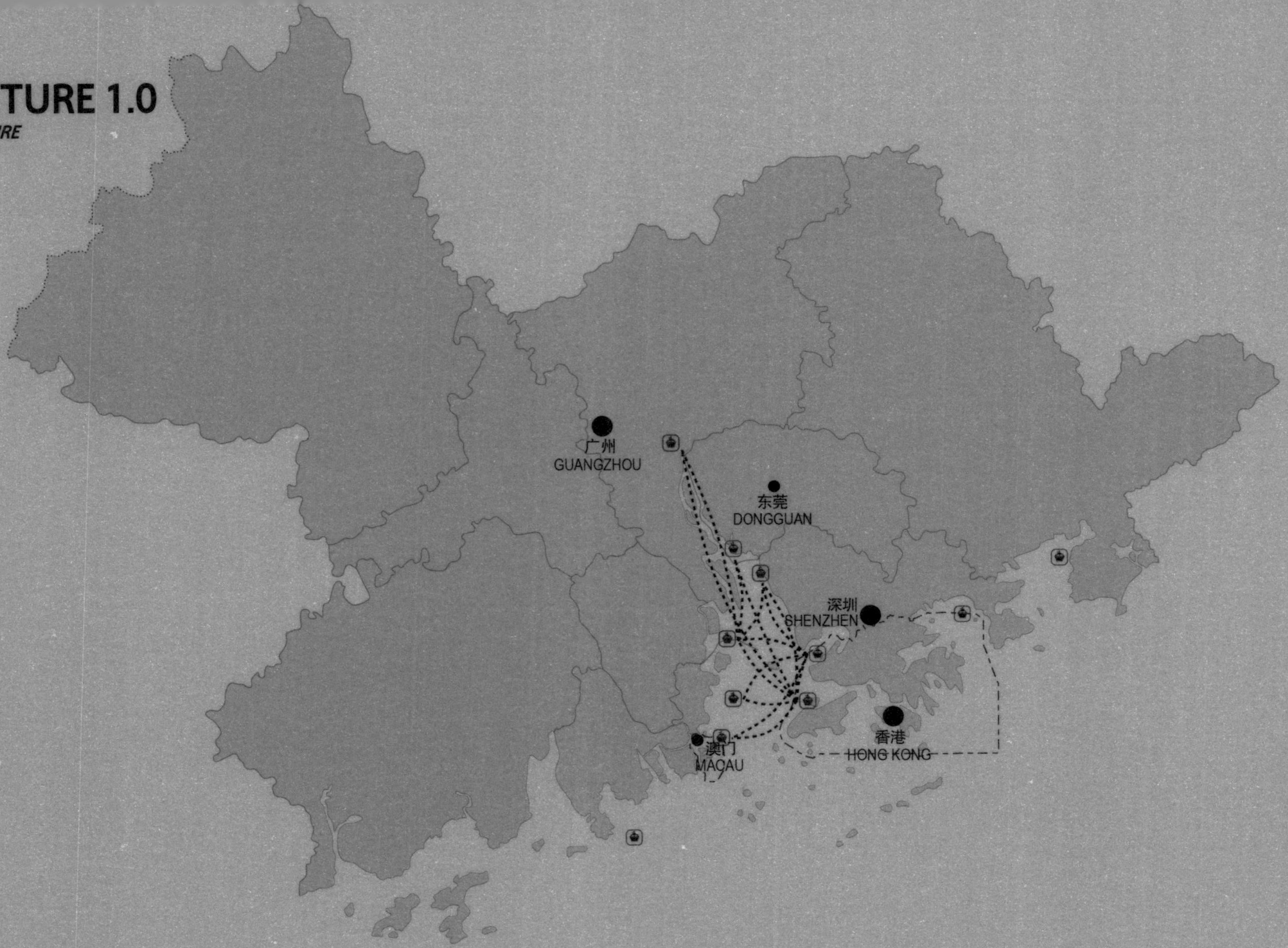

INFRASTRUCTURE 1.0

WATER WAY INFRASTRUCTURE

基础设施1.0

水路基础设施

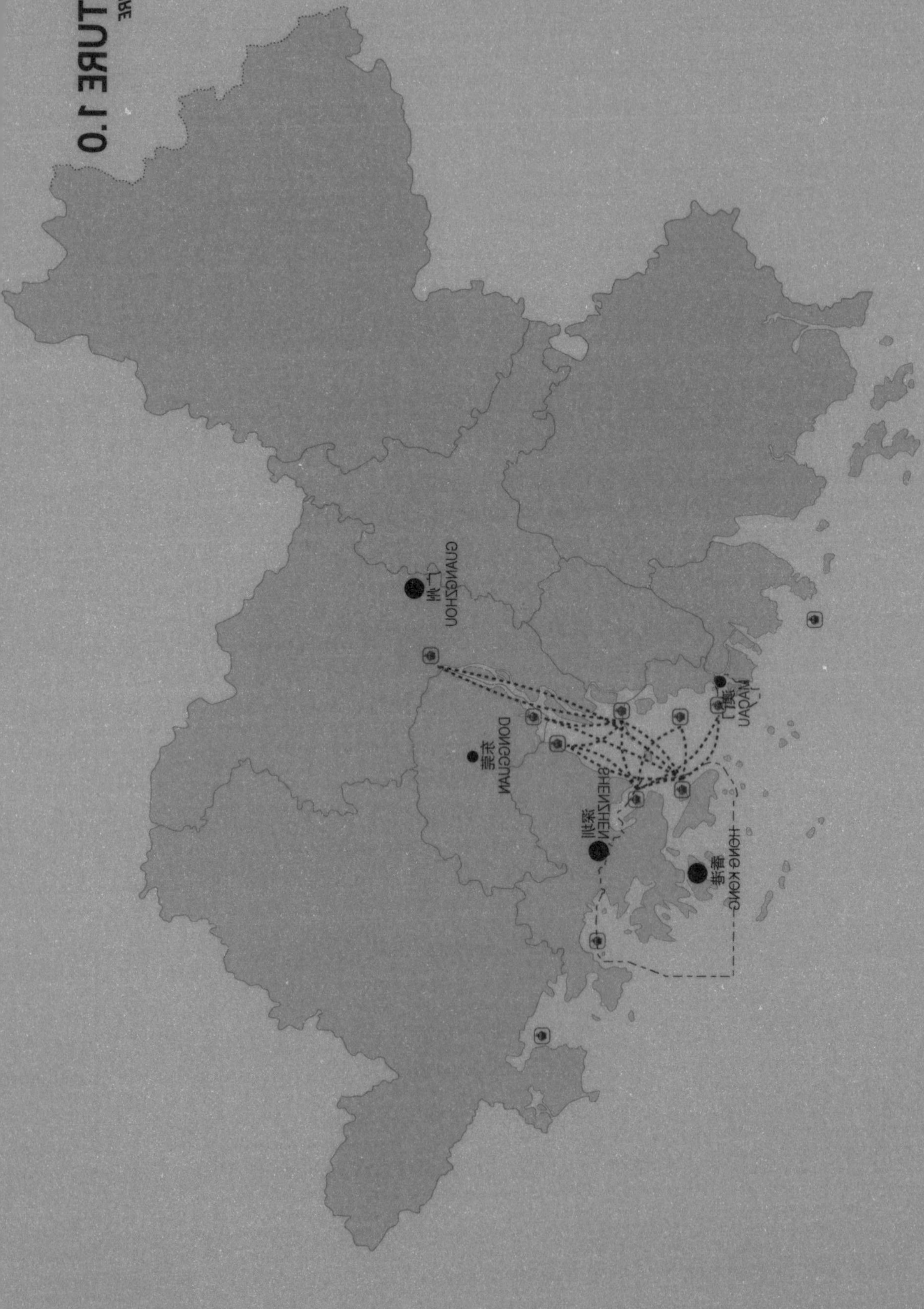

INFRASTRUCTURE 1.0

ROAD WAY INFRASTRUCTURE

基础设施1.0

道路基础设施

INFRASTRUCTURE 1.0
ROAD WAY INFRASTRUCTURE

基础设施1.0
道路基础设施

INFRASTRUCTURE 1.0

RAIL WAY INFRASTRUCTURE

基础设施1.0

铁路基础设施

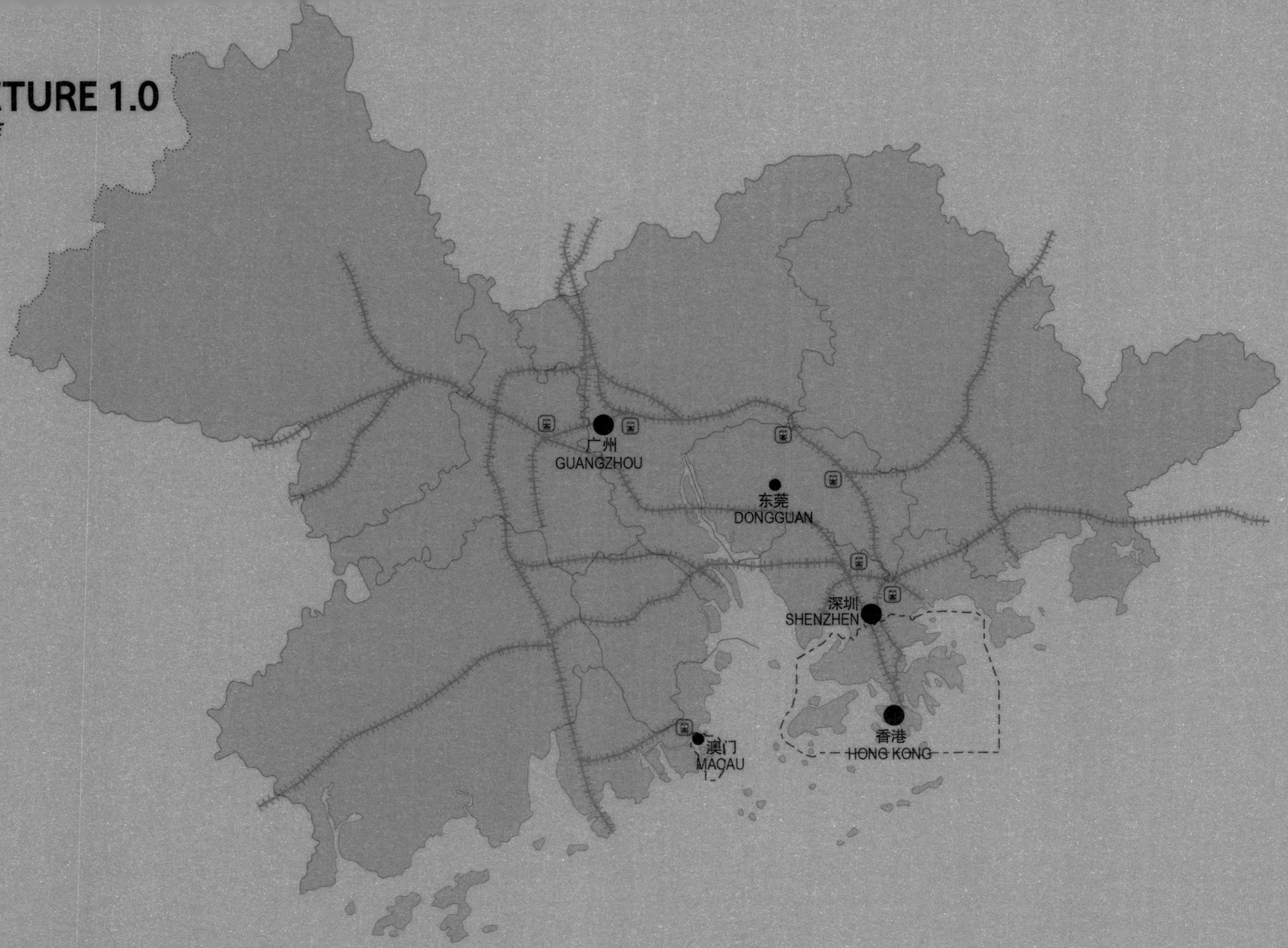

INFRASTRUCTURE 1.0

RAIL WAY INFRASTRUCTURE

基础设施1.0

铁路基础设施

INFRASTRUCTURE 1.0

AIR WAY INFRASTRUCTURE

基础设施1.0

航空基础设施

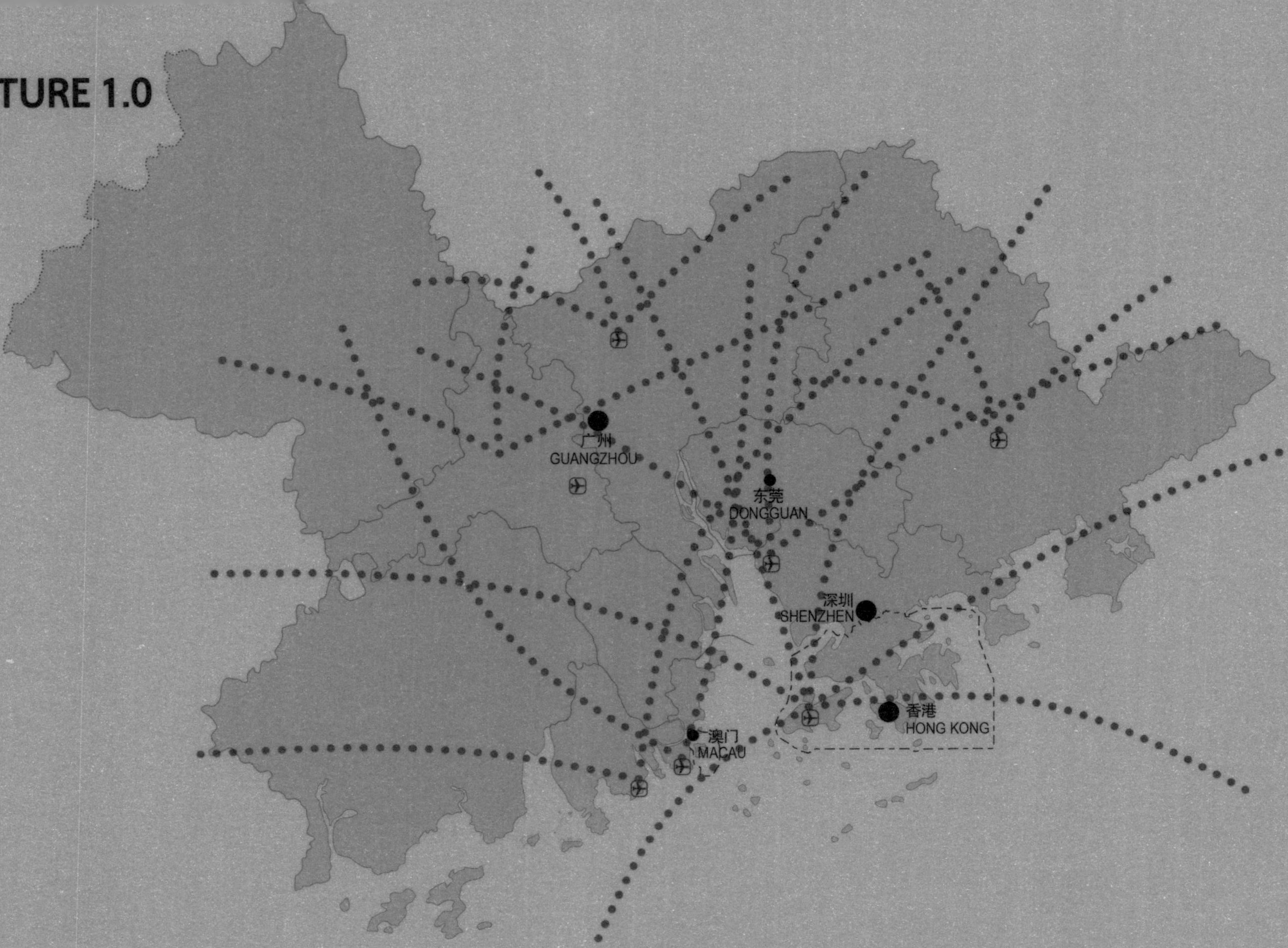

INFRASTRUCTURE 1.0

AIR WAY INFRASTRUCTURE

基础设施1.0

航空基础设施

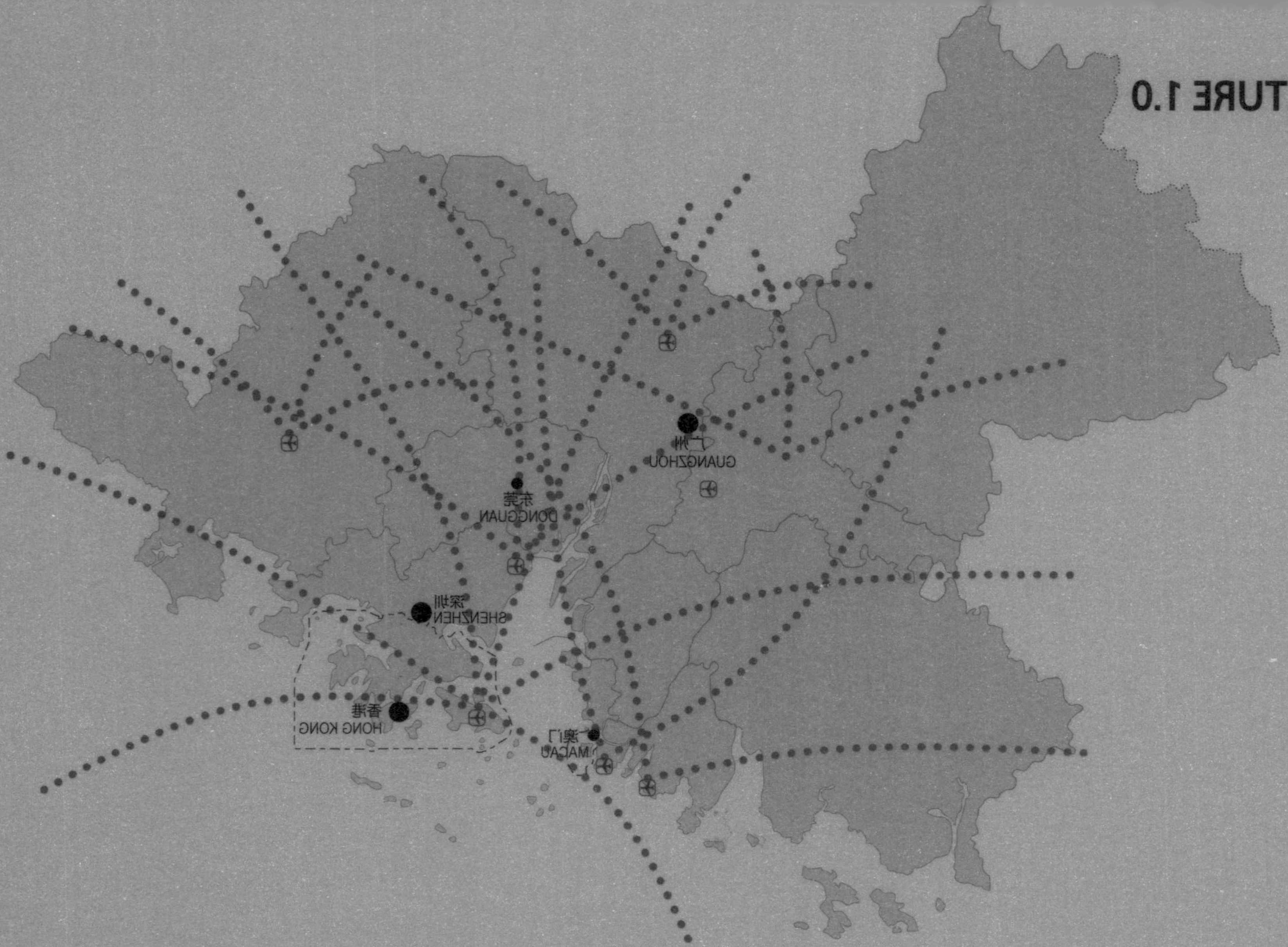

INFRASTRUCTURE 1.0

PHYSICAL WIRED CONNECTIVITY

基础设施1.0

实体连接

INFRASTRUCTURE 1.0

PHYSICAL WIRED CONNECTIVITY

基础设施1.0

实体连接

INFRASTRUCTURE 1.5

VIRTUAL WIRED CONNECTIVITY (FIX PHONE & INTERNET)

基础设施1.5

虚拟连接（固定电话&互联网）

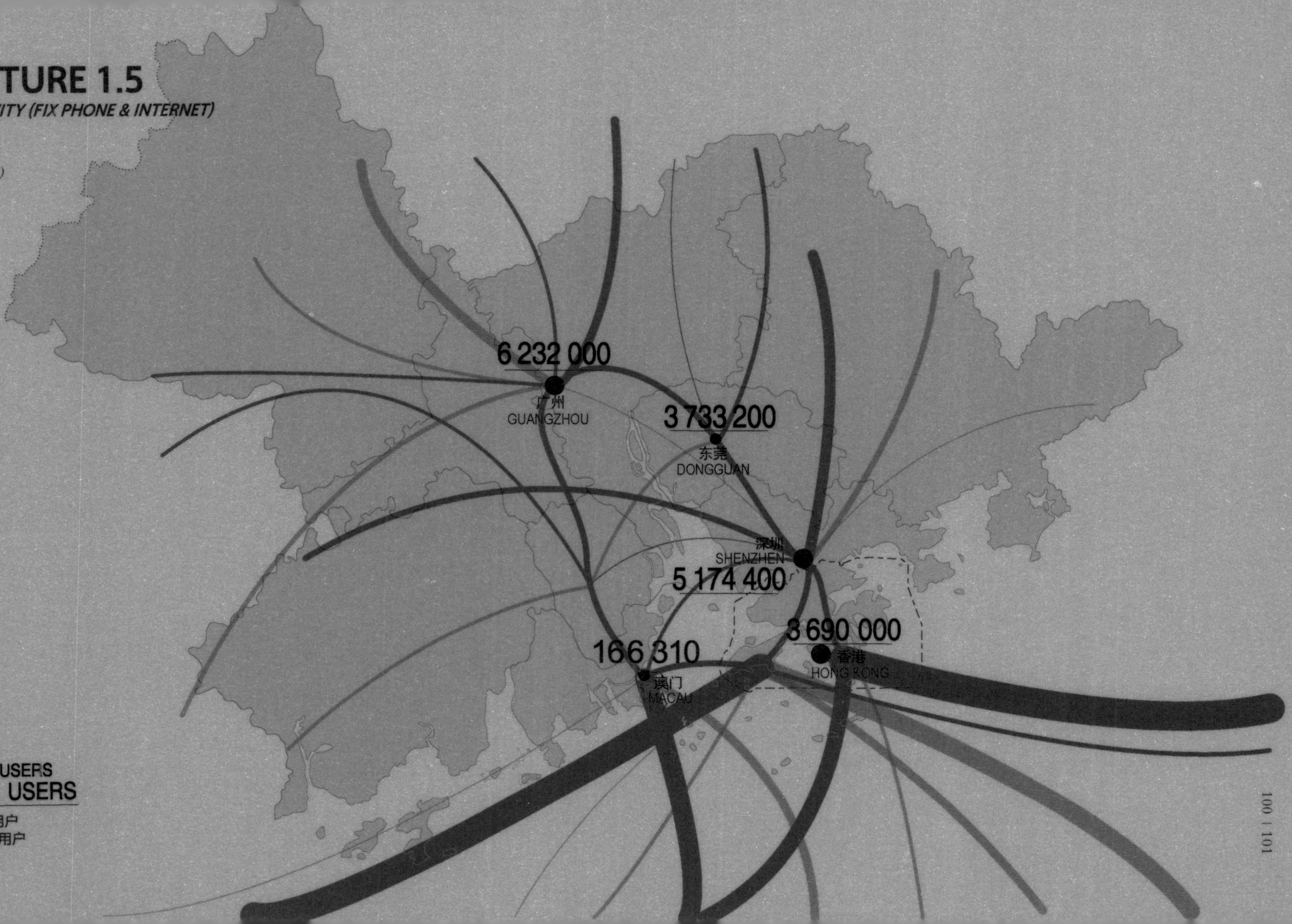

INTERNET USERS

FIX PHONE USERS

互联网用户

固定电话用户

INFRASTRUCTURE 1.5

VIRTUAL WIRED CONNECTIVITY (FIX PHONE & INTERNET)

基础设施1.5

虚拟连接（固定电话&互联网）

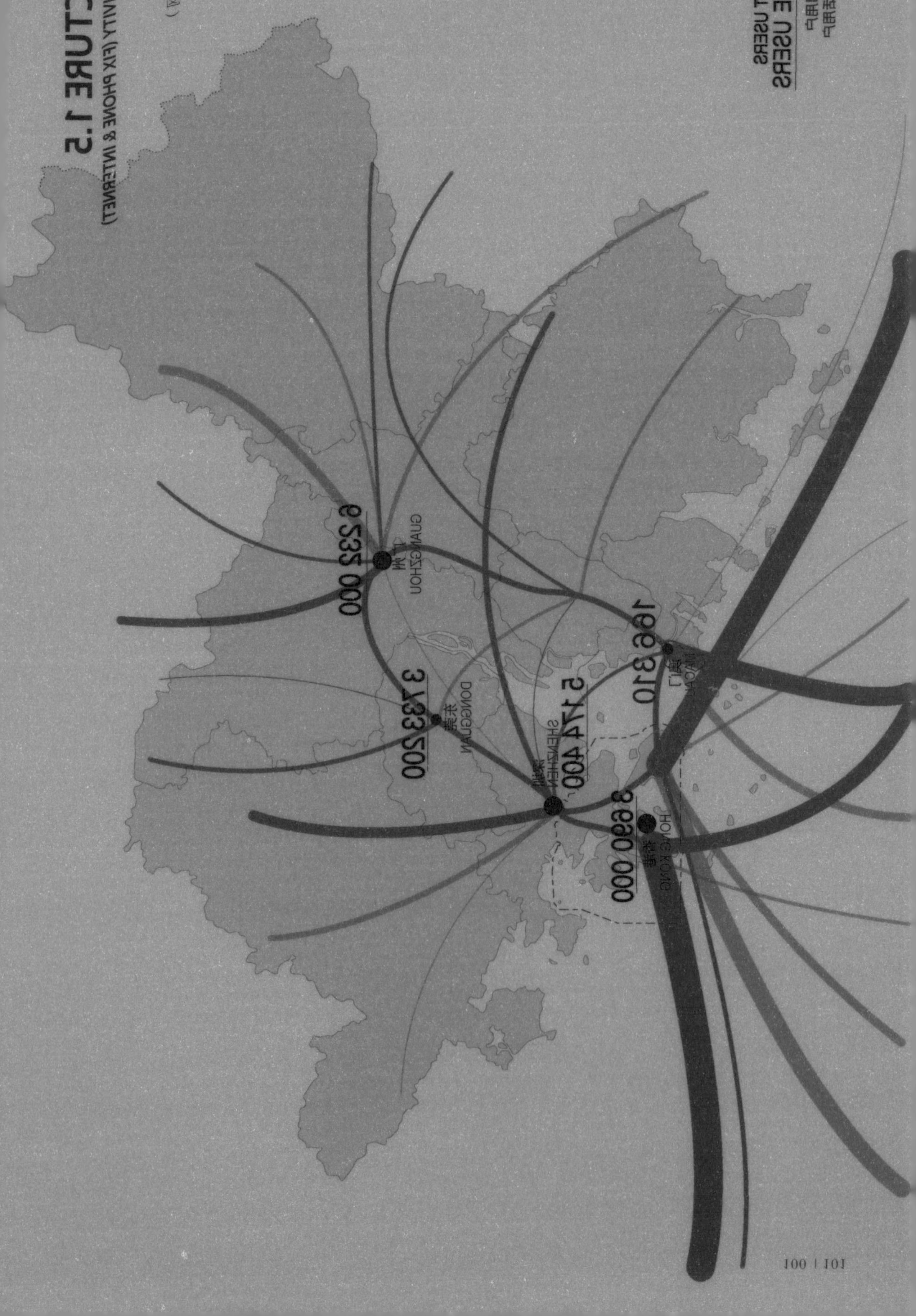

2011年统计数据 Statistics

INFRASTRUCTURE 2.0

VIRTUAL WIRELESS CONNECTIVITY (MOBILE PHONES)

基础设施2.0

虚拟无线连接（移动电话）

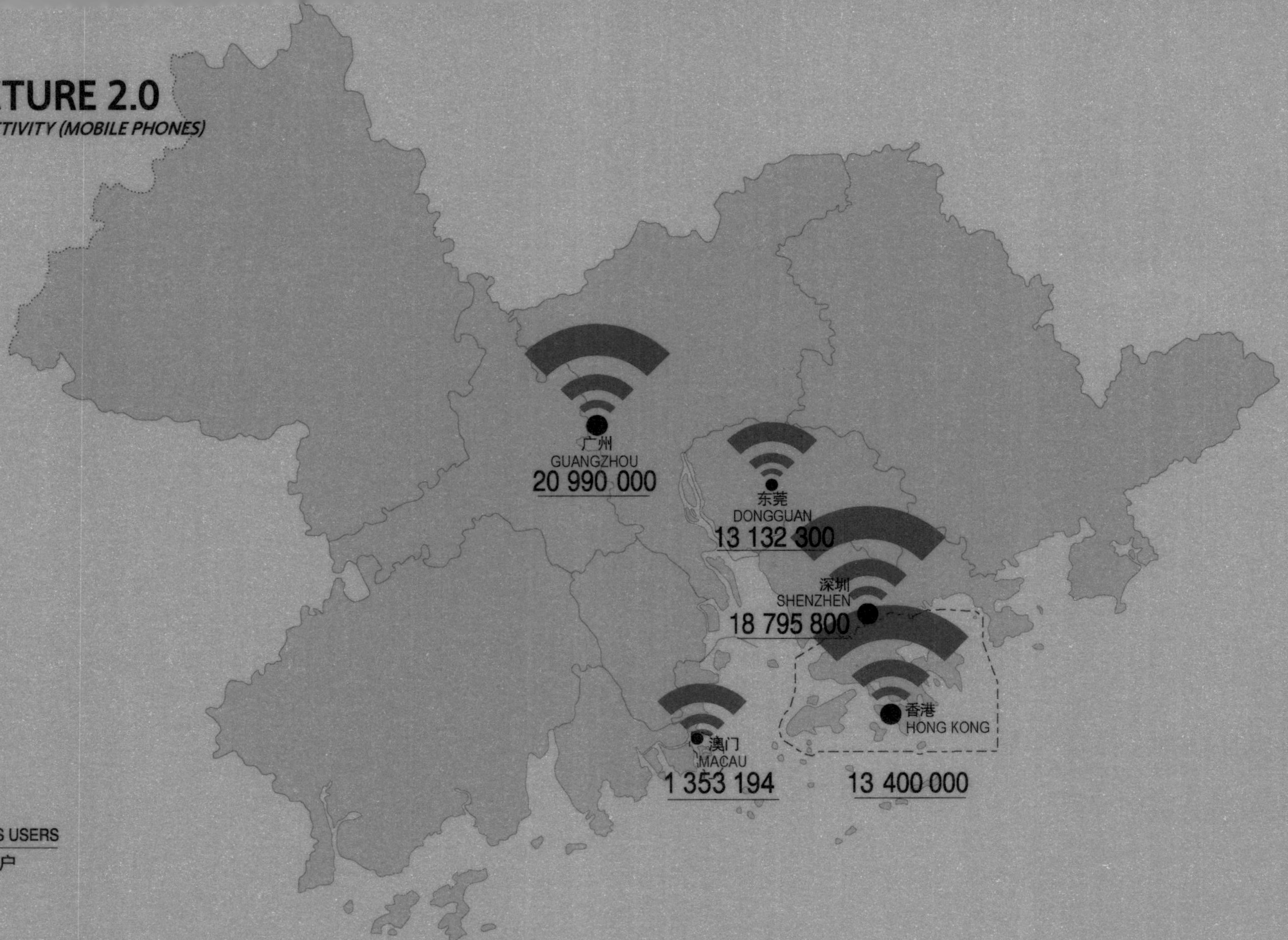

MOBILE PHONES USERS

移动电话用户

INFRASTRUCTURE 2.0

VIRTUAL WIRELESS CONNECTIVITY (MOBILE PHONES)

基础设施2.0

虚拟无线连接（移动电话）

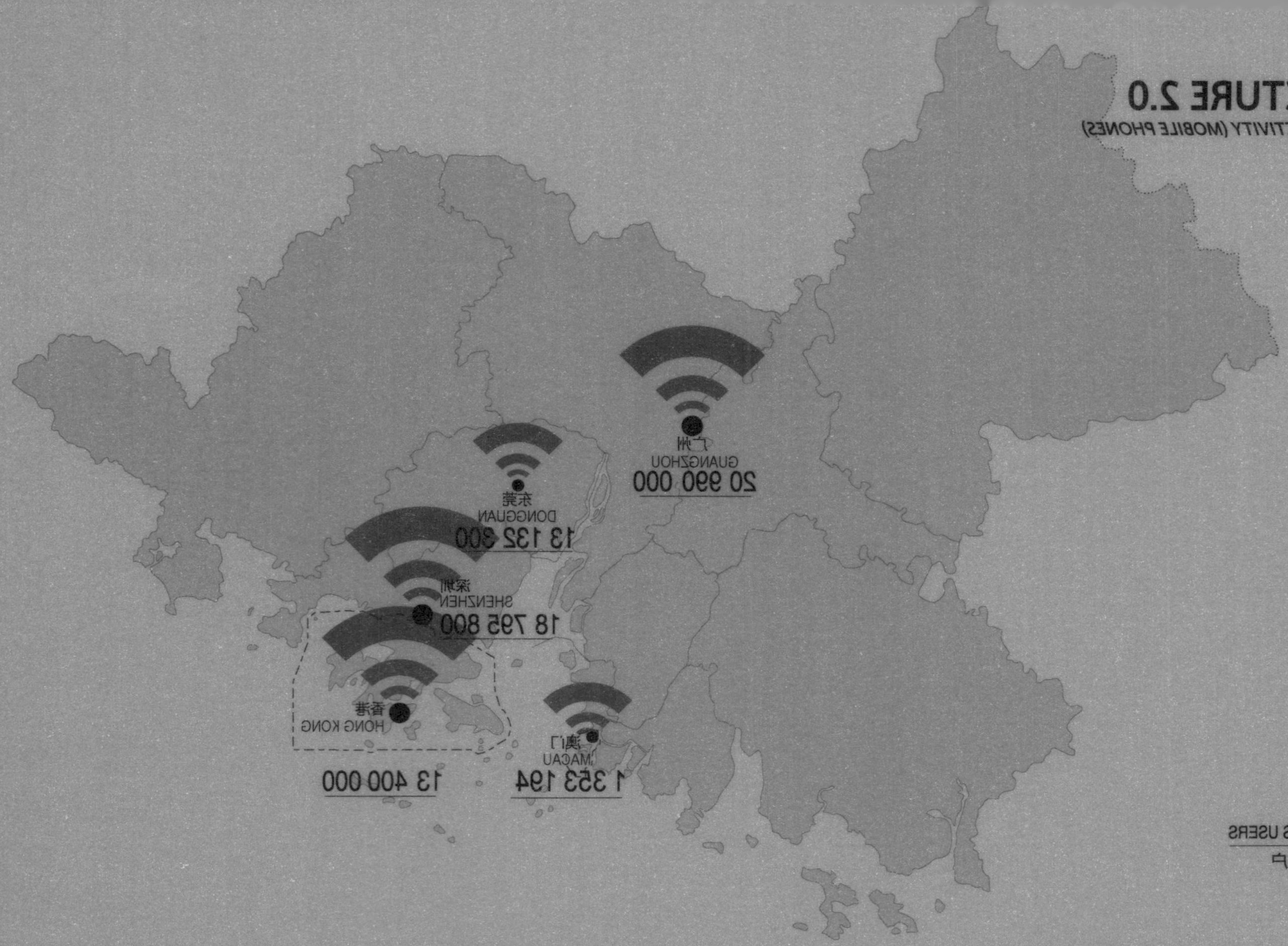

2011年统计年鉴 Statistics

INFRASTRUCTURE 3.0

PHYSICAL + VIRTUAL CONNECTIVITY = ?

基础设施3.0

实体+虚拟连接=?

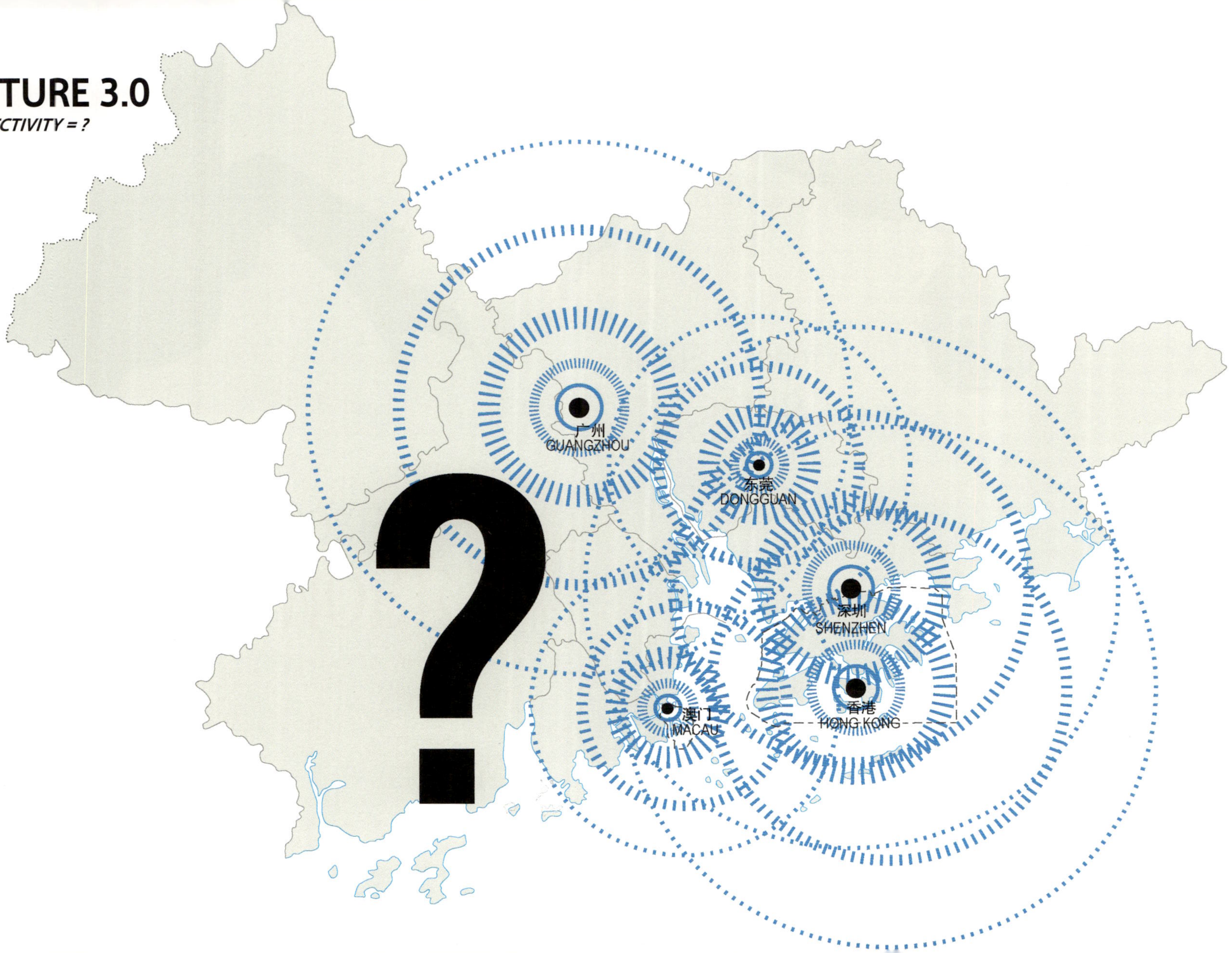

WHAT IS MORE?

什么是“多”？

《Domus国际中文版》，2011年9月，第 57期

关于珠三角的未来

刘珩 + 雷姆·库哈斯

15年前，库哈斯的《大跃进：哈佛大学设计学院的城市项目》和《普通城市》为珠三角地区带来了全新的思考模式，之后OMA在这一地区获得了一系列的成功。他与刘珩的这次对话揭示了他近来的思考。

刘珩：你早先的作品谈论了许多关于未来的内容；近些年，你开始对保护（preservation）产生兴趣了。你认为未来和保护之间存在着什么样的关联呢？

雷姆·库哈斯：这是两个矛盾因素。一方面在于保护本身——它本身是一个怀着对20世纪60—90年代社会化建筑的憎恨而产生的大型运动。有意思的是，和保护一样，这种憎恨也全球化了，可是它不过是代表了我们对建筑意识形态的一种愤恨。鉴别这一现象十分重要，因为它影响着每一个国家，包括中国。它的影响同样会波及到建筑师工作的多种可能性上—— 一旦社会化建筑被消除，就没有人能够说“这里曾经有人在做社会住宅”了。另一方面，保护的范围竟是如此巨大，大到已然成为决定我们未来的最重要因素之一。因而我认为，保护作为未来的元素之一，是十分重要的。在最近一次以保护为主题、名为“Cronocaos”的展览中，我曾明确表明：我们的未来一方面将会表现为彻底的变革，另一方面则会带有彻底的停滞和凝固。因此对我们而言，认真思考如何能够去适应这样一种某些部分保持不变、某些部分又不断变化的建成环境是非常重要的。通过研究，我们已发现地球12%的表面是存在于某种保护体制下的。由此，这些地方便与“日常的”世界隔绝了，而这在历史上是从没有发生过的。因此必须要有理论来支持这种现象。

刘珩：这也是我们3月在广州举办“三角四方”学术论坛的初衷。如何看待保护问题？前30年快速城市化让中国许多城市的历史风貌归零。无论是经过2000年发展历史的广州还是经历30年建设的深圳，都属于你讲的“彻底的变革”、颠覆性的30年，而近几年“保护”的声音越来越响亮，是因为大家过了这么多年，突然觉得好像又缺了什么。但是否是“彻底的停滞和凝固”呢？30年后更多是有旧有新，而且是一种无秩序的“匀质”状态。我们也对这种“半新半旧”状态提出了用“行进中的历史博物馆”立场去看待。是否把动态的保护与保护中的发展作为设计策略去应对未来呢？（在西方）是什么时候开始，保护运动开始变得如此重要了呢？

雷姆·库哈斯：作为一个全球体系，它始于20世纪70年代，与市场经济的急速扩张同一时期。保护运动的爆炸式迸发是经济爆炸式发展的一部分。这也是我们现在正在探寻的一种关联。

刘珩：在中国过去的30年似乎并没有关联性。“彻底的变革”似乎源于对建筑意识形态的愤恨和反弹。对中国发生的关于保护的讨论，你有什么样的看法？

雷姆·库哈斯：我不得不承认我对这个并不是特别的了解，不足以发表评论。我曾试图参与其中，到现在而言，参与其中也仍是有趣有益的。从某种程度上讲，在尝试用理论来阐释之前，我们一直是用实践者的角度来思考的。香港西九龙文化区项目便反映了我们所构建的理论，可以提供相关联的参考。

刘珩：在保护工程中，你觉得什么是最具挑战性的？

雷姆·库哈斯：对于保护而言，最大的困难之一就是人们从不讨论如何保护某种生活方式，或是某一社会维度，或是某种互动形式。而且很多人还没准备好接受这样的想法。

刘珩：你们的西九龙文化区项目已明确开始往这个方向努力。但内地还依然停留在物质形态和硬件的保护上，也许“保护”作为整体的课题在中国需要系统的讨论。现在让我们回到你早期的珠三角研究中来，15年前你写作了《大跃进：哈佛大学设计学院的城市项目》和《普通城市》，这两本书对阐明你对这个地区的理解十分重要。现在我们所看到的大多是那时发展的成果。在你眼里真正的发展有多少呢？

雷姆·库哈斯：基本上所有的案例给我的印象都很深刻，特别是在中国，最初的规划已经产生了良好的效果。你可以看看深圳，15年前深圳规划局的办公室就像间店面一样，里面只有4个人，加上几辆自行

车。现在呢？他们在都市实践事务所设计的光鲜亮丽的大楼里办公， 而且他们的确对这个城市产生了巨大的影响。在这15年的时间里，当时看来很疯狂、看似可能失控的珠三角地区如今已借由规划师扳回一局。在我所知的城市里，深圳是一座规划能起到极大作用的城市，并且城市能在很大程度上控制什么会发生、什么不会。

刘珩：深圳规划局被誉为是中国最有进取心、相对独立开明的政府规划部门。

雷姆·库哈斯：我只是将现在的情况和当年对珠三角地区的第一印象相对比。珠三角地区已开始出现一种连续性，开始出现内部的相互调整，而且已经有越来越多的基础设施。所有的这一切都源于规划，以及规划的执行。多年以前，珠江三角洲只是一个没有明确意图的“偶然出现”，而现在它却是有意图、刻意规划了的。

刘珩：你觉得这样好吗？

雷姆·库哈斯：那两本书里我都对城市规划的能力十分怀疑，而现在的情形在一定程度上与那些怀疑相悖，因为你看到了规划成功的证据。不过，规划在很多时候总是缺乏一些远见。

刘珩：中国和珠三角地区发生的一些大事件，如奥运会、亚运会和大运会，都为城市带来了“做新规划”的好理由。但是赛事结束后，下一步又将如何规划呢？每个人都有着不同程度的困惑。如果普通城市是不受限制发展的产物，那么接下去又会发生什么呢？

雷姆·库哈斯：我需要澄清的是，深圳已经不再是一个“普通城市”了。它被规划为具有某种特性的城市，现在已经上升到了另外一个高度了。

刘珩：在中国，建筑师总是认为自己很关键，我们也看到了中国某些城市建筑实践的后果。你怎样看待建筑师在实践中的责任问题？

雷姆·库哈斯：首先，我认为这是个全球性问题，即建筑师只能生产所有建造量中非常少的一部分。在西方，只有大概1.5%的建造量是由建筑师完成的。我不知道在中国这个比例是多少。

刘珩：在中国这个数额肯定略高一些。在《大跃进：哈佛大学设计学院的城市项目》中你谈到了“炒更”，也就是很多建筑师在就职事务所的项目之外，还自己从事其他项目。现在可没有什么“炒更”了，只是这种情形发展得更加极端。国有设计机构控制了二三线城市中的大部分工程项目，独立事务所更加难以生存。可以预测在不远的将来，大城市中的建筑将达到饱和，实践活动必然会向中小城市转移，这就会产生另外一种危机。你是怎样看待建筑师实践中的危机呢？

雷姆·库哈斯：我认为这可以作两方面解释：一方面大型事务所挤掉了小事务所，小事务所项目的质量可能会下降，然而就另外一方面而言，小事务所本身可能并不具备从事大规模项目的能力。这与市场经济分不开，然而我们现在确实还没有能力发展出一个替代选择。问题在于，建筑师做小一点的、具体一点的或者独特的项目时往往会具有更多的优势，而那些具有重大意义、关于多变的未来的大专案，则是我们的劣势。大型事务所便可能产生向外“殖民”的趋势，因为它们的规模太大了，而且本身又缺乏敏锐的洞察力来制订好的项目规划。

刘珩：我们的确还没有准备好替代的选择，但是你曾参加过一些意义重大的工程，例如香港西九龙文化区你尝试进行跨学科融合。你认为在中国发展这种工作方式是否有意义？

雷姆·库哈斯：可以说对于CCTV这个项目的严格关注，让我们觉得在中国尝试新的项目比较困难。

刘珩：可是对于你在中国的其他项目，比如深圳的“水晶岛”，或是广州的时代美术馆，你已将刚才说的那种“替代选择”逐步影响、渗透到中国的建筑行业中。

雷姆·库哈斯：深圳证券交易所是另外一个例外，我们感到非常骄傲。它是OMA所作的 “普通”建筑系列的首个产物——作为办公室场所的新潮流，力图创造一种“非标志性”（non-iconic）的建筑。

刘珩：对我们来说，深圳证券交易所却更象是普通与标志性的统一体，这似乎很具讽刺性。 话说回来，在《普通城市》中，你注意到了珠三角地区基础设施的快速发展。如今，随着高速铁路的建设，基础设施建设似乎起到了十分重要的作用。

雷姆·库哈斯：《普通城市》中我提到了基础设施属性的一个很关键的变化。基础设施通常用来平衡社会之间的差异。例如，在大城市和小城市之间有条河，因此建一座桥将有助于这两座城市的沟通和发展。但是现在，基础设施反倒是会带来不平衡。这是很激进的一种变化，我想这样的情形有一天可能也会发生在中国。

刘珩：珠三角地区的问题是，如果某些地区桥梁或者道路都无法到达，他们该怎么办呢？飞过去？

雷姆·库哈斯：我认为这会不可避免地产生问题，不过这些问题也可以变成好事，比如生活在小城市中就是件好事。当然你会感到不同的自由、不同的花费和不同的压力。这两年来，我不再关注城市，而是在考虑乡村发展。在某种程度上说，乡村和城市一样，它们的未来都拥有同样多的发展机遇。就像通过后视镜看城市，能看到巨大的变化——也许乡村正是最能描述当下之处。中国的好处在于，政府把乡村看作一个整体，确保不是所有人都涌向城市。对我来说，留下的这部分“人”更有意思。

刘珩：到2010年为止，农村人口和城市人口比例是对半平分，预期在未来5年内，城市人口将升至60%~70%，那是一个很大的数字。这将意味着大批来自农村的人口将需要安置到城市中。

雷姆·库哈斯：其影响将会是现有城市继续扩大；但与农村居住率降低的问题相比，那问题简直微不足道。

刘珩：中国已经阐明，将有相当数量的土地（18亿亩）会被保持农业用地性质，剩余的部分供地方政府和开发商使用。这是计划经济对市场经济的有力影响。

雷姆·库哈斯：你可以看到同样的事发生在俄罗斯。由于市场经济具有风险，人们都移居到了莫斯科和圣彼德堡。随后，出现了一些地区，或脱离城市化，或停滞发展，真正地陷入了完全不同的境况中。现在他们要开始处理这些遗留问题。我认为这是一个十分重要的议题，它为建筑师提供了新的机会。我们曾经都努力去考虑事情的密度和复杂度，同样的，我们也需要怀有一个不同的心态去看待这片开阔且开放的土地。你可以注意一下瑞士，人们利用土地进行不同种类的农业发展，或是进行其他目的的使用。食品生产现在看起来象是工厂流水线作业。这是对城市之外土地另一种方式的占用，但是它同样也是工业化的。

刘珩：对你而言，被遗留的是“开阔且开放”的土地，但是对中国来说，这些土地掌握在谁的手里是一个关键的问题。中国对土地使用的历史和意识形态，与俄罗斯或瑞士完全不同； 当然，这可能也与我们正处在不同的农村与城市发展阶段有关。上个月我与李欧梵教授曾有过一次探讨，他提到了中西方文学的差异，很大程度上是源于乡村文化与城市文化的区别。这肯定是有什么原因的，而这个原因很可能会导致中国农村地区与西方国家所形成的意识形态和物质观念的终极差异。你怎么看？

雷姆·库哈斯：西方文学中很多著名的作品，也许是最好的作品，或是在乡村写作，或者写的就是乡村地区，从歌德、卢梭到蜜雪儿、乌洛贝克等。我也说不清这是为什么。

刘珩：让我们关注回城市吧。普通城市中也存在着被遗留的“空洞”（void）。我们关注的是如何来填补这些城市中的空洞。这也是当下一些中国城市和建筑师所关心的问题。

雷姆·库哈斯：作为一名建筑师，我经常会去思考接下去发生的事情。就目前而言，我认为去填补那些城市中的空洞，是建筑师应尽的义务。然而，就某些时刻来讲，我希望我们能重新拿回主动权，成为城市行动的首要阶层而不是次要阶层，并不是单单去做修正，而是去掌握主动权。在20世纪70年代的西方，建筑师是主导，那时建筑师所扮演的角色更受尊重。

刘珩：但是主动权一定是积极的、好的吗？假设我们从另一端考虑，例如：后果。

雷姆·库哈斯：过去这一做法被证实很有效，例如日本的新陈代谢运动。这是最后一批现代主义先锋运动，动员政府和公众，得到大量的支持来支撑其对未来的设想。

刘珩：我们再回到珠三角地区，产业重组将会给这个地区带来什么影响呢？特别是在人口学和城市或乡村状况上？

雷姆·库哈斯：我对于珠三角地区的经济与产业了解的并不多，但是我有兴趣去重新思考一下这个问题。我经常说，中国没有别的选择，必须拯救这个世界。我现在也仍然确信这个说法。中国也确实具有能力和资源做到这一切。从这个方面说，我当初对中国所保有的乐观仍然合乎情理。

刘珩：最后一个问题，关于能源：你的评论文章大部分都是基于对已经融入珠三角地区的实体结构的观察，而世界所要面对的下一个挑战是能源。你会将城市化——无论是表现为何种形式——看成分配和消耗能源的方式吗？就城市而言，能源的标准是什么？那些更加无形的能源形式，如社会能源，在构建未来中又将扮演什么样的角色呢？

雷姆·库哈斯：作为一家事务所，我们认识到一件事：对于能量交换，建立相互依存的关系是至关重要的。与智囊团AMO一起，我们起草了一份计划，希望能够整合欧洲能源网络，从而促进国家间可持续能源形式的交换，甚至可以连接到非洲。非洲的太阳能可以形成一种双赢局面，一方面使非洲可以从这项投资中获益，而另一方面也帮助欧洲实现了可持续发展。

雷姆·库哈斯，荷兰建筑师，1975年创立大都会建筑事务所（OMA），2000年获得普利兹克建筑奖。

Domus China, Sept 2011, Vol. 57

THE FUTURE OF THE PEARL RIVER DELTA

Doreen Heng Liu + Rem Koolhaas

15 years ago, Rem Koolhaas and his *The Great Leap Forward: Harvard Design School Project on the City* and *Generic City* offered a fresh mindset to the PRD region. Since then, OMA has been actively involved with the area. This conversation between Rem Koolhaas an Doreen Heng Liu reveals some of Koolhaas' recent thoughts.

Doreen: In your previous works, you have talked extensively about the future; over the last few years, you have shifted your focus to preservation. What is the relationship between the future and preservation, according to you?

Rem: There are two contradictory reasons. One lies in preservation, which is a large movement that shows its hatred for the particular period of social architecture from the 1960s to the 1990s. The interesting thing is that like preservation, this hatred is also global. It simply represents our hatred for ideology in architecture. This phenomenon itself is extremely important to identify, because it affects every country, including China. It affects also the possibilities of architects to do that kind of work – if it is erased, nobody could say there used to be architects who did this kind of social housing. Secondly, the scale of preservation is so enormous that it is one of the key elements that will determine our future. For this reason, I think preservation is a crucial element of the future. In a recent exhibition about preservation called Cronocaos, I formulated that the future will be, on the one hand, about radical changes, and on the other, about radical stasis and radical immobility. Thus it is very important to think how we can adapt to the situation where certain sections of the living environment do not change and certain sections do change. What we found is that 12% of the world's surface is under certain systems of preservation. For this reason, it is simply excluded from the "regular" world, and this has never happened before in history. It has to be theorized.

Doreen: When did preservation as a movement start to be significant?

Rem: It started in the 1970s as a global system, coinciding with the rapid expansion of the market economy. The explosion of preservation is part of the explosion of the economy. It is also a kind of connection we are exploring.

Doreen: How do you see the discussion of preservation in China?

Rem: I have to admit that I don't know it well enough to give comments. I have tried to get involved and it will still be interesting to be involved. In a way we were thinking about it as practitioners, before we tried to formulate theories around it. West Kowloon Cultural District project reflects the theory that we constructed to give a coherence of reference.

Doreen: What do you find challenging in a preservation project?

Rem: One of the biggest difficulties of a preservation project lies in the fact that it never talks about the preservation of a way of life, or a social dimension, or a form of interaction. But many are not up for that kind of thinking yet.

Doreen: It seems that your WKCD project has started to move towards this direction. But at the moment preservation means nothing more than physical forms or objects in China. Preservation still needs to be discussed systematically. But now let's go back to your early research studies focusing on the PRD highlighted in the publications The Great Leap Forward: Harvard Design School Project on the City and Generic City, begun 15 years ago, as they are important for your understanding of the region. For the most part, what we see right now are the consequences of the past 15 years. How much has the situation developed?

Rem: I'm impressed in all cases by how much initiative urban planning has been able to regain, especially in China. If you look at Shenzhen, 15 years ago the Shenzhen Urban Planning Bureau planning office was in a shop-like house, and in the office were four people and a few bicycles. Now they are in a sleek office building designed by Urbanus, and they really exercise a huge influence on the city. In 15 years, what looked like a wild and uncontrolled development of the PRD region has regained ground in planning thanks to planners. Shenzhen is one of the cities I know where planning has a significant role and where the city can control, to a large extent, what can happen to it.

Doreen: The Shenzhen Urban Planning Bureau is considered the best in China.

Rem: I'm simply comparing now to my first impressions of the PRD. Now I see a beginning of coherence, of mutual adjustments, and there is more and more infrastructure. All of this is attributed to planning and its execution. Years ago, the PRD was "happening" but not really with an intention. Now it is intentional.

Doreen: Do you consider it good?

Rem: Compared to what was described in the two books, both skeptical about the ability of planning, the situation now partly contradicts them, because you see evidence of successful planning. But planning sometimes lacks a vision.

Doreen: Big events in the PRD such as the Olympic Games, the Asian Games and Universiade all gave the cities a good excuse for the implementation of new urban planning. But after these events are over, what will be planned next? Everybody is somehow confused. If the generic city is the consequence of uncontrolled development, what comes next?

Rem: To make it clear, Shenzhen is no longer a generic city, it is planned with a certain character, and it is now at another level.

Doreen: Architects think they are important in China. We see the consequences of their practice in Chinese cities. How do you regard the issue of responsibility in the field of architecture?

Rem: First of all, I think it is a global issue. Architects by themselves only produce a very small percentage of the total built substance. In the West, about 1.5% of the total amount of built substance is done by architects. I don't know the percentage in China.

Doreen: It must be higher in China. You described the phenomenon of "moonlighting" in The Great Leap Forward: Harvard Design School Project on the City, that is architects working on other projects apart from their office projects. Now that the phenomenon of "moonlighting" has disappeared, the situation has become more extreme. State-owned design institutes control most of the projects in the second-and-third-tier cities, and for independent offices it is getting more difficult to survive. I can see that not far in the future when big cities are saturated with buildings, the practice of architecture is going to move to smaller cities. This will create another danger. How do you see the danger and crisis of architectural practice?

Rem: For me it's a double-edged situation. On the one hand, you can see the big firms squeeze out the small ones and the quality of work goes down; on the other hand, we ourselves have not been able to project a vision of a large-scale development. This lack of vision is connected to the market economy, and we haven't been able to develop an alternative yet. The problem is that architects are much better as small, specific or unique operations; we are all weak at making projects about a relevant and viable kind of future on a larger scale. Big offices may have a colonizing tendency, because they are so big, but at the same time they seldom have a sharp vision in terms of planning.

Doreen: We are not ready for alternatives, but you have already worked on some projects of relevant significance, the West Kowloon Cultural District project for example, where you try to develop an interdisciplinary practice. Is it relevant to develop this work method in China?

Rem: The sheer attention that CCTV brought us makes it hard to try another work in China.

Doreen: Yet with your other Chinese projects,Crystal Island in Shenzhen, Times Museum in Guangzhou to list a few, you have started to insert your influence in terms of that kind of alternative in China.

Rem: The Shenzhen Stock Exchange is another exception of which we are very proud. It's OMA's first in a series of "generic" buildings – a stream in the office dedicated to creating non-iconic architecture.

Doreen: Generic but iconic at the same time. Is it kind of cynical? I also can see it in the Times Museum in Guangzhou. In Generic City, you noticed the fast development of infrastructures in the PRD region. Today, with the building of high-speed rails, infrastructure seems to still play an important role here.

Rem: In *Generic City* I noted a very important change in the nature of infrastructure. Infrastructure is typically used to undo inequalities. For instance, there is a river setting apart a big city and a small city, so building a bridge in between will help both the cities. But now infrastructure is creating inequalities. And that's a radical change and I think it will happen in China, too.

Doreen: In the PRD region, the question is what happens to those areas that bridges or roads do not reach? Shall we simply decide to fly over?

Rem: I think it leads to inevitable problems, but maybe the problems will also be advantages, i.e. not being in a big city will be an advantage. That mean could be different kinds of freedom, different costs, currency and pressures. For two years I'm not thinking about cities anymore, but I'm thinking about the countryside. In a way the countryside has as much a future as the city. It's looking in the rear view mirror of the city, seeing tremendous amounts of change – probably the countryside is the best metaphor for our current times. One good thing in China is that the governors are looking at the country as a whole, making sure not everybody moves to the city. For me, the areas "left behind" are very interesting.

Doreen: In the last year, urban and rural populations were exactly equal at 50% each of the global population; in 5 years we expect urban population to increase to 60% or even to 70%. These numbers are huge. that number is huge. That means mass relocation of people to the city from the countryside.

Rem: The effect will be that the existing cities grow bigger, but this effect is almost negligible compared to all the countryside becoming less inhabited.

Doreen: China has set out that a certain amount of land (1.8 billion Chinese acres land) will be reserved purely for agriculture. The rest is for the local government and developers to use. In this case, the centrally planned economic system produces a more beneficial effect in the management of the land than the market economy.

Rem: You could see this happening in Russia. With the rise of the market economy, everybody moved to Moscow and St. Petersburg. But then there are areas that are de-urbanized, de-developed, and really falling into completely different situations. And they have to deal with areas that are left behind now. I think this is an important discussion that opens new opportunities for architects. We have all worked to make things dense, with issues like density and complexity in mind, but similarly we might need a different mindset and look at the vast and open land. If you look at Switzerland, they are already using the land for a different kind of agriculture or other manipulated purposes. Food production now is like factory work. It's a different kind of occupation of the land outside cities, but it is also industrial.

Doreen: What is "left behind" as you say is the vast and open land. But in whose hands is this land is an important issue in China. From the ideological point of view, China has a very different understanding of the land in comparison to Russia or Switzerland; perhaps it is also at a different stage of its rural and urban development. In the course of a conversation I had with Prof. Leo LEE last month, he mentioned the difference between Western and Chinese literature when it comes to understanding rural and urban culture. So there must be a reason for this. Perhaps rural China will embrace an ideological and pragmatic future that is totally different from the West. What is your opinion?

Rem: In Western literature, many famous books – perhaps the best ones, were written either in the countryside or about the countryside. Take the works of Goethe, Rousseau, even Michel Houellebecq for example. I don't have a theory to explain this phenomenon yet.

Doreen: Going back to the topic of cities, generic cities have also created voids from within. We are interested in how to fill in these urban voids. This is what some Chinese architects are concerned at the moment.

Rem: As an architect, I'm always thinking what the next thing will be. For the moment, I think that it is an architect's duty to take care of urban voids. However, at some point, I hope we can regain the initiative to be the first layer instead of the second layer of action on the city, not to merely do corrections but to take the initiative. In the 1970s architects were in charge, and being an architect was more honorable a role then.

Doreen: But is the initiative necessarily positive and good? If we are looking at the other end, for example, the consequences.

Rem: In the past it proved very productive for instance in the case of the Metabolist movement in Japan. They were the last avant-garde movement able to mobilize huge support from the government and the public in order to speculate on the future.

Doreen: Coming back to the PRD region, what will be the impact of industrial transformations in the PRD area, especially on demography and the urban or rural situation?

Rem: I don't know so much about the economics and industry in the PRD area, but I'm interested in re-engaging with these issues. I have always said that China has no choice but to save the world. I'm still convinced of this. The sheer ingenuity and energy of China will lead the country towards success. On that level, my initial optimism about China is still justified.

Doreen: My last question is about energy: your critical essays are largely based on the observation of the physical structures that have merged in the PRD, while the world's next big challenge lies in energy. Do you think that urbanization plays an important role in the distribution and consumption of energy? What standards should we embrace in relation to energy in the urban realm? What role do the less tangible forms of energy, e.g. social energy, play in shaping the future?

Rem: As an office, we have realized one thing: whenever it comes to energy exchange, we must be aware that we are interconnected. With AMO, our think tank, we drafted a plan to integrate the European energy grid to enable and accelerate exchange in sustainable energy forms between nation states, possibly even connecting to Africa. In Africa solar energy could become a kind of win-win situation where they would benefit from the investment and Europe would become sustainable.

Rem Koolhaas, Dutch architect, founder of the Metropolitan Office of Architecture (OMA), winner of the Pritzker Prize in 2000.

UNBALANCED GROWTH

INCREASES AND DECREASES

不均衡增长

增长与减少

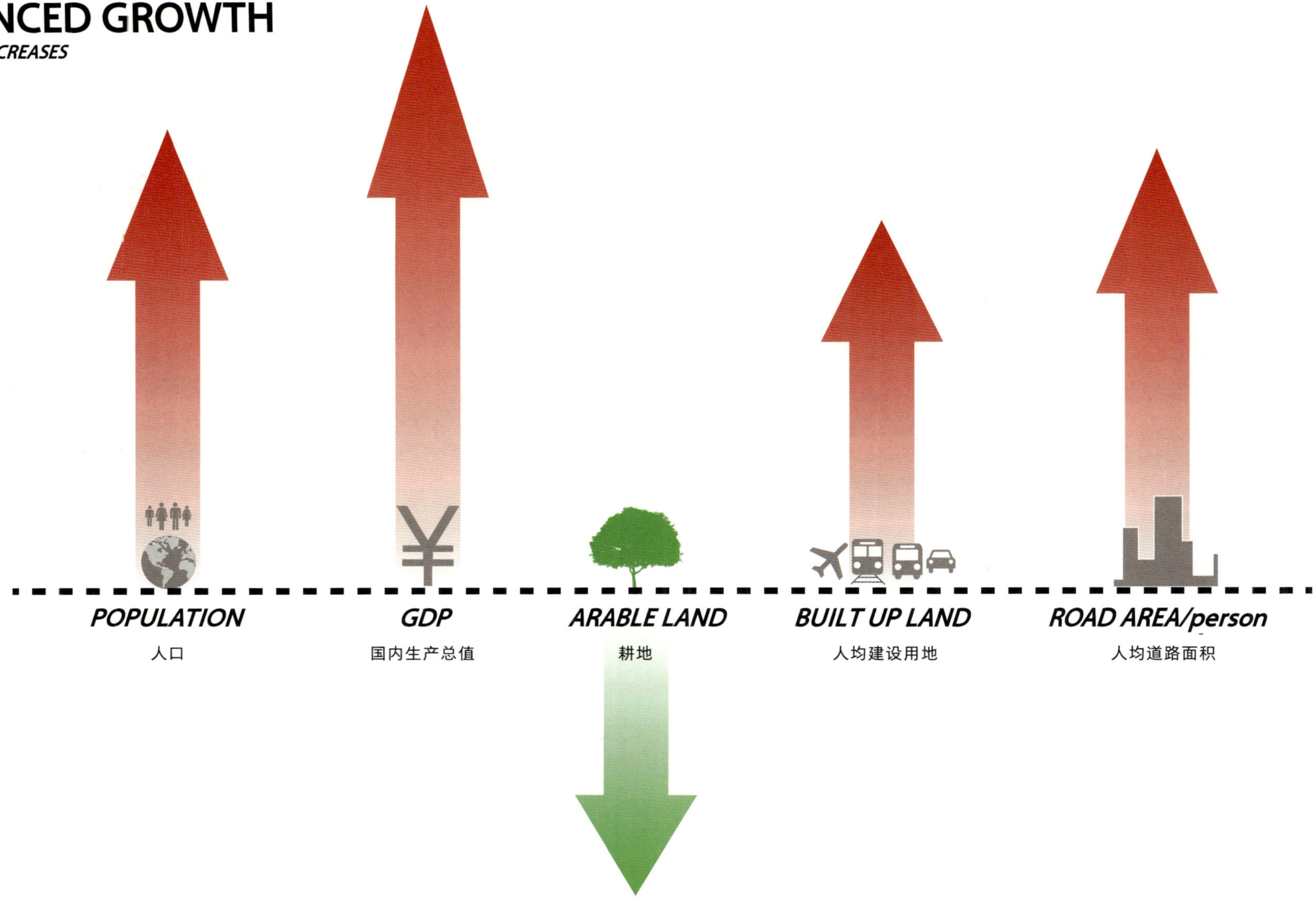

WHAT 什么是珠三角地区?
IS THE PEARL RIVER DELTA?

WHAT 我们是谁?
IS NODE?

WHERE 我们在哪里?
ARE WE?

WHAT 基础设施的角色是什么?
IS THE ROLE OF THE INFRASTRUCTURE?

WHAT 现在的问题是什么?
ARE THE ISSUES NOW?

WHAT 我们的愿景是什么?
ARE OUR VISIONS FOR THE IMMEDIATE FUTURE?

INFRASTRUCTURE ROLE IN MOBILITY

TRANSPORT + INFRASTRUCTURE + ENERGY

基础设施在流动性中的作用

交通运输+基础设施+能源

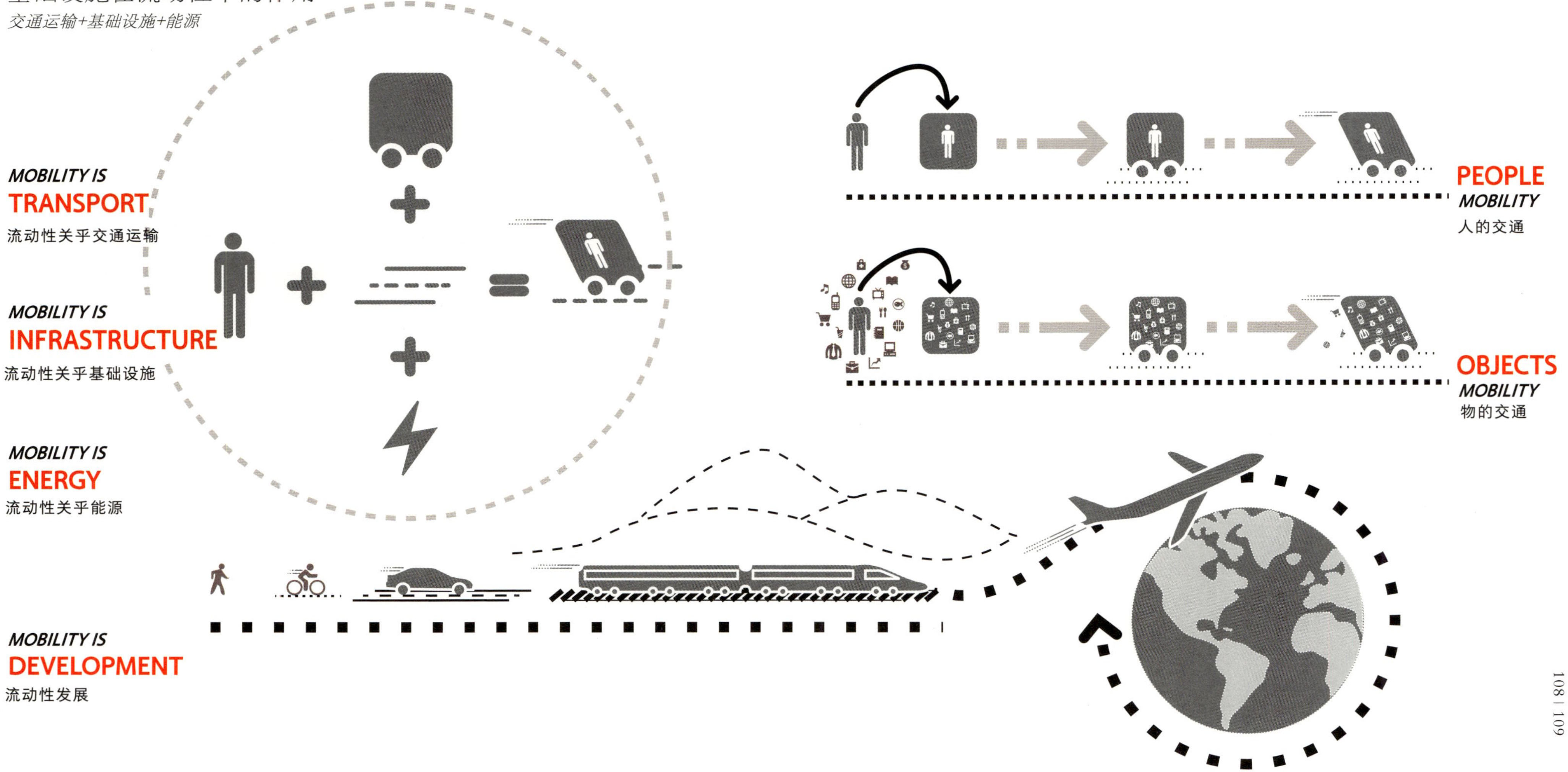

BALANCED INFRASTRUCTURE SYSTEM

SUSTAINABLE MODE IN MANAGEMENT OF INFRASTRUCTURE

平衡的基础设施系统 *可持续的基础设施管理模式*

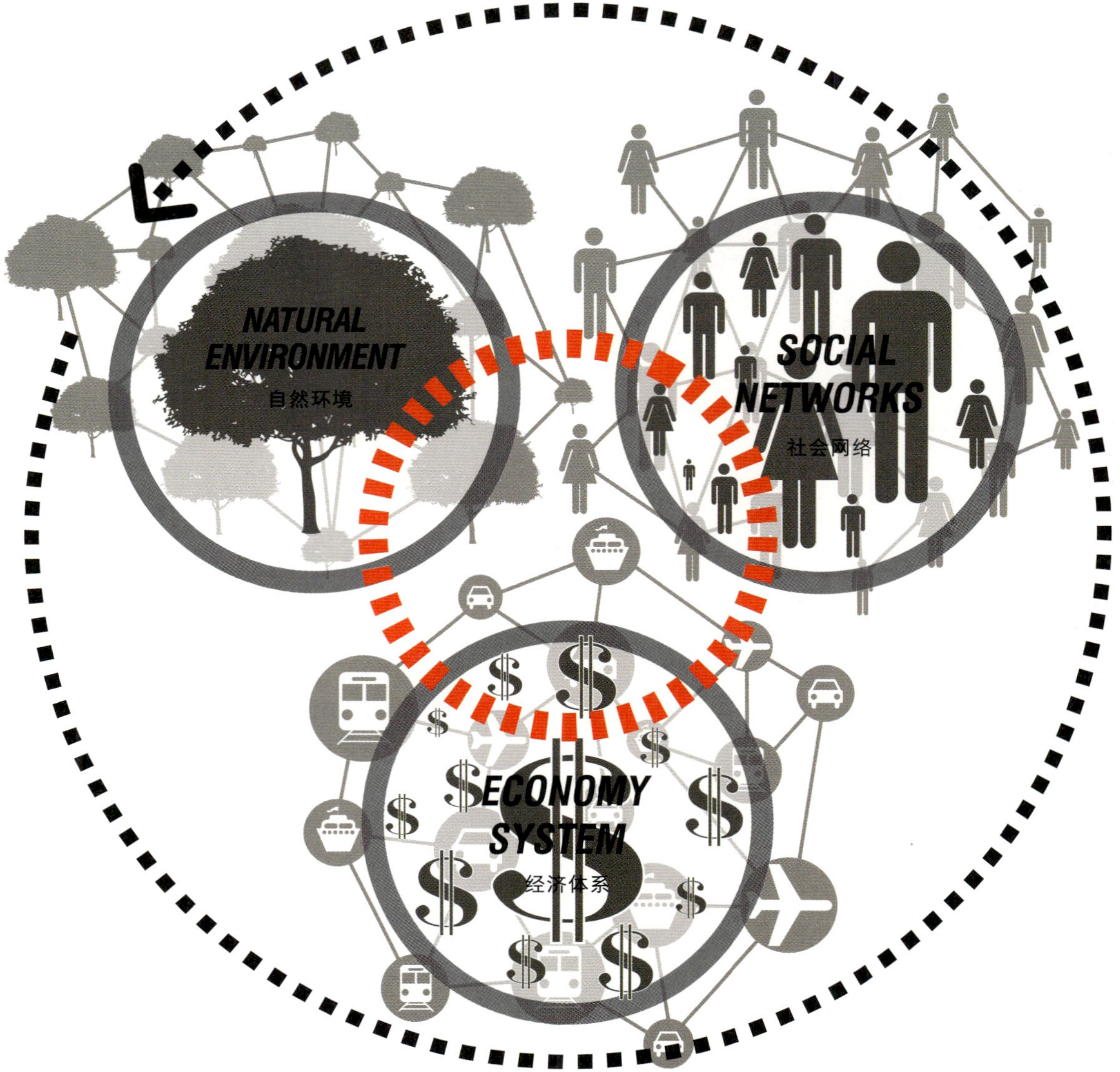

UNBALANCED INFRASTRUCTURE SYSTEM

UNSUSTAINABLE MODE IN MANAGEMENT OF INFRASTRUCTURE

不平衡的基础设施系统 *不可持续的基础设施管理模式*

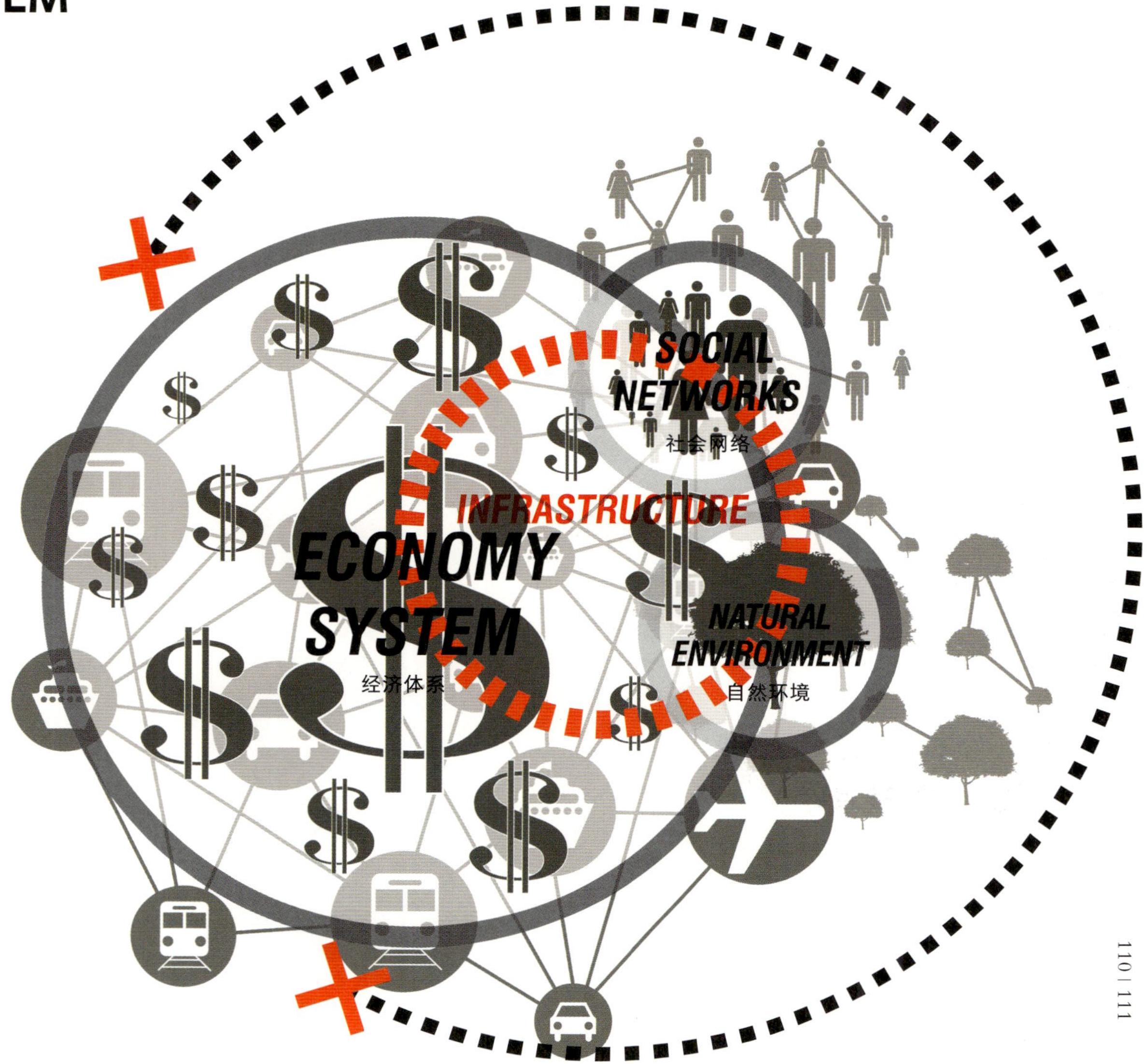

WHAT 什么是珠三角地区？
IS THE PEARL RIVER DELTA?

WHAT 我们是谁？
IS NODE?

WHERE 我们在哪里？
ARE WE?

WHAT 基础设施的角色是什么？
IS THE ROLE OF THE INFRASTRUCTURE?

WHAT 现在的问题是什么？
ARE THE ISSUES NOW?

WHAT 我们的愿景是什么？
ARE OUR VISIONS FOR THE IMMEDIATE FUTURE?

哈佛大学+香港中文大学联合出版物《深圳：设计一座永不停歇的变化之城》，2010年

权宜城市：向华强北学习

刘珩

“乱”的困惑

华强北作为课程的选题是赞助方的愿望。它30年的土地使用权很快就要到期了，因而产业的转型和城市更新迫在眉睫。赞助方需要一些有别于中国传统套路的策略和设计思路去重新审视这块区域。但是华强北，对我的研究生而言，是个很复杂的选题。它空间呈现出的表象很乱：密集的人群、烦杂的噪声、错综的流线、缭乱的产品和争先夺后的广告充斥在看起来整齐划一的商业建筑群。这是一个开放的服务生产线，疯狂的交易市场和拥挤不堪的生活场景。这么直观、赤裸裸地呈现在你的眼前，让人措手不及。就在如此混乱的条件下，居然也能成就电子产品GDP的全国第一，令人瞠目。这就是拥挤的华强北文化——颠疯的密集城市，但同时也是给深圳这座只有30年的年轻城市带来巨大产值的一块风水宝地。

华强北的奇迹带给我们的思考是矛盾的：如何保持其活力和产值，同时又能改变城市空间和面貌的“脏乱差”？提升这个矛盾的共生体不言而喻地成了大家共同期望的权宜策略。但理清眼前这个“乱”已不是一个简单的研究课题，更不用说，我们能否拿出适时适地的设计策略或策略设计。当下的学生，包括中国大多数的实践建筑师往往只是知道城市化结果，而不知道它是如何被城市化的；甚至连城市的管理者们也天真地认为解决表象的人车拥堵，就能够缓解华强北的乱。但直觉告诉我们，它的“乱”是有一定的铺垫，是有前提和条件的。首先，我们不得不从承载着华强北板块的这座城市的地缘性开始……

“乱”的由来

深圳：珠三角地区的一块飞地

30年前，当邓小平选择了深圳的时候，它只是一个普通的、毫不起眼的南方小渔村。没有人关心过它的命运，它所以被选中，只是因为它是香港的邻居。邓小平在考虑，外国人能在异邦创造出一个繁华的华人国际大都市，难道我们中国人不能创造出自己的繁华城市吗？虽然深圳还一无所有，但有中国的国力作为后盾，难道还扶它不起来？

邓小平的一句话，深圳的命运就从此被改变。政治的历史选择了有地缘优势的深圳去迈出经济宏略的冒险一大步。有战略也有战术，政府给予了深圳有别于计划经济调控外的特殊政策，以保证它能毫无阻力地按市场规律自由发展。深圳成为中国第一个经济特区。借着这春风，在国家和政策的双重支持推动下，短短30年，原本不到3万人、规划人口为100万的边陲小镇到2006年人口翻了规划的8倍，已发展成为千万人口的大都市，GDP跃居全国第一。

深圳的奇迹一方面的确来源于地缘政治自上而下的推动；但另一方面显然也离不开承载这个奇迹的一方土壤和文化自下而上的滋养和宽容。作为岭南文化发源地的这一方土壤和文化，珠三角地区有着与正统的中原文化不同的发展历史，因为珠三角地区也曾是中国的一块飞地。

珠三角地处五岭以南，简称岭南。由于这五岭之隔，岭南在中原版图上一直处在边缘的地带，历史上从来就不是兵家必争之地。所谓“山高皇帝远”，一方面，中原权势和文化影响力到此已弱化不少，因为没人关心，岭南文化从一开始就是在一种自由自在的状态中孕育起来的。这种几乎在无政府状态下发展出来的文化体系到今天某种程度上已成为中华民族特有的包容、创新和开放的代名词。另一方面，由于同样的逻辑，岭南地理的边缘性也符合理想中实验场的概念。决策者在不肯定一件决策是否能成功之前会小心谨慎，可以选择在此地试着做做看。即使失败了，它的负面影响也不会波及全国、威胁到政局的稳定。岭南历史上几乎是所有当权者的权宜之地。

地缘的边缘化和若即若离的状态给了岭南有了更多向外寻求发展和交换的机会。密集的河网、临海的地理条件和宽松的社会政治环境，符合世界近代史上工业革命发展所必备的一些客观条件。在18世纪和19世纪，珠三角地区毫无悬念地成了世界列强必争的一块资源和通商宝地。在西方工业革命的高峰期，以广州为主打贸易城市的珠三角地区顺理成章地切入了当时世界的产业链上，成就了中国第一和最大的通商口岸。“时势造英雄”，应该说，经济和工业的历史选择了有地缘优势的珠三角地区。即使是1949年之后，包括开放改革的这30年，珠三角地区在很长的一段时间里始终保持着经济发展佼佼者的地位。然而珠三角地区有着宽松的政治氛围和地缘文化，但对着深圳跨越时空的突然空降，这么猛，这么“无厘头”，这么义无反顾，的确没有充足的思想准备，但也毫无怨言地接受了。深圳作为新一轮的实验场具有强烈的发展野心，是在地缘的逻辑框架下的必然选择。被作为中央指定的实验田，深圳一开始就是命运的宠儿，她不能失败也不可能失败；她没有过去，只有现在和未来；她只有结果，没有过程。“不管黑猫白猫，抓住老鼠就是好猫。”只要达到目的，手段和铺垫并不重要。

华强北：深圳的一块飞地

华强北就是这样发展的结果；在地缘政治逻辑和地缘散漫文化的影响下，城市产业和形态直接呈现。它的一夜成名完全是在政府无意识扶持下自发成长起来的产物。华强北如今有了个很炫耀的名声——“中国电子第一街”。经过近30年产业的自主发展、演变和巅峰阶段，现在已成为中国最大的电子产品集散地：首先是电子产业，所有商品应有尽有，然后由产业带来一系列配套服务——包装、物流；当这些物物流通日益加聚的时候，于是服务于这些产业人群的生活配套也开始活跃起来，廉价酒店和宿舍、廉价快餐和娱乐、廉价服装、廉价超市的植入……华强北这1.5平方公里的区域成为深圳中心商业区里一个有着完整产业/生活链的微型城市，一块自给自足的飞地。

然而华强北这种生产、交换、消费一体化的产业和空间模式，某种意义上存在也违背了现代城市规划中土地利用的一些基本分配原则。例如工业和商业的分离，工业与居住的分离，居住和商业的可能分离等……华强北不仅在“平面”上功能混合，在“剖面”上也功能交织，共同打造了高效立体全方位的“拥挤文化”和“普通城市”：一个是空间形式和内容功能的随意分离和随意搭配；另一个是“每个星期一起来都有一个新的身份”的自生自灭的实时集群，这两者无所顾忌的组合就是我们眼前这座真实的城市：活力和密度。只是来得太直接、太另类、太赤裸裸。这是座十足的权宜城市：因需要而存在，因存在便合理。

但无可否认，短短30年，华强北就完成了从农业用地转变为工业生产到今天的都市状态，成为深圳中心城区的重要一部分，这堪称是都市生产的一个神话。也许用“完成”这词并不确切，华强北用30年就几乎浓缩了西方工业城市300年的发展历史和内容。这种压缩版城市模式是发育不良的产物，还是有可能首创了未来城市空间或生活方式的某种原型呢?

“乱”的拆解和重组

言归正传，不管是悲观的发育不良论，还是乐观的未来原型论，华强北由于这种混合的便利，人、物和事越聚越多，彼此在空间的竞争也越演越烈，原来的空间越来越堵，越来越乱……华强北终于成了

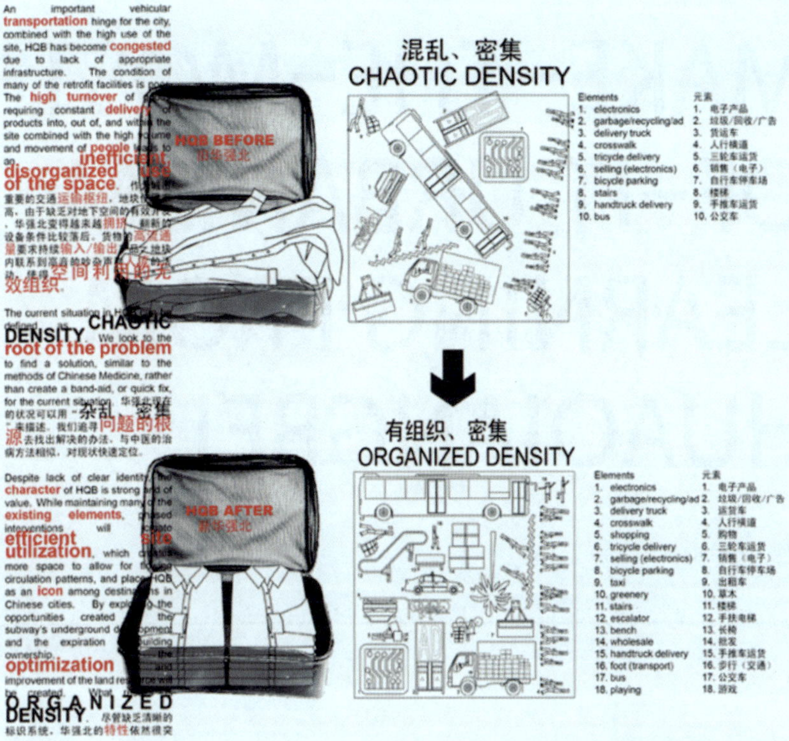

一个忍无可忍的城市问题。为了解决这个“堵”，当地政府想尽一切办法疏通交通问题，包括有超过4条不同的地铁线在此设站。但正如前面所说的，乱只是一个表象，它的问题可能是自内而外的。研究需要从表象形成的原因、过程和规律入手，以谋用设计手段探讨未来物质空间形态发展的多种可能性，我认为是针对华强北设计课程的出发点。首先尝试采用的是“案件重组”的元素观察分析法，拆解造成华强北城市空间错纵复杂的物质构成元素，理解它们各自的游戏规则和生存原则，以及形成“乱”的动力方向；这样的分析过程让我们理解了这个城市的过去和现在；然后通过“拨乱反正”的策略和设计手法，推理出这个城市在未来发展的“顺变”和“突变”（例如地铁的开挖、政府的政策转变等）情况下可能引发的空间发展的多种可能性：让这些原有元素在“顺变”或“突变”的规则下重组再生，自由发展。在体量不变的情况下，可能生出更多的面积；而新的容积率需要的时候，也可以从容地衍生出新的体量和空间。总而言之，更高密度、更强GDP、更具活力的华强北需要对空间形式和内容功能的未来分配和布局原则有着一如既往的创造性和想象力。

走向权宜城市

虽然华强北只是个案研究，但它的产生和发展在珠三角地区具有普通性和普适性，因而对它未来的预测也将是个很有意义的设计尝试。在中国快速城市化过程中空间形态几乎都象是自上而下一个模子塑造出来的今天，华强北存在和演变无疑展示出了城市发展的另一面：自主选择和积极适应造就了城市产业和城市空间的多元性、复杂性和生动性。不管多乱多堵，它毕竟代表了城市发展的多向可能性，它的影响力是值得关注的。

30年不仅是一个数字，也像是正在结束或即将开始的一个完整体系。俗语曰：“三十而立”，前30年的华强北立足于创造一个全球化和被动的“权宜城市”，而“无心插柳”却也同时“插”出了一个地域和主动的“权宜城市”。以后的30年，华强北和深圳还能否以“不变”或“善变”应万变的姿态抵抗和领先于外部一切无法预测的变量，保持城市在空间和产业的竞争力呢？对此目标，我们希望用研究和设计贡献我们一点有效的想象力。

SHENZHEN: Designing the Non-stop Transformation City,
Harvard + CUHK joint studio publication, 2010

MAKE-THE-MOST-OF-IT URBANISM: LEARNING FROM HUAQIANGBEI

Doreen Heng Liu

Puzzle of Chaos

It was the sponsor's wish that we chose Huaqiangbei as our research focus. With its 30-year land-use-right soon to expire, and its need for industrial transformation and urban renewal ever more urgent, Huaqiangbei calls for an unconventional way of re-design. Our sponsor understood this perfectly. Yet Huaqiangbei to me and my students is a complex case, as it presents itself in constantly accumulating chaos, in which we find a great number of people and noise, multiplex flow, and a perplexing assortment of advertising billboards all in a rather decently arranged neighborhood of towers. It is an open assembly-and-service-line, it is where trade meets day-to-day life, in a way so blatant and multi-dimensional that it leaves one bewildered. Still, Huaqiangbei scores No. 1 in the electronic products GDP in China. Huaqiangbei – a delirious stacking city and a money machine, which has brought and continues to bring great fortune to the young city of Shenzhen.

The phenomena of Huaqiangbei pose a paradox to us. How can we re-organize such accumulating chaos in space and improve its look while keeping its urban vigor and output value unspoiled becomes the shared vision of our sponsor and us? Understanding the cause of the Chaos suffices as a research project itself, before we ever go into strategic design. Most students and even many architects nowadays in China take only the demand and desired outcome of a project into consideration, without necessarily knowing how the project comes about. Even the administrators of Huaqiangbei are naive enough to believe that solving traffic and human flow problems will solve it all for Huaqiangbei. We sense that, however, the Chaos happens from within, which has its cause and process. By understanding it fully, first we may take a look at the geopolitical characteristics of the city and the region that embraces the extremities such as that of Huaqiangbei.

Condition of Chaos

Shenzhen: Enclave or Exclave of the PRD

30 years ago, Shenzhen was a little-known fishing village, the impoverished neighbor to Hong Kong. Deng Xiaoping designated it as the first Special Economic Zone in China, holding that if the Westerners could build Hong Kong into a world-class cosmopolitan away from their homeland, the Chinese could build its own within China.

The political moment favored Shenzhen, a place with geo-political advantage, granting it special policies outside the frame of the planned economy, allowing it to develop freely according to the rules of the market economy. Backed by the political powerhouse of China, in 30 years, Shenzhen's population grew almost eight-fold from the originally planned one million to nearly ten million, generating the No.1 GDP among all Chinese cities.

Shenzhen's miracle owes its root not only to the political choice from the top and its policy implementation, but also to the particular culture from the ground that nurtures and tolerates the process of such implementation – the region of the Pearl River Delta (the PRD). The PRD, the birthplace of Lingnan culture and a world apart from the orthodox Chinese culture, was once an enclave in China.

The PRD lies south of Wu Ling (Five Mountains) and the area is thus called Lingnan (South of Mountains). As an idom says, "The Mountains are high, the emperor is far away". On one side, far from the reach of former emperors, Lingnan in history has never carried much geopolitical significance. This, in turn, proved to be the cradle for the somewhat anarchic and careless culture of the South. On the other side, this marginal status was used to the convenience of those in power, when they exercised policies and were yet unsure of the outcome of such experiments. Even when it failed, it wouldn't affect the rest of the country. Lingnan has always been make-the-most-of-it for those in power. Lingnan culture has long been the forefront of experiments.

The geopolitical marginality to the central and proximity to the sea afford Lingnan a chance often to look outward for exchange and opportunity for development With unique advantage of a dense network of waterways, in the 18th and 19th centuries during the Western Industrial Revolution, Guangzhou (Canton), a capital of the PRD and the gateway to China, had been fully integrated into the chain of global industry and became the first and biggest trade portal of China. Economy and industry made the PRD the pioneer of its time. All the way into the new China, including the recent 30 years of Open Reform, the PRD has always taken the lead in economical development. Given this, the "forced delivery" of Shenzhen was a shocking one even to the PRD.

Shenzhen, as a new round of experiment lab, is a "must" choice of political power of the moment, conceived under the same geo-political logic. As the designated favourite, Shenzhen cannot and will not fail. It has no past, only present and future. It aims only at the goals, it concerns itself with no methods or process.

Huaqiangbei: "Enclave" of Shenzhen

Huaqiangbei represents outcome of such go-to-any-length attitude of development, fertilized by geopolitical policies and somewhat anarchic but spontaneous drive, in industry and urban form. 30 years has earned Huaqiangbei the title "China's No.1 Electronics Street", and it is indeed China's biggest electronics distribution center. In the beginning there were only a great variety of electronic products, ranging from original goods and copied versions, then the ancillary market, such as packaging and logistics, boomed. This, in turn, led to living and leisure development for the people working there, which includes budget hotels, dormitories, fast food, entertainment business, and soon clothing markets and department stores moved in. Huaqiangbei has become a micro-city or enclave with a complete industry and living chain packed in its 1.5 km^2.

As much as Huaqiangbei's industry model and spatial form is efficient, with production, trade and consumer linked in line with each other, Huaqiangbei contradicts some basic land use rules in that the industrial and commercial areas are not separate, industrial and residential areas are not separate, as well as residential and commercial not potentially separate. Huaqiangbei is not only congested on the horizontal level, but also has a mixture of functions on the vertical level, thus forming an efficient and 4 "culture of congestion" and "generic city". One reveals the total randomness of the allocation of spatial form and program, the other encapsulates an instant cluster that "can produce a new identity every Monday morning". The reality of the mini city Huaqiangbei lies in a random combination of the two. It's vigorous and intense, if not a little strange and blatant. This is the make-the-most-of-it urbanism, it exists upon need, therefore its existence makes sense.

In 30 years, Huaqiangbei completed the cycle of transformation from agricultural land, to industrial production house, to what it looks like now an urban reality, as a key part of Shenzhen's central business district. But "completed" may not be the right word to describe it. Huaqiangbei as a mini-city of 30 years in existence has compressed 300 years of western urban transformation. The question is, is Huaqiangbei an undernourished product of a highly compact process, or could it provide a prototype type of China's future urban form and lifestyle?

De/Re-constructing Chaos

Be it the "undernourished product" or "future prototype" viewpoint we hold, the congestion of Huaqiangbei is ever heavier that the area begins to feel like "survival of the fittest". Local government has taken all measures to solve the problem of "survival", including building more than four subway lines. Still, as said before, congestion is merely a superficial expression, it must take place from within. Our research, like a detective, should go into the cause, rules and process of the formation of the phenomenon, in hope to shed light on possibilities of future forms. That's the pretext for Huaqiangbei studio.

As the design detectives investigating the dynamics of the area, we first observe, then analyze and then deconstruct the complicated phenomena into its core elements to understand the rules and tactics of survival. In considering reconstructing the system we utilize outside opportunities such as subway development and unexpected policy shift to explore the internal relationship between all the elements (people, things activities). Only then have the proper tools to reconfigure and reorganize the area to its most efficient use by developing optimal kinds of scenarios for all the core elements. We then deduct two future threads, the "consequential" and the "mutant", and their respective possible consequences with a focus of how they might interact. Within the same volume of space, this could result in better efficiency of space consumption and meet new demand for higher plot ratio. In short, the future of a denser, more vigorous and higher GDP generating Huaqiangbei must celebrate a creative way, if not more than ever, to allocate spatial form, program and function.

Make-the-Most-of-It Urbanism

Although Huaqiangbei is only an individual case study, the coming into being and development of Huaqiangbei bears general and universal characteristics in the Pearl River Delta. In a time of rapid urbanization and top-down decision-making taking place in almost all cases, Huaqiangbei's existence and evolution showcases otherwise – self-choice and adaptability make possible the multiplex and vigorous industries and spatial forms of a city. Its positive influence should be acknowledged.

Thirty years, more than just a number in Chinese notion, could be taken as how long it takes for a thorough transformation to complete its cycle. Confucius held that "a man should be independent at the age of thirty". We may see Huaqiangbei in its first 30 years as a passive make-the-most-of-it urbanism under the influence of globalization, what remains to observe is whether it will transform into an active make-the-most-of-it urbanism of regional integrity, and whether Huaqiangbei and Shenzhen will continue to stride across time of changes, to remain competitive in its geopolitical standpoint and industries. To this goal, we would like to contribute our share of imagination through this research and design.

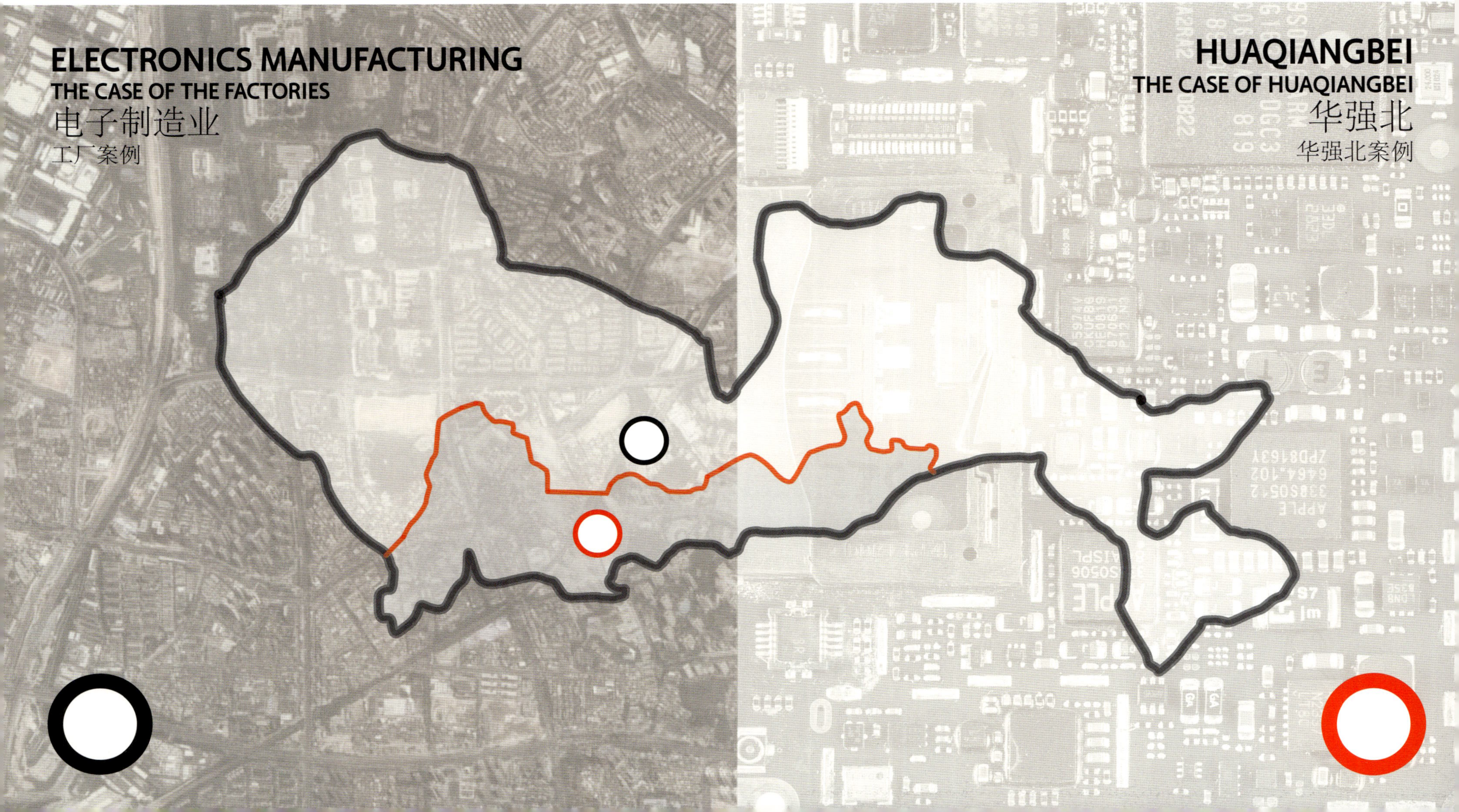
ELECTRONICS MANUFACTURING
THE CASE OF THE FACTORIES
电子制造业
工厂案例
HUAQIANGBEI
THE CASE OF HUAQIANGBEI
华强北
华强北案例

LOCATION

PRD ELECTRONIC MANUFACTURING FACTORY

位置 *珠三角电子制造业工厂*

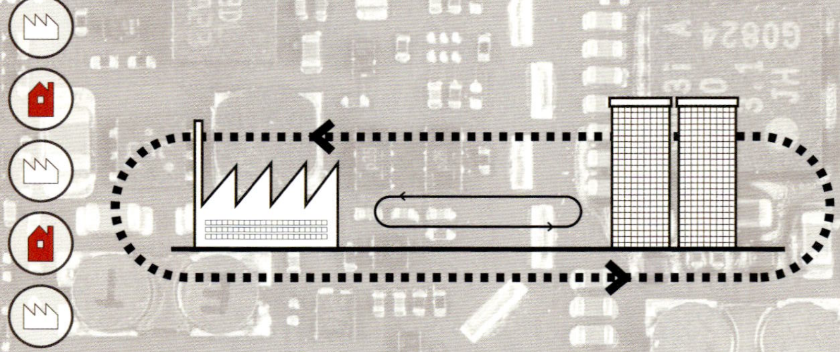

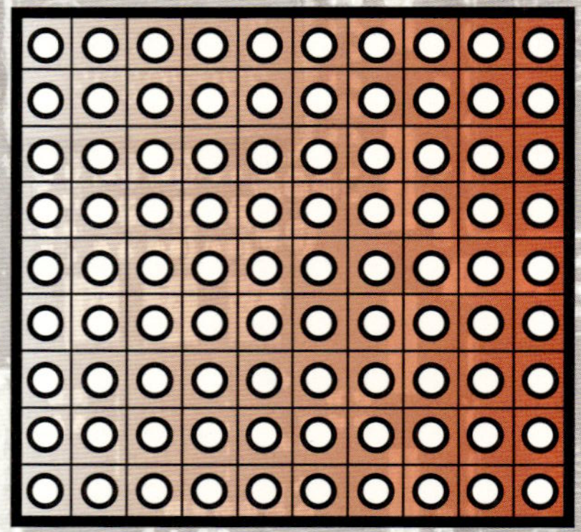

工厂修筑围墙，将42万人集中在仅3平方公里的弹丸之地

THE FACTORY WALLED IN 0.42 MILLION PEOPLE IN A TINY PLACE: OF 3 km^2

大部分工人每天工作12小时，每周工作6天

MOST OF THE WORKERS WORK 12 HOURS A DAY AND 6 DAYS A WEEK

恶劣的工作条件、对工人的歧视，以及与世隔绝的生活环境，甚至带来悲剧事件的发生

POOR WORKING CONDITIONS, DISCRIMINATION AGAINST WORKERS AND ISOLATED LIVING ENVIRONMENT EVEN BRING ABOUT TRAGIC EVENTS

MORE IS LESS
多即是少

HUAQIANGBEI

THE CASE OF HUAQIANGBEI

华强北

华强北案例

商业繁荣，附近街区道路拥挤堵塞

MONEY MACHINE WITH A JAMMED CONGESTED NEIGHBORHOOD STREET

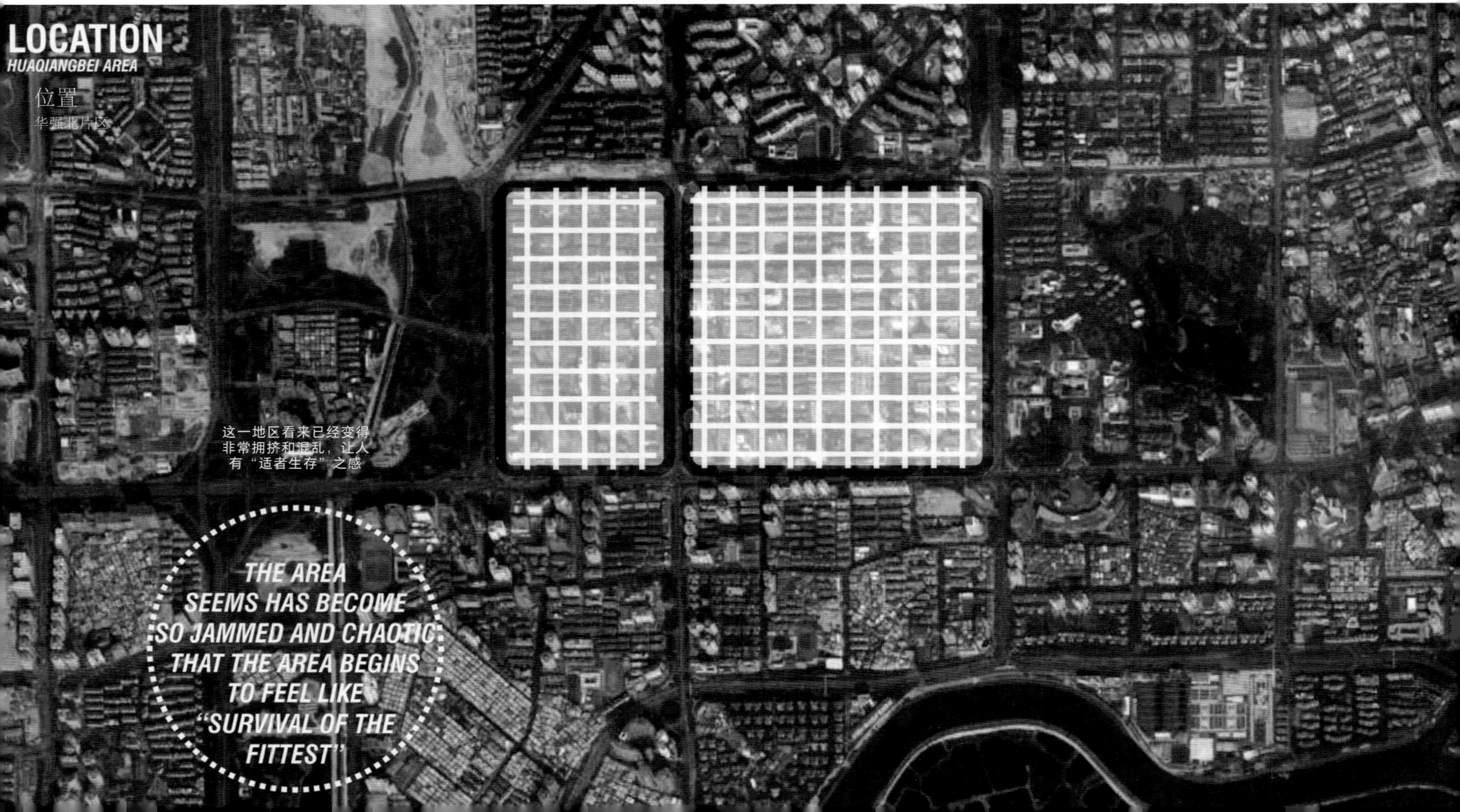
LOCATION
HUAQIANGBEI AREA
位置
华强北片区
这一地区看来已经变得
非常拥挤和混乱，让人
有“适者生存”之感
THE AREA
SEEMS HAS BECOME
SO JAMMED AND CHAOTIC
THAT THE AREA BEGINS
TO FEEL LIKE
“SURVIVAL OF THE
FITTEST”

INDUSTRY
MADE IN HUAQIANGBEI
行业
华强北制造

INDUSTRY 行业
MADE IN HUAQIANBEI 华强北制造
PRODUCED in 生产
FIXED in 修理
BOUGHT in 购买
TRADED in 交易
SOLD 销售 in
ASSEMBLED in 组装
DESIGNED in 设计
REPLACED 更换 in
COPIED 仿制 in

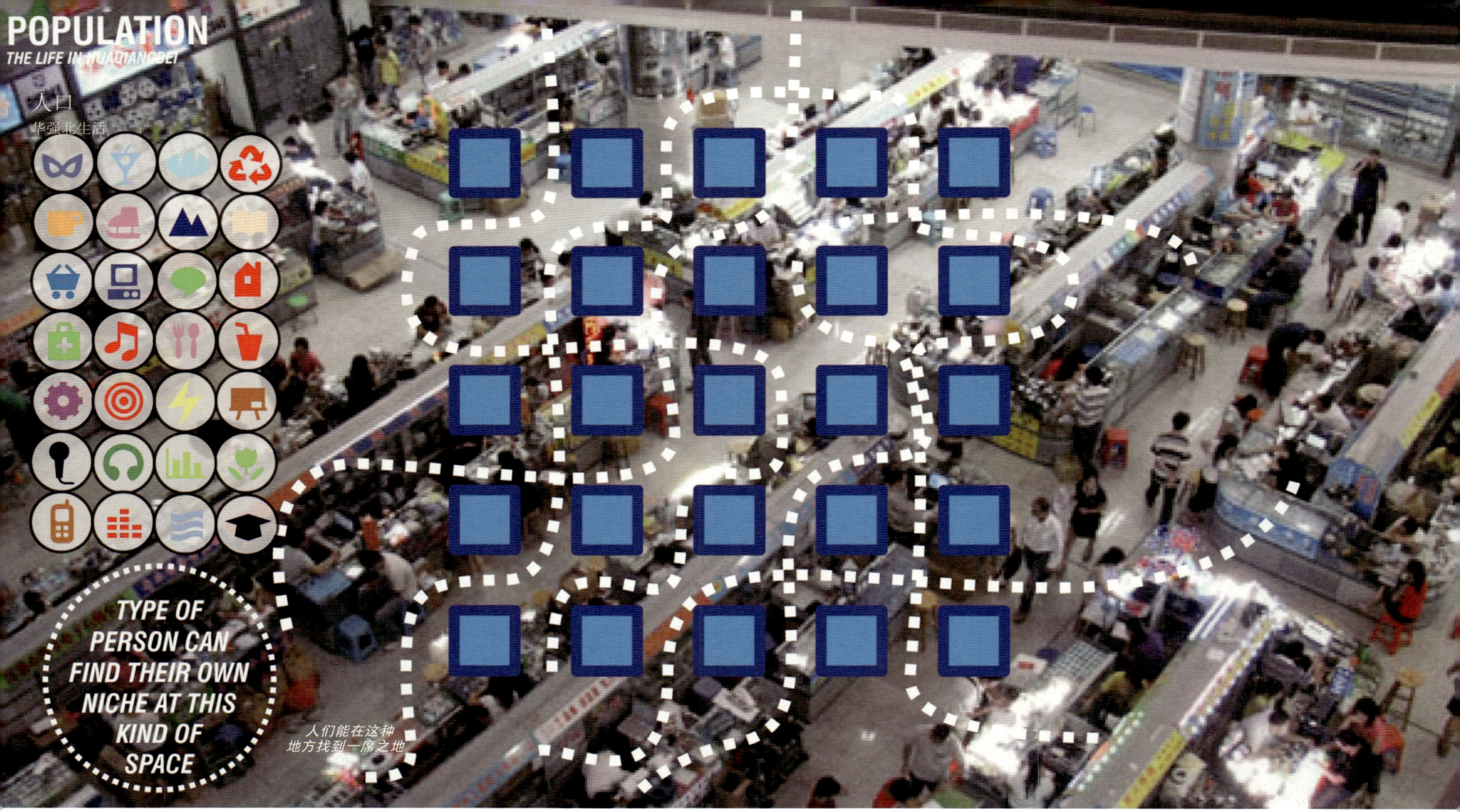
POPULATION
THE LIFE IN HUAQIANGBEI
人口
华强北生活
TYPE OF PERSON CAN FIND THEIR OWN NICHE AT THIS KIND OF SPACE
人们能在这种
地方找到一席之地

不过，华强北也是自由、活力、灵活之地

BUT IT IS ALSO A PLACE OF FREEDOM, VITALITY AND FLEXIBILITY

MORE IS MORE

多即是多

WHAT 什么是珠三角地区？
IS THE PEARL RIVER DELTA?

WHAT 我们是谁？
IS NODE?

WHERE 我们在哪里？
ARE WE?

WHAT 基础设施的角色是什么？
IS THE ROLE OF THE INFRASTRUCTURE?

WHAT 现在的问题是什么？
ARE THE ISSUES NOW?

WHAT 我们的愿景是什么？
ARE OUR VISIONS FOR THE IMMEDIATE FUTURE?

FRAGMENTS OF LOSE

负面的片段

BALANCING THE INFRASTRUCTURE

BALANCING THE GROWTHS OF INFRASTRUCTURE 平衡基础设施 *平衡基础设施的平衡发展*

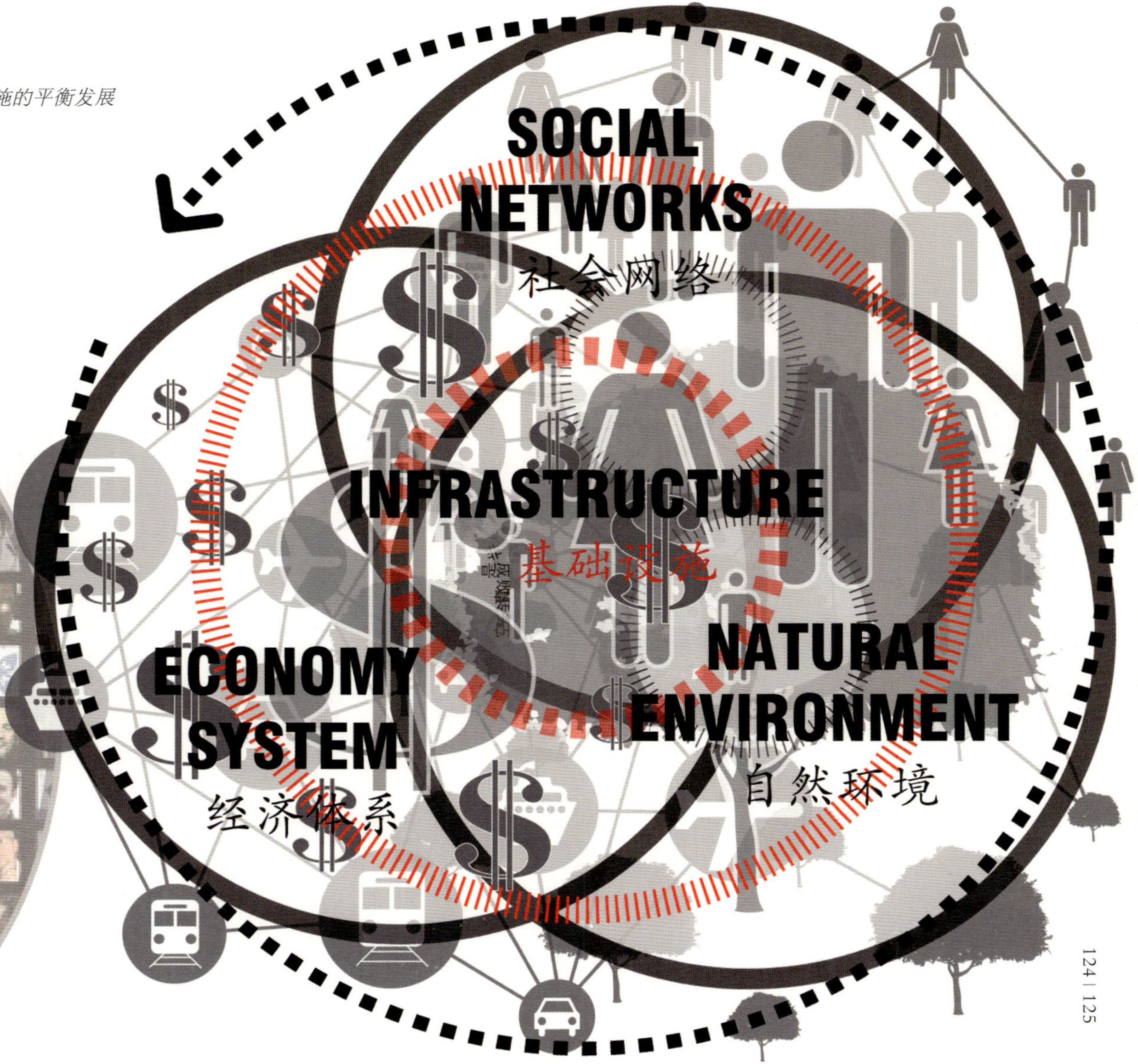

BALANCED INFRASTRUCTURE

BALANCED GROWTHS OF INFRASTRUCTURE

平衡基础设施

基础设施的平衡发展

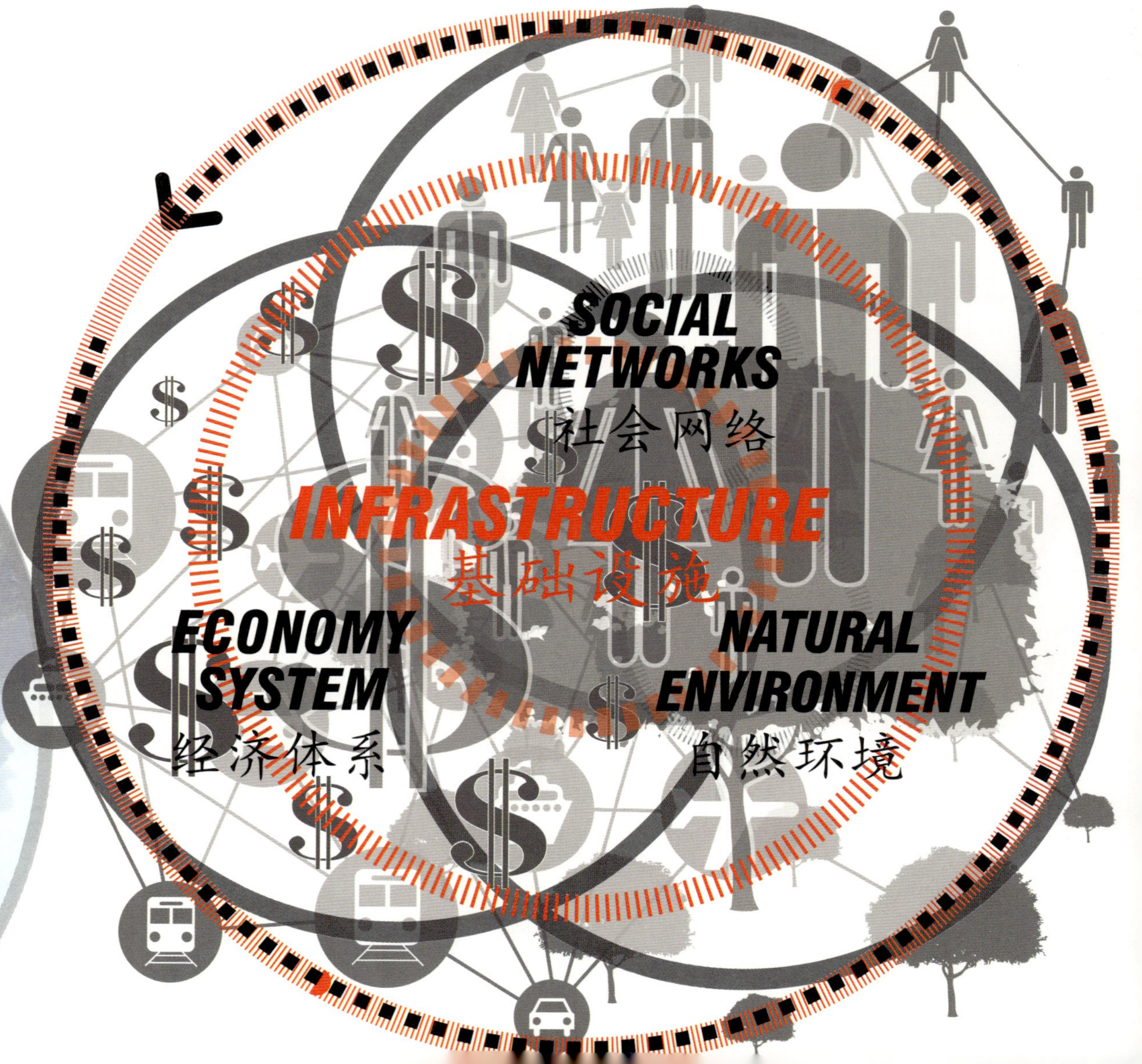

《住 · Abitare》，2009年1月/2月，第7期

后“普通城市”——当一个城市就要“过期”的时候

刘珩

“历史是一张无缝的网，一个打不开的戈耳迪之结。总是需要或多或少的一些随意的撕裂，才能找到突破口。”

—— 彼得 · 霍尔，《明日城市》

“不论是否涵盖复杂的人类关系或生态系统平衡，区域批判主义都反对以一致性为借口盲目采取自我陶醉的信条，最终导致经济成本高、对人类社区生态环境造成极大破坏。我们所称的批判性地域主义设计方式以及身份构建认识到了在某些力量、社会和文化限制下，一些单个项目或限制性项目的价值，其目标就是要既从一致性中获益，又维持可持续的多样性。”

—— 亚历山大 · 佐尼思，《批判性地域主义》

九月的南方还是盛夏，沿江堤坝路两侧一边是南方独有的骑楼，另一边是泛黄的老厂区，带着明显的20世纪五六十年代的痕迹；江中行驶着我幼时常坐的摆渡船……时间好像凝固了。熟悉的乡土气息让我想起了与和外婆一起在雷州半岛糖厂里度过的童年……

应顺德市文化主管部门的邀请，我跟随几个热衷于岭南文化研究的学者朋友来到了顺德沿江老镇容桂。据当地官员说，水利部门为保护水源决定停止沿江工业生产，并将拆除所有老厂区，改建为公共绿地。这些热心的朋友希望我们建筑师想想办法，能否用专业的意见说服政府尽可能把厂房保留下来，然后再考虑它们的新用途——比如引进像北京798这样的文化艺术产业区。尽管国内千篇一律的沿江绿地已让我感觉几近麻木，但体验着容桂依然故我的慢节奏生活，带着挥之不去的童年记忆，我觉得自己有责任——作为建筑师也好、学者也好，或是南方人也好——让这个即将被抛弃的地方和久违了的生活方式重新引起些必要的关注。这种关注或由此引发的关于城市身份课题在当下珠三角地区产业转型时代具有普遍的意义。

“岭南城市”

历史上的顺德是个典型的岭南水乡，密布的河网有条不紊地组织着人们日常的生活和工作。亦家亦店的骑楼，配上湿热气候下特有的植被，勾勒出岭南人似闲散又忙碌的《清明上河图》，伴随着桑基鱼塘诞生的丝绸工业时代演绎出了一个缓慢而热闹的早期生态绿色城市的雏型。

专栏7-2

“工业城市”

1958年的“大跃进”把顺德推上了另一轮工业化进程。借助珠江发达的水系运输而大力发展起来的沿江工业区便成了那个时代最先进的生产力代表和最典型的城市空间，特别是沿江的城市景观，有如18世纪中叶刚刚进入工业社会的欧洲城市。

“普通城市”

在经历了早期生态工业和“大跃进”的强制性工业化，顺德在改革开放带来的空前机会中一跃成为广东经济“四小虎”之一。珠三角地区成功的经济模式标志着中国乡镇全面进入工业化、全球化和城市化的高速发展时代：在单一追求高GDP的价值导向下，城市在瞬间肆意地扩张、删除和添加，令城市管理者束手无策。不仅顺德，整个珠三角地区也在短短几年的随意和混乱中发展出“千城一面”的城市景观——一个4000万人口的超级“普通城市”。这现象被西方学者和建筑师雷姆·库哈斯一针见血地戏称为“普通城市”：“它什么都不是，只是当下需求和目前能力的一种反映……它很随意，不需要保养。如过它太小，它就扩张；如果太旧，它就自我摧毁和更新。每个星期一早上它都可以制造出新的身份。”

“后普通城市”= 新岭南城市?

然而，这种“变脸”游戏能玩多久？以牺牲珍贵的土地资源和环境换取的快速工业化、全球化和城市化，在珠三角地区“拿来主义”和“模仿型”经济模式下滑的今天难以为继，而容桂沿江工业让位于净化水源和建立公共绿地的可持续策略的出炉在所难免，也势在必行。

等各种层次的道路和高速公路变得像江河一样密布的时候，沿江工业区也到了寿终正寝的时候，这些产业又得面临着新一轮的转型危机：在考虑产业竞争力的同时，当地政府可以以建设可持续城市保护水源防止进一步污染为由，不仅顺理成章地废除了沿江工业生产，而且“连根拔去”这些旧厂房；沿江工业用地在顺德最新的五年总体规划图上换成了今天在中国大肆推广的“千河一景”的公共绿地。如果所有的历史空间真能如此轻易地被抹掉，中国城市的身份更新岂不是太简单了吗?

迫不及待的工业化和全球化利用规模和速度所带来的混乱几乎横扫了珠三角地区所有的一线、二线和三线城市。当一片狼藉之后，城市中残留的历史痕迹作为城市的活标本进入新一轮“变脸”游戏时，我们是否有机会去重新解构和定义新的游戏规则?

保护水源一定要拆除工业遗址吗？公共绿地或是含工业遗址的公共空间是否是沿江区域的唯一选择？如果工业遗址作为公共空间保留下来，它可否再次作为非水源污染的“生产空间”还原给社区或提升社区的产业结构和社区空间？如果沿江工业遗址可以作为“生产空间”，当下流行的创意产业园模式是否又成为单一的选择，陷入危险的“千厂一园”的循环游戏中？

正所谓“三十年河东，三十年河西”，保护工业遗产和借址而起的创意产业园的全球化趋势在西方已是老生常谈，但在中国，特别是在珠三角地区对产业结构调整和城市空间更新问题的深层研究和质问才刚刚开始。创意产业园区自身有哪些更新问题？在以创意产业园和公共绿地为代表的自上而下的城市更新趋势之间，是否还有其他植根于当地文化自下而上的城市产业、地方文化和城市设计的创新可能？公共空间是否等同于公共绿地或社区空间？公共空间、社区空间和生产空间能否复合，创造出更有效的土地利用空间？

后续

从工业的全球化到可持续发展观念的全球化，中国的城市永远都在疲惫地跟随着世界的步伐，纵然不能超前（其实也不知如何超前），也希望一夜之间就能完成从工业城市到生态绿色城市的转换，似乎在停、拆、建这三个简单的机械运动中就能完成“变脸”以至“脱胎换骨”的全过程。中国人永远习惯于在破旧立新中“明白”自己的崭新身份，但是每一次的“变脸”或“脱胎换骨”之后，是否我们都真的有了新的身份？或者，也不过是“皇帝的新衣”？

“后普通城市”既代表了时间上的节点划分，也代表了“普通城市”概念特指的珠三角地区。面对全球的动荡经济和能源危机，以及中国产业转型的大时代，“普通城市”是继续“普通化”、全球化，还是考虑回归原本并不普通的地方身份？2007年深圳双年展提出了“城市过期”的问题，“普通城市”在无数次“变脸”之后的骨架是否能以不变应万变，承接不可预测的未知和风险？对这些问题的思考都要回归到城市的生成本质和发展策略上。沿江工业遗址保护与发展只是珠三角地区“后普通城市”时代首先面临的困惑。

在所有问题都反复问了许多遍之后，我相信答案总比没有问题的结论要来得真实和谨慎，也相信由此而来的再生城市更能抵御未来未知的危机。在慌乱和失控中忘却了自己身份的人是否能在缓慢中能找回自己？缓慢至少是一个机会，就像30年前的快速一样。

Abitare, *Jan/Feb 2009, Vol.07*

POST "GENERIC CITY" – WHEN A CITY IS NEARLY "EXPIRED"

Doreen Heng Liu

"As usual, history is a seamless web, a Gordian knot, requiring some more or less arbitrary unpickings in order to get started."

– Peter Hall, *Cities of Tomorrow*

"Whether this involves complex human ties or the balance of the ecosystem, it is opposed to mindlessly adopting the narcissistic dogmas in the name of universality, leading to environments that are economically costly and ecologically destructive to the human community. What we call the critical regionalist approach to design and the architecture of identity recognizes the value of the singular, circumscribes projects within the physical, social, and cultural constraints of the particular, aiming at sustaining diversity while benefiting from universality."

– Alexander Tzonis, *Critical Regionalism*

In September, which was still summer in southern China, I drove slowly along the riverbank. On the river side, there were factory buildings, painted yellow with a flavor of 1950s and 60s; on the other side, there were typical southern arcade buildings. On the river, small boats were busy carrying people traveling across...The time seemed to stop, and familiar smell reminded me of my childhood in Leizhou peninsula when I lived with my grandma who worked in a sugar factory.

With an invitation from the Cultural Bureau of the Shunde government, I, together with some friends who were fond of southern culture, came to Ronggui, an old county in the southern part of Shunde. According to the local officials, the water resources department, in order to protect water resources from further pollution, had decided to close down all the factories along the waterfront, and soon would demolish these decades-old factory buildings. Eventually, the waterfront would be transformed into the public green parks. My friends turned to us, hoping that we, the architects, can come up with a professional point of view to persuade the local government to save these buildings for other uses, like Beijing's 798, or other creative industry.

After visiting so many similar waterfront green parks across the country, I became senseless. Now, experiencing the slow pace in Ronggui, with the inerasable memory of childhood, I felt a sense of responsibility, either as an architect, or as a scholar or as a southerner, to bring the nearly abandoned place back to the attention...What's more important, this attention or the subject of "city identity" at the age of the industrial transformation in the Pearl River Delta region would be put under the spot light.

Lingnan City

Before industrial globalization, Shunde was a typical waterfront town in southern China. The network of waterways helped people organize their daily life, and unique arcade buildings together with the vegetables and plants, which only grow in the humid and hot environment in southern China, constituted a relaxed and yet busy urban life image. The mulberry plantation and fish pound led to scaled production of silk. By that time, a prototype of a busy yet leisurely ecological green city had come into shape.

Industrial City

The "Great Leap Forward" movement in 1958 forced Shunde to enter another round of industrialization. The waterfront industrial zones, which were developed by taking the transportation advantage brought by the dense waterways in the Pearl River, became the model of the most advanced productivity and most typical urban space at that time. Especially the city scene along the river looked just like European cities in the mid-eighteenth century when they became industrialized society.

Generic City

After the early ecological industry and the top-down mandatory industrialization in "Great Leap Forward", by taking advantage of the unprecedented opportunities brought up by the "reform and opening up", Shunde successfully landed itself among the "four tigers" in Guangdong's economy. The successful economic model in the Pearl River Delta region ushered in a time of speedy development when townships in China all entered into all-round industrialization, globalization and urbanization: guided by the sole pursuit of high GDP, cities, in an instant, arbitrarily spanned, deleted and pasted, leaving no room for city managers to deal with; for a time, with a mindset of seeking for immediate interests, arbitrariness and chaos, not only Shunde but the whole Pearl River Delta region was reduced to a universal city scene – a super "generic city" with a population of 40 million.

This phenomenon was pinpointed by Rem Koolhaas as "Generic City". Just as he said: "It is nothing but a reflection of present need and present ability. It is easy, and it does not need maintenance. If it gets too small it just expands. If it gets old it just self-destructs and renews. It is equally exciting, or unexciting everywhere. It can produce a new identity every Monday morning".

Post "Generic City" = New Lingnan City

However, how long can this "face-changing" game last? The rapid industrialization, globalization and urbanization at the expense of treasured land resources and environment appear unsustainable, especially at a time when the PRD region's "take in" and "copying" economic model is on the down-turn. Thus it became inevitable that Ronggui's waterfront industry had to be replaced by sustainable policies such as cleaning water resources and building public green land.

When the network of highways and roads at various levels became as intense as that of the waterways, waterfront industrial zones were bonded to reach their final days. Those industries were put into a new round of transformation crisis: while considering preserving industrial competitiveness, the local government, in the name of protecting water resources from pollution and building a sustainable city, not only shut down all the waterfront production, but also demolished the old factory buildings. Shunde's waterfront industrial site is replaced by today's popular "public green land" in Shunde's five-year plan. If it's true that all the historical dimensions can so easily be erased, isn't it too simple in renewing city identity?

The scale and speed developed in industrialization and urbanization almost swept all the cities in the Pearl River Delta region, no matter the first tier, second tier or third tier. After the chaos, When the historical urban residues have been regarded as the living memories of the city and get involved in the next round of "face-changing" game, do we have an opportunity to reconstruct and redefine them?

– Does the protection of water resources make it impossible to keep these industrial sites? Is it necessary that waterfront public space has to be the form of public green land; can it be public space with industrial sites in it?
– If the industrial site is preserved as the public space, is it possible to be reused as "communal space" to upgrade the community's industrial structure and social space?
– If the waterfront industrial site can be saved as "production space", then is the model of creative industry of Beijing's 798 or Shanghai's Suzhou River the only choice they have? Are they going to be trapped in the cycling game of "thousand factories but with the same face"?

Already becoming cliché in the Western world, the industrial preservation and protection, together with the creative industrial parks built on the sites, is just about to sweep across China, especially in researching and questioning the issues of industrial reconstruction and city space renewal. As a form of globalization, how can creative industry parks regenerate themselves in globalization itself is a tough question. Between the globalization represented by creative industrial parks and the sustainable cities represented by waterfront public green lands, are there other possibilities for bottom-up approaches for renovating city industry and city design based on local culture? Finally, does public space means public green lands or community space? Can we integrate them to make more efficient use of land?

Epilogue

From industrial globalization to sustainable development, Chinese cities have always been busy catching up with the world's pace, even though they can not over take (and they do not know how to). Chinese cities hope to complete the transformation from industrial cities to ecological green cities overnight, and believe that they can accomplish the "face changing" and even "rebuild" simply through repeating the three actions – shutting down, demolishing and reconstruction. Chinese people are accustomed to "understanding" their new identity by dismantling the past. But each time, after the "face changing" and "rebuilding", do we really get a new identity? Or maybe it is only an illusion.

"Generic city" is a concept particularly referred to the Pearl River Delta region, and a time divider to mark nearly the end of the current industrial age. Facing the global economic turmoil and China's industrial transformation, will "generic city" continue to stay generic, become more globalized, or return to its unique local identity? In a biennial exhibition held in Shenzhen in 2007, the question of "city of expiration" was put forward. After so many rounds of "expiration", should cities like "generic city" re-invent themselves in the way we demolish all the waterfront factories and replace them by public green lands? To think about these questions, we have to go back to the essence of a city. The waterfront preservation and development is perhaps the first of a series of questions that "generic city" has to answer.

When all the questions have been asked so many times, I believe the answer is more prudent and real than the unquestionable conclusion. I also believe the city of regeneration can be better coped with future's unknown challenges. Can the one who has lost his identity in chaos find himself again in a slow-paced life? Slowness at least is an opportunity, just like fastness three decades ago.

FRAGMENTS OF HOPE
希望的片段
Musée d' art et d'h
归家团圆的节日
FESTIVALS FOR
HOMECOMING REUNION
全球化的文化交流
GLOBALIZED
CULTURALEXCHANGE
消费繁荣的时期
CONSUMPTION BOOMS

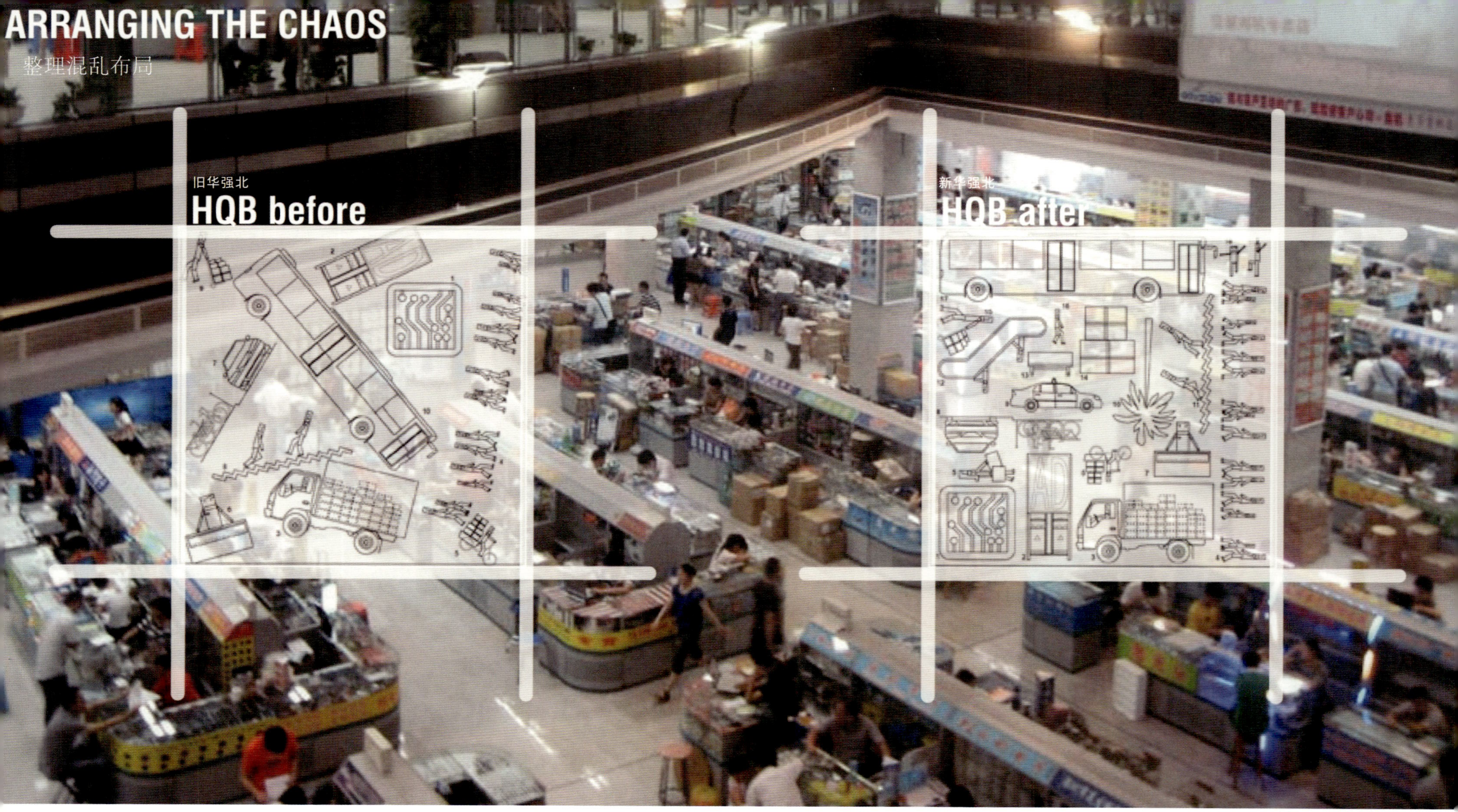

ARRANGING THE CHAOS
整理混乱布局
旧华强北
HQB before
新华强北
HQB after

CHAOS ARRANGED

整理混乱

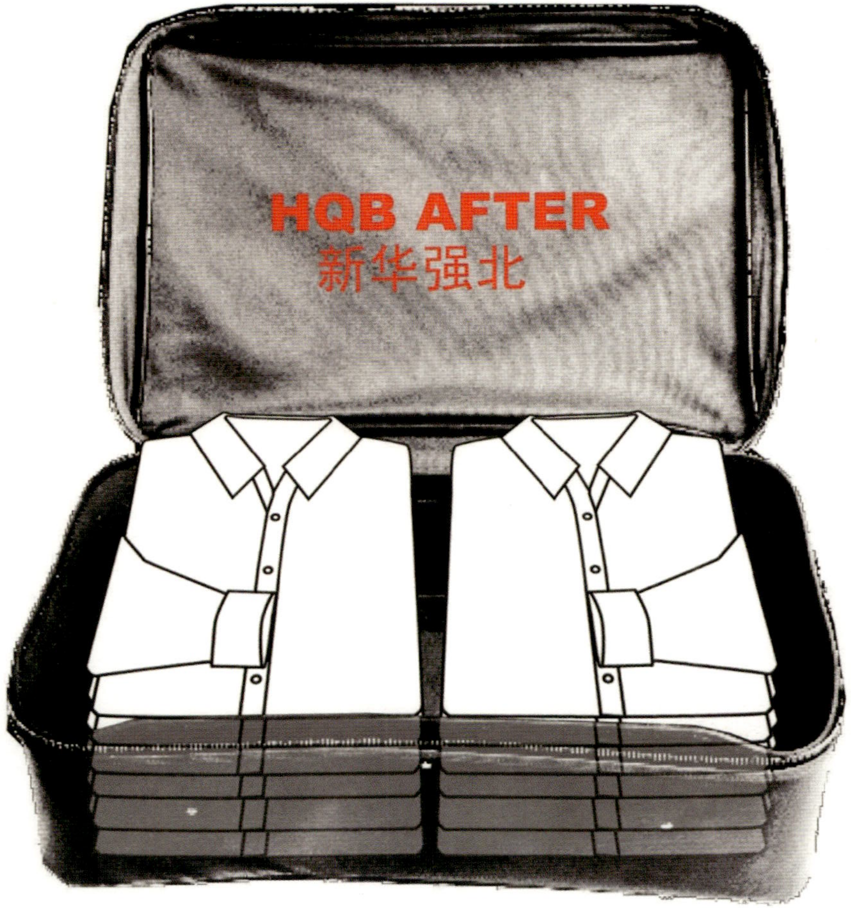

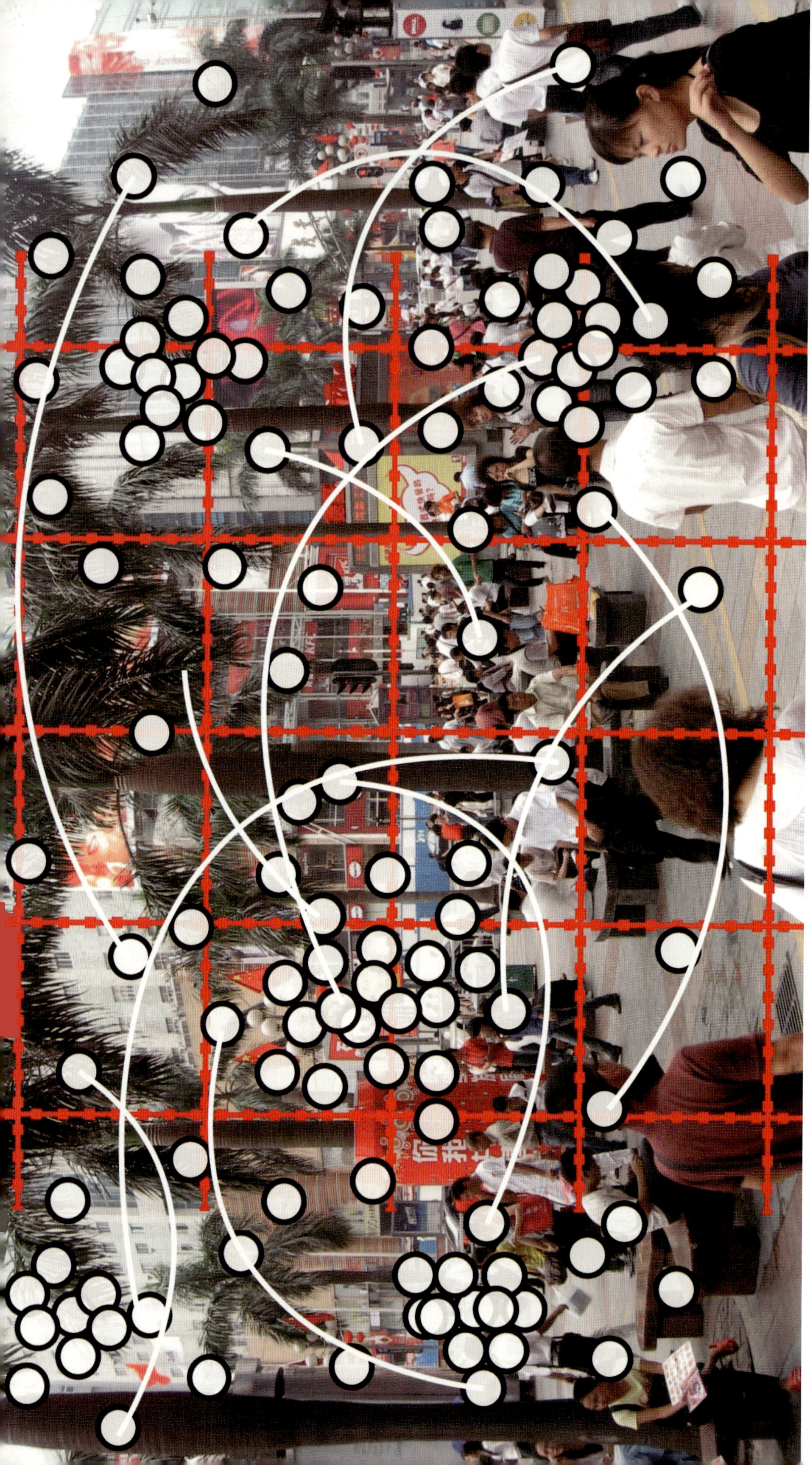

MORE & MORE

越来越多

ENERGY FLOWS

EQUILIBRUIUM

能量流动 *均衡*

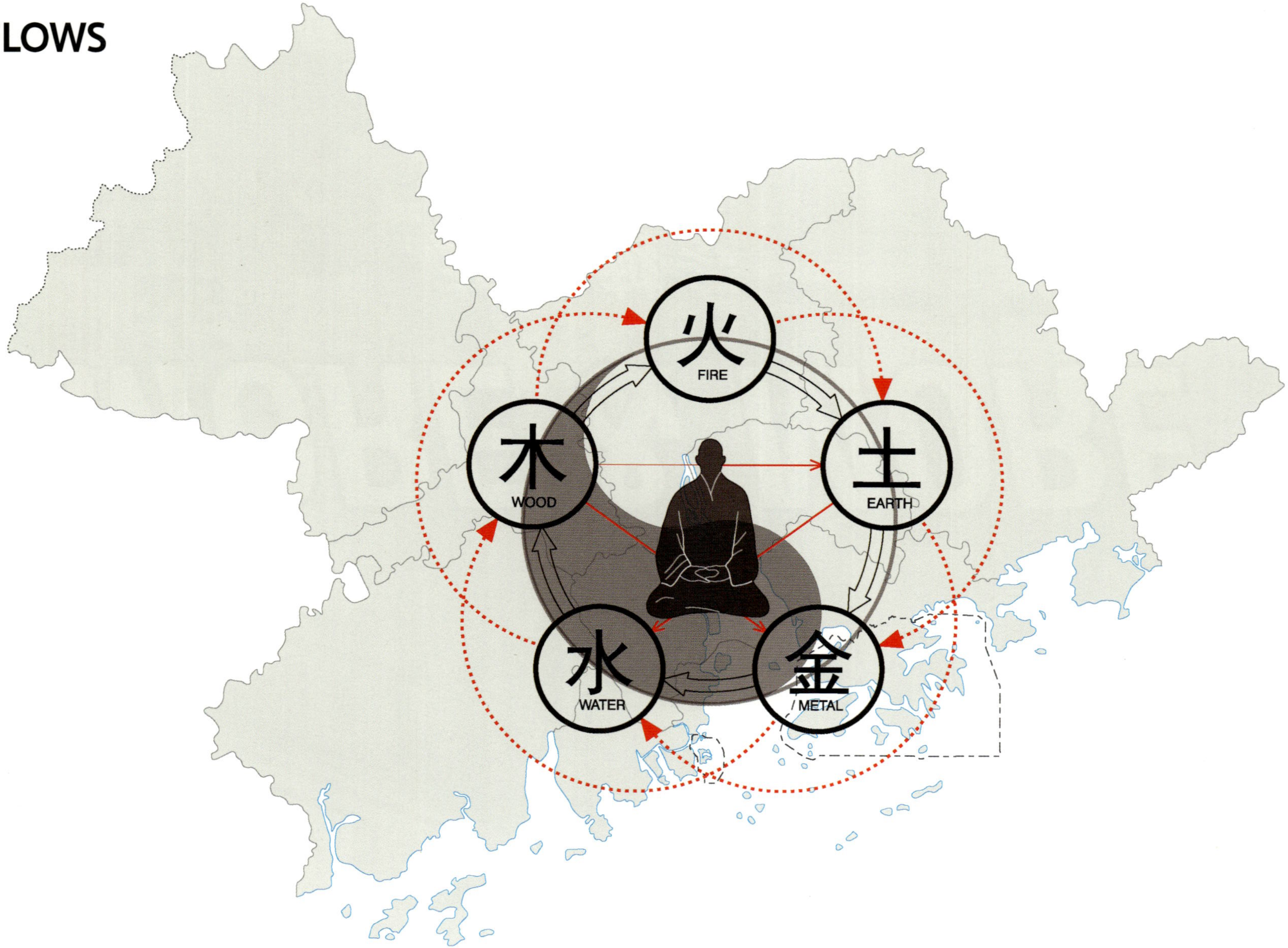

《今天》，2009年夏季刊02，第85期

另一个珠三角

刘珩 + 姜珺

刘珩：很久没见，南方朋友很多都北上了，似乎大家也越来越少关注南方的发展. 是否珠三角的问题已过时了？作为中国改革开放最早城市化的地区，这几年其势头显然没有长三角地区和环渤海经济圈来得猛。“三十年河东三十年河西”，这也很正常。但南方的城市化到底何去何从？也许我们今天可以围绕着这个话题展开讨论。

姜珺：这应该还是地缘政治经济的问题。我们的政体曾经是一个内向的政体，在不需要太多国际贸易的时期，珠三角地区就相对显得不是那么重要；而在全球贸易萌发的时期，如海上丝绸之路的开拓、殖民主义的全球化，由于东西方之间的海路更多是自西向东通过南中国海进入中国的，珠三角地区就相对于中国的东部更早地受到全球化的影响。珠三角地区的城市化比较特别，相对来说比较自发，比如老广州，老城和沙面本身是自觉的，但之间因一口通商而产生的城市格局都是自发的；而今天，改革开放以后的广州城市空间也存在两种动力机制，一种是内生的框架，另一种是来自其他城市的影响，尤其是来自香港的影响。所以历史上，南方城市就更多地受到内生型政治和外向型经济的交互作用。

香港对珠三角地区的影响很大。香港政府对于市场经济的管治比较规范：深圳向香港学习，在某些制度层面成功了，就向全国推广，在外向型经济体制和相关行政管理体制上做了“试验田”。它的城市化如果说有什么必然性的话，事实上跟整个国家的政治经济环境，还有它所处的地缘位置有关。在内向经济时期它处于边缘，但在外向经济时期就变成了前沿，成为“排头兵”，在中国的城市化中起到向内传递的作用。如果它成功的话，它的经验就很快会被内地的城市学习并追赶。今天的珠三角地区在城市化和现代化上如果要继续有所作为，必须在其他方面继续走在其他城市的前面。

刘珩：我觉得城市化的问题，应从两方面来谈，一方面是社会经济，另一方面是城市空间。现在的中国城市化还在走向“普通城市”，城市空间趋于均质化。前30年这种快速均质化带来了巨大的经济效益，但经济发展现在已经到了另外一个阶段，就是求变。求变的过程中，以深圳和广州这两个城市为例，深圳是很典型按照西方现代主义的模型进行规划和建设的城市，它非常有秩序，非常具有逻辑和理性，所以带来了整个城市的空间质量，与西方的现代城市有很多的相似性，很多新空间甚至控制得更理性、更极致，像深南大道。西方人特别喜欢和认同深圳，因为深圳有一种可识别性的质量。但来到广州，他们就有一种迷路的感觉。广州喜欢按照自己那种惯性方式，想怎么改变就怎么改变，广州人觉得这些改变跟其他人没什么关系，因为其他人都不生活在这个城市里，只有他们自己才生活在这个城市里，所以他们觉得城市就是他的家，想怎样就怎样。深圳其实还不是南方的城市，它是一个北方的城市，或者是在西方规划体系下造就的城市。广州才是一个真正南方的城市，很生活化、很随意。

姜珺：广州是一个南方和东方的城市，深圳是一个北方和西方的城市。如果说地域性的话，深圳和广州的差异性是非常大的。深圳更多以年轻外来移民为主体，体制转型和个人家庭方面的负担相对来说比广州要少。广州的主体是本地人，历史上这里就有“土客矛盾”。两地在城市规划的制定上，肯定有大的区别。在建筑单体空间上，两个城市差异并不大；但在建筑之间的关系或社区之间的格局上，两地差异就很大。这是不同潜规则导致的不同区域性。

刘珩：是什么样的潜规则？

姜珺：就是空间的潜规则，它不是已经画成图纸的建筑空间，而是在图纸之间没有被画出来的，或者说画出来没有被执行的或者被错误执行的地方，能够反映出一种集体意识，其实就是甲乙双方的相互翻译。这是两个城市之间的差别。

刘珩：我觉得这种潜规则很有意思。我觉得这件事还是可以再谈一下。就是说南方和北方的城市拿到同一套图纸、同一套规划，出来的结果是不一样的。

姜珺：很可能是不一样的。

刘珩：如果把广州的珠江新城和深圳的深南大道CBD作一下比较，我觉得还是有相似性。

姜珺：中国各级地方政府的发展战略和行为模式都比较相似，因而在城市空间上也就可能比较相似。差异性则存在于一些更为自下而上的空间，比如东莞的一些村庄，它们之间可能有一些产业链，这些产业链是它们原住民村落之间的一种默契，或者是历史上不同宗族之间遵守的一些潜规则。它们会联合起来做鞋、手机，这就是超出传统城市空间的、没有规划师去规划、由当地人自己产生出来的东西。这些东

西虽然在深圳也存在，但不是主流。

刘珩：像深圳华强北这个例子就非常有意思，因为它是全国电子产品交易最活跃的市场。似乎各种人群、物流在这个地段也在遵守一些潜规则，但感觉与珠三角地区其他城市又很不同。

姜珺：我觉得华强北是一个比较典型的自我升级、向香港学习的结果。它的自我升级主要是产业升级，在空间上主要是向香港学习。在深圳稀有的空间里面如何让它加密，这一点应该是向香港学习的，香港做得比较好。深圳华强北产生了一批比较有名的高科技企业，在一个比较低端的产业环境中竞争，整个业态可能不健康，现在是通过空间加密的方式对整个业态进行重新选择。它不完全是自然选择，带有人工的性质，来促进它内部的某些更加优秀的企业进行良性竞争。我完全理解华强北的这个状况，虽然我还没看竞赛的结果。

刘珩：华强北这个项目的设计竞赛只是想解决形式上的一些事情，竞赛本身探讨的余地不是太大，但怎么去看待华强北本身是非常有意义的。竞赛的命题纯粹在于设计立体式的街道，这样也许临时解决了目前诸如交通流量、人车矛盾等问题，但实际上许多事务所，包括我们南沙原创的方案，发现华强北的问题不是简单地靠这种形式的东西就可以解决的，像人跟车之间的矛盾等。其实要从更加深层的像后街这种物流区着手，是从产业开始，看业态是怎么形成、怎么运转的，只有了解这个方面，最后才会回到城市空间的问题上。华强北这个案例表现的其实是当下解决问题的一个基本倾向，没用很多时间去深究它的前缘，去研究它是如何来的、怎么发展的。事情一急，就很自然地把责任放在建筑师的身上，希望建筑师用最直接的、可视的一种形式解决当下迫于眉睫的问题。形式能带来表面的改变，但是不能根治问题，或深层地解决问题。

姜珺：你刚才说的其实是比较普遍的问题。政府在主导规划的时候，通常会把规划看做是一种空间目的，而不是调控手段。当然规划作为一种空间调控的手段，目的是宏观调控城市的经济、产业结构，重新制定或者更新整个城市的战略，确定战略方向到底是向哪块倾斜。先有战略，再有资源的配置、产业的梳理、产业链的整合，然后再是空间，以及在新的空间上再进行项目设立，然后再进行项目管理。而现在的城市规划很单薄，过于倚重一种先入为主的空间规划，对产业的解读并不是那么专业，甚至有时候比较武断；另外，实施也不是彻底地调动整个社会力量的通力合作。我觉得这是中国很多城市非常典型的规划过程。

刘珩：我觉得这个无可厚非，深圳规划局是全国最好的规划局之一，他们的做法很规范，也很理性。现在我们谈的是整个珠三角地区规划带有普遍性的问题，特别是二三线城市，甚至包括广州这些城市。广州本来就是大家说不清楚的城市，对它的发展都不清楚的时候，必须要有新的形态、新的东西来说明它的规划是有成绩的，建筑就扮演了一个很重要的角色。正如雷姆·库哈斯所说，现在大地上出现了很多物体（objects），实际上物体间是没有关联的，它不能够形成有机体（organism），它应该还有另外是一些动力（dynamics）的东西，促成这些物体变成一个主题（subject）和城市。这些东西是不是当下我们要考虑的一些事情？但我觉得在很多层面上都没有把这些事情谈清楚。加上政策的执行缺乏一种连续性，使得人根本没办法深层次去探讨软性的东西，还是必须把建筑与形态的东西摆在第一位，从长线来说，可能对整个城市的发展和社区的形成产生一些很消极的影响。深圳，像你所说的，本身能发展的空间已经很有限了，必须靠加密的方式，去推动城市的发展。但是广州一下子从1000多平方公里扩展到7000平方公里，突然间有很多的土地用于建设。所以在这种情况下，加密不是广州要考虑的基本问题，它还是在不断地扩展，但是我相信，这种无节制的城市化给后人带来的危害会很大，因为土地的自然状态是不可逆转的。我不知道我们的这些思考会对城市有什么帮助。

姜珺：我觉得这种主动思考，不如产业链上的被动改变对城市化造成的影响大。像东莞，它也在“中国制造”如日中天时以所谓的高新产业园区推动产业转型，其实在落成以后几年基本上还是一个壳。东莞在目前产业结构比较单一的情况下，想通过单个的项目去推动东莞的产业升级并不现实。而在这一轮的外向经济倍受打击的情况下，大量中小企业的扩展，或者是很低端的产业会被排挤出市场；而原来是自主创业的企业，会影响整个东莞的未来格局。

刘珩：我现在对一个问题很有兴趣，因为你说30年以后，城市堆出了很多建筑物，其实很多都空了，可能土地也闲置了。所以闲置这个问题变得非常突出，可能跟产业升级也有关系。像南沙新区东部，经过了这么多年的发展，现在还是一块处女地，很多的土地没有发展起来，最主要的问题是发展商没有想到放什么项目在上面，才能起到一种带动的作用。所以在没想清楚的情况下，就让土地放在那儿。现在大家都在讨论提高土地利用率和土地效益问题，政府也在推动这种土地的利用。但在永久的项目没办法具体化和落地之前，还有一个时间差。这个时间差里，我们是否可以考虑一种中间状态规划，所谓临时规划和临时建筑这种灵活的策略去填充这个时间差，去适应当下城市化过程中的不预测性，将来把它拆了，也不觉得可惜。

姜珺：投入成本与经济效应之间有一个边际效应问题。但是在某些地区或者在某些项目的初期阶段，可能没有能力、没有财力，甚至连耐心都没有去等待企业化的发生。如果它提前占用了那些土地，在后来会越来越成为负担，因为空间是很难被摧毁的。它往往会以实体的方式约束整个产业的发展，以旧空间的发展约束了新的活力的产生。南沙这个项目可能还算是少数的、能够通过长期规划和大规模投入整合产业链，进而产生相应的城市格局的一个例子。

刘珩：我觉得南沙新区比较特殊，因为它是一个由外资的发展商来发展的新城，而且这个发展商没有发展新城的经验。南沙东部这块土地22平方公里，相当于一个澳门主岛的面积。在新城的事情上，我觉得发展商并没有想得比较全面和透彻，而是过于简单化和乌托邦化，他对新城的理解还是建立在一种建筑形态的创造方面。因为没想清楚，所以在迫于发展的时候就必须靠建筑不同形态的项目去引起别人的注意，这方面太类似其他地区了。南沙早期的发展只有总规划图，这个总图还是由一个在后现代建筑时期有很高知名度的西班牙建筑师与他的助手做出来的，实施过程中基本上就是现代主义的规划加上一些后现代建筑，结果也就是一个平面和多种建筑形式拼贴的一层皮。但这种纯建筑的设计和实施并没有带来人气，也没有引发一个社区正常成长的机制。这是建筑师基本上无能为力的问题，十多年前看是这个问题，十多年后再看还是这个问题。说到新城社区的成长机制，我觉得这个讨论会很有意义。以南沙为例，南沙发展很慢，但这种慢并没有带来很多的危害，那种矛盾的反差还没有变得那么突出。但像大学城，就很有意思，其实大学城的面积跟南沙东部的面积是相当的，它是18平方公里，南沙是22平方公里。它在18个月的时间内建成了几百万平方米建设量的“城市”，并且把几万的学生引到这个“城市”来。虽然空间上有这么多的建筑面积，也有少量的人口，但它也还不是一个正常的社区。俗语说：“罗马不是一天建成的”。这道理在哪？番禺的社区经过不长的时间就已经建立起来了，很便宜的地价和住宅，看市场的需要而建，慢慢经过这么多年以后，形成一个比较良性的社区发展，然后才考虑社区质量的提升。我觉得像大学城这种新城模型的发展，经过多年以后再看是不是会与番禺卧城有同样的结果，还是说会有其他情况发生？你怎么看？

姜珺：我想这三个案例还是有点不一样的，在广州，大部分人都在城里就业，番禺一部分还是一个“卧城”，有比较好的公共交通将两者联系起来。广州不需要每天去上班、在家里就能赚钱的人挺多的。他们可以在城里收租，然后到乡下去买个房子。这些人很多是那些在茶餐厅喝茶的老人，他们的子女大多在海外，有自己稳定的收入来源。我觉得这种情况在其他城市可能不完全是这样。其他城市在老龄化以后会有危机，但是在广州不是那么严重。多少也是因为它属于外向型经济，他们可能通过某些贸易渠道做一些小生意，能够养活自己，所以他们的养老就不是大问题。我觉得这些人口是社区活力的主体。因为地价的缘故，番禺当时的房子卖得很便宜，因此人们的生活压力也不是那么大。大学城的功能看上去很单一，就是一个“教学城”。里面的流动人口也在不断更新，但它能形成一个比较稳定的消费群。学生可以完全不用进城，他们只要每天去图书馆看看书、在篮球场打打球，基本上就可以了；而且很多大学之间可以有参与性，学生可以到其他学校去听课。这种城市结构其实很单一，它的学生主体有非常明确的目标，流动比较稳定，能够每年有进有出；而且还能够养活大学城里的几个城中村，这些城中村能够提供一些学校没办法提供的服务。南沙的问题，我觉得目前主要是交通问题，计划中的一小时经济圈目前还没有完全实现。如果能够实现一小时经济圈，甚至时间更短的话，人口还是会继续流入南沙。另外，进驻的企业也没有完全落成，落成的企业也没有真正形成规模生产；流入的人口不能马上在这里找到工作，或者找到工作的人也不能够形成南沙的主要人口，这些都需要一个孵化的过程，因为南沙作为一个新城是比较独立的。

刘珩：南沙作为一小时生活圈的几何中心，它应该是什么样的城市？我觉得这与对日常生活的理解很有关系，我到深圳、广州、香港都是一小时，但我到这些城市都有不同的目的。我到深圳很多时候是公务，不在深圳住；我在香港住，但我的事务所主力又在南沙，其实目前在南沙又没有业务，没有正常的生活内容，所以我觉得南沙只是一个想象中的中心，但实际上它又是可有可无的、没有承担一个城市所需要的任何一个重要功能。从深圳到广州，要经虎门大桥，必须要在南沙经过，但你不需要在南沙逗留。这种情形下，南沙作为一个地理几何中心和想象的中心，跟它作为一个不可缺少的、实际上的生活中心，存在着很大的距离，它会是怎样的一座城市？

姜珺：未来南沙的主体人口，是由目前设计的产业结构和产业配套形成的就业主力。产业要有承上启下的作用，承上就是珠三角地区传统的转口贸易、出口加工，启下就是比较独立的制造业、加工业；这些产业必须要靠一小时经济圈的区位优势来展开物流，它的服务也可以相应围绕这个经济圈展开。

刘珩：但目前我感觉到，你刚才谈到一小时经济圈，把产业物流放在南沙其实是最合理的，因为从最短距离的运输可能性来考虑，这是最合理的产业地点。但是如果把人放到生活圈这个位置上，我觉得又会产生另一个可能性。如果把南沙想象成一个卧城，或许一个人住在南沙，工作地点可以是在深圳，可以在广州、香港、珠海。会不会还有这种反向的可能性，把所有的工作都放在南沙，而人可以住在深圳、广州、香港。人不过于就是工作和生活两个头嘛，你怎么去分配这一小时？这是个想象了，你可以把中心想象成一个卧城，你的工作地点是在一小时经济圈之外。这是一个空间分配的问题。另外还有第三个可能性，在广州有自己的工作、生活圈，深圳或珠海也有自己的工作、生活圈，大家都不需要南沙。其实这是另外一种场景，现在就是按照第二种情况发生，所以南沙最后可能只是一个物流中心或是换乘中心，而不能够成为一种生活方式的中心。

姜珺：生活方式还是要培育的，需要有一定的住户。如果只是把南沙当成一个工作地点的话，到了晚上基本上就没有活力了。南沙的规模尺度决定它必须是一个混合型的、相对独立的卫星城。城市的吸引力很多来自第三产业，尽管它的第二产业可能非常好，但不会特别吸引人，只不过是生产工具而已；而第三产业是很有吸引力的，但这个不能去规划它，只能去引导和培育，并继而形成一个有质量的社区环境和公共空间，然后人们可能才会觉得南沙值得待，值得在这里生活、工作。这肯定是需要时间的。

刘珩：对，我觉得这个是三四年以后的事情。大家也在讲差异化的发展，就是说广州跟深圳的发展肯定是不同的，澳门跟香港的发展肯定也是不同的。深圳跟香港一体化发展，广州跟佛山一体化发展。无形中又把南沙边缘化了。即使是有一种培养的机制，慢慢地发展起来一种社区，其实这种社区的身份是很模糊的。现在想，南沙可以是怎样的城市？现在大家在谈深圳、谈广州，但你去这些城市，都需要经过南沙。大家都经过它，但它还是在继续边缘化。在空间上怎么去考虑南沙的地位，大家都没有把这件事情想得很清楚。就像你刚才说的，通过一种产业来带动生活社区的形成，也许这是最直接的方法，其实也不用考虑得太多，到底它会是一种什么东西。

姜珺：广东省如果真的要把广州南沙变成一个重要的轴线，区别于广深港轴线或者是广珠澳轴线，它其实要做的还是要整合这两条轴线，以及现在正在做的港澳这一条轴线。当珠三角地区的三边都完型了，三条轴线的关系都理清楚了、分工很明确的时候，南沙的重要性一下子就体现出来了。过去很多年里，珠三角地区是各自为政的，有很多重复建设；这些年开始鼓励优势互补、错位竞争、联动发展。广州跟东莞有一定的分工了，广州与佛山开始实现同城化了，深圳和香港开始加大合作了，广州和香港的关系也开始摆正了；广佛、深港这两个珠三角东翼的城市圈定位逐渐浮出水面了。当这条链上的产业分工和城市定位都明确的时候，南沙的作用就清楚了。另一条轴线就是广佛到珠澳，目前也在整合。下一步港珠澳大桥通车以后，这条线会慢慢地热起来。“环南沙”这个城市圈完型以后，南沙的作用就浮现出来了。我觉得霍英东看到的主要是这一点。他看到的是一个几何空间，这个几何空间起作用是建立在整个环南沙城市带成型，它才能真正作为一小时经济圈的几何中心，对周边资源起到一个调配作用。到时从南沙经过，你很明确它能够为经过的人起到怎样的中介和调配作用。那些想调配整个城市带上资源的产业能够留在南沙。现在东边这条已经趋于成型，西边和南面的两条边也在成型当中，指日可待。

刘珩：珠三角地区的这种同城化，随着快速铁路的形成，到2011年基本都已经完成。珠三角地区的这种模式，与长三角地区和环渤海经济圈是不是还有很不一样的东西？其实我不了解其他两个圈的情况。你觉得这三个圈相比起来差异是不是很大？

姜珺：很大，主要是行政上的差异非常大，地缘上的差异也很大。地缘差异，如果是讲外向型经济的话，环渤海经济圈就不是那么明显，反而是内源型经济占主体。珠三角地区和长三角地区相对来说比较近。环渤海经济圈作为一个后发的经济圈，行政关系上是完全不一样的。行政关系上，珠三角地区既简单又复杂，简单的是涉及省份比较少，复杂的是有两个特别行政区；长三角地区涉及的省份比较多，却有个直辖市作龙头；环渤海经济圈有两个直辖市和几个大省。这三者比较起来，长三角地区应该是比较好操作的。它有一个直辖市、两个省，直辖市的级别高一点，它在统筹两个省的过程当中，相对来说比较有执行力。珠三角地区的情况不大一样，理论上谁都不服谁的。东莞不一定服广州，广州也不特别服香港，深圳作为经济特区也不服广州，根源是谁都不服谁。但是经过一段时间的痛苦教训，它们之间慢慢地形成了共识。在环渤海经济圈，理论上北京是可以统筹的，操作起来主要在于中央决定要在环渤海这个大的经济圈里面，以“举国之力”要施加多少力量。这力量大到南水北调、西气东送，大到可以统筹北方很大范围里面的几个省，这个范围比长三角地区要大很多。它的力量也在于和俄罗斯、韩国、日本等附近的几个大国之间的利益分配。它自己内部的几个城市之间，目前来说有很多定位上的不稳定。譬如说北京作为政治、经济、文化中心的全能定位；目前定位看上去比较清晰的天津，在工业和港口方面又跟唐山有重合。我觉得这些都是定位不够清晰的方面。北京的角色在于，它可能需要以行政规划的手段来统筹谁先做什么事，谁之后做什么事。首钢必须要搬迁到哪个地方，煤必须要从哪出去，铁矿石必须从哪出去，挖湖要先做哪一块，循环经济先在哪里实验等等。这些都是宏观调控。北京需要有首都的实力，平衡各个地方的关系。

刘珩：现在回到珠三角地区的问题上，我们讲一下对“后普通城市”的理解，其实这个名字是源于我前段时间对顺德沿江工厂厂区改造的课题。既然库哈斯讲到普通城市，我们再讲“后普通城市”的珠三角会是什么样的情形。它是产业升级版的普通城市，还是珠三角的城市会走向一种差异化，形成一种更加有意思、更加生猛的城市群体？或者其实这两种可能性是不是都存在着？

姜珺：我觉得差异化肯定还是存在的。以前的这种差异同时又在恶性竞争，以前的问题是同质竞争，慢慢变成差异竞争。然后又变成一种差异的联合，就是错位竞争。这种联合导致共赢的局面可能会使得这种差异化加剧。其实是越有差异就越有竞争力的。

刘珩：这种差异会给城市空间带来一种什么关系呢？作为建筑师，我们总想三年后我们再接手这些案例的时候，在做城市设计、建筑设计的时候，我们该如何面对，我觉得目前的这种差异并没有给城市空间带来直观的不同感。

姜珺：我觉得还是有的，首先比如说香港，我觉得整个珠三角地区没有一个城市像香港那样，其他城市没办法跟它竞争。广州肯定是华南的中心城市，华南的大部分资源都往广州跑。深圳肯定是跟香港捆绑起来，而且为香港提供它的文化、经济价值，然后把香港行政、金融方面的经验，以及其他国际经验吸收进来。深圳跟广州和香港很不一样，它掺入了大量的北方文化的因素，可能它更有创造力。这种创造力可能会弥补香港在文化上的千篇一律。在香港的城市空间漫游还是很有趣味的，每次去都觉得很好玩。虽然在空间内部其实没有太多的内容，但是整个城市空间有非常强的创造力。香港的核心竞争力是它有一个行政特区的身份，所以有很多从北方过去的精英。如果东莞未来还是走制造业这条路，它依然还是一个世界工厂，必须要很快地走向自我转型。我觉得东莞在很长一段时间内都将是一个以制造业为主的城市。

刘珩：你刚才说香港，我觉得以会展这个功能来展开谈这个问题会很有意思。香港本身汇聚东方和西方的两种文化，有不同的制度，有开放的机制，它自动引发了空间的某种活力，跟内地是不一样的；像充分借用机场这个基础设施空间来拓展，能够带动其他社会功能、旅游功能，它已经朝这个方向发展了。这些附属功能是依附于基础设施而引发的新的城市空间，再加上一种灵活的制度，使得香港的会展中心能够带有多元性。反观深圳和广州，现在都在搞会展，像白云会议中心、琶洲会展中心，但还是以一个孤立的和单一的“岛”的观念来建设，大家都在拼“大”，拼有几个五星级酒店。深圳在会展功能上和广州没有太大的差异，还是存在对同一种资源的单纯竞争。它所带来的城市空间也是比较相近的。所以从长远来说，你所说的差异化，我觉得是在同样资源的竞争上去体现和理解附加功能的差异化而产生的综合竞争力。我觉得将来在珠三角地区还是要通过综合竞争力来寻找差异化，而不是这种单一功能上的差异。

姜珺：刚才说的这三个经济中心，还是有各自的综合竞争力的。广州主要是广交会（中国进出口商品交易会）；深圳的高交会（中国国际高新技术成果交易会）是华南的高新技术中心；香港的会展相对来说比较综合，但没有像广交会、高交会那样的规模，所以在短期内没办法取代广交会的某些功能和作用或者高交会的储含量，是以第三产业为主的会展。所以这三者还是各自有竞争性的，都代表了自己城市的核心定位，还是属于综合竞争力的部分。不过香港经历了这么多年的发展，基础设施肯定已经是高度发达了，而且很多方面要比内地城市做得细，所以在体现综合竞争力方面显得比较突出。我觉得关于“后普通城市”，雷姆·库哈斯的观点对于某些亚洲国家可能并不大适用。在中国这样的国家，你想普通，有些城市还普通不了，不承认这么一个条件。这与受西方文化影响较大的上海不大一样。空间在一个很难被同化的城市里面，其实并不是那么重要。空间摆在那里，更重要的是在空间里进行的事情，这些事情有能量的话，它可能从使用上能够反映到这个空间。文化对全球化其实是有一种反抗作用的。它在全球化的过程当中，也完成了当地化，未来越具有全球化可能性的城市将越当地化，因为它不得不与其他全球化、普通化的城市相互区别来实现它的全球化，它身份的取得是与当地文化不脱节的。

刘珩：如果把建筑看成一种符号，符号的全球化跟文化的当地性有效地结合，其实就形成了这个城市的地域化。

姜珺：我把它说成是建筑的符号化。

刘珩：我觉得符号不是太好的词，只有一层表皮。全球化的建筑还体现在项目选择上的趋同性，这些项目有同样的体量、同样的规模、同样的材料和形式。这些项目也是符号，是全球化的硬性指标。

姜珺：像会展中心、码头、机场这些直属全球化功能的设施又往往是非常有限度的全球化。没有充分的余力去完成全球化的进程，它们大部分都是自我更新、自我完善。我觉得未来的文化，当它需要重新推广的时候，必须要完成一种当地化，才能完成推广。当时我去蒙古，发现恰恰是当时的蒙古音乐濒临灭绝，蒙古人才能够到处巡演，寻求到了经验。而当年那些模仿欧美乐队的可能已经消失了。

刘珩：我觉得像你这样去定义文化，可能反映在对公共空间的认同和使用上。当你说到机场、码头、会展中心这些由功能来定位的城市空间，它们有自己功能的界定，在这些界定的功能空间里，大家有共同的目的和模式语言，甚至连装修都是一样……如麦当劳。只是现在换成了丽思卡尔顿酒店、古根海姆博物馆、扎哈·哈迪德设计的歌剧院或诺曼·福斯特设计的机场，等等。只有这些全球化语境空间或符号以外的公共空间才似乎存在地域化的可能性，才能够引发人们跟当地结合得很紧的一种生活。

姜珺：国内的很多功夫没起到作用，但事实上从结果来看还是有很多公共空间让大家来唱歌跳舞，完全不了解中国的人是没办法想象的。

刘珩：是的，规划做得再好、再复杂、再超前，也没有中国人自主的创作性来得及时和有效。到头来就是乱改一气，最后得到的往往是一个对于管理者事与愿违，但老百姓们喜闻乐见的结果。要知道，我们中国人很善于也很乐意自发地决定如何使用这些公共空间，这也是中国人为什么外表看似乎容易接受全球化，但骨子里根深蒂固地追求着自己觉得舒服的生活方式。我想这种随意性和变通性就是地域文化得以保留的基础，也是城市空间地域化、个性化的再生前提。明白这些本地的需求，我想是决定未来中国城市规划和发展走势的关键所在。所以，目前我们急需的中国式或者地域化的规划应该是一个更加简单、更加框架式的游戏规则，像临时规划、临时建筑或临时发展策略等，我想可以成为当下一个设计尝试，也许这种尝试可以给我们带来一个有别于前30年的更自在、更有生命力、更具全球传播力的另一个珠三角。

姜珺，设计师，评论家，时任《城市中国》主编。

Today, No.02/2009/Summer, Vol. 85

THE OTHER PRD

Doreen Heng Liu + Jun Jiang

Doreen: It's been quite a while since we last met. Nowadays many friends have moved from south to north, and there seems to be less concern about the development in the south. Does this mean that the Pearl River Delta (PRD) is really an outdated topic? As a forerunner of the earliest urbanization in China since the country's reform and opening up, the PRD region has been overshadowed in recent years by the strong development momentum in the Yangtze River Delta region (YRD) and the Bohai Economic Rim (BER). As "the pendulum swings backwards and forwards", this ever-travelled cycle is indeed nothing unusual. But where shall the urbanization of the southern cities head? Maybe, that's something worth our discussion today.

Jun: This, more or less, has something to do with the geopolitical economy. Our political system used to be domestically-oriented. At a time when international trade was not much needed, the PRD region did not really play a prominent role. However, with the emergence of global trade, such as the development of the Maritime Silk Road and the globalization of colonialism, the PRD region was exposed to globalization earlier than the eastern part of China, as the sea routes to China primarily extended from the west to east via the South China Sea. In fact, urbanization in the PRD region is quite different and spontaneous. Take the old city of Guangzhou for example. The Canton System facilitated the urbanization of the old downtown and Shamian, while the urban patterns there were generated spontaneously. Nowadays, since the reform and opening up, the urban spaces in Guangzhou have been shaped by two dynamic mechanisms. One is the city's inherent structure, and the other is the external influence from the other cities, especially the influence from Hong Kong. For this reason, throughout the history, cities in the south have long been more exposed to the interactions of endogenous politics and export-oriented economy.

Hong Kong has exerted a significant impact on the PRD region. In fact, Shenzhen has tried to learn from Hong Kong government about the relatively standard management over the market economy, and brought some of the successful learning results at the institutional level across the country. In this sense, Shenzhen has become a pilot for the export-oriented economy and its corresponding administrative system. If there should be anything accounting for its inevitability in urbanization, I'd say, it must have something to do with the country's entire political and economic environment, as well as the city's geographical location. In the era of a domestically-oriented economy, Shenzhen was marginalized; while in the era of export-oriented economy, it became the frontier and a "vanguard" that conveys information and experience to inland cities during the urbanization process in China. Once Shenzhen attains success in a certain aspect, the successful experience would be quickly copied and overtaken by the inland cities. So to continue playing a prominent role in urbanization and modernization, the PRD region has to maintain its leading position in more aspects.

Doreen: Our discussion on urbanization, I think, should involve two aspects. One is the socioeconomic aspect, and the other is urban space. At present, China's urbanization still keeps producing "generic cities" with homogenous urban spaces. In the past three decades, this rapid homogenization delivered huge economic benefits, but now the economy has evolved into another stage, a stage of change. Let's take Shenzhen and Guangzhou for example. Shenzhen is a typical city planned and built following the Western modernism models. It is orderly, logical and rational. As a result, the spatial quality of the whole city bears much resemblance to that of modern cities in the West. Many newly built spaces are even more rational and extremely controlled, such as the Shennan Avenue. Westerners, in particular, highly favor and recognize Shenzhen because of its recognizable quality. But when they get to Guangzhou, they feel totally lost. Guangzhou more tends to follow its own way and change as it wants. People in Guangzhou think that the changes they make have nothing to do with others, since the city is their own home and they can do whatever they want with their home. Actually, Shenzhen is not a southern city in the real sense, but rather a northern city, or a city created under the Western planning system, whereas Guangzhou is a real southern city, a city that cares about everyday life and stays at a relaxed status.

Jun: Guangzhou is a city of the south and the east, while Shenzhen a city of the north and the west. In respect of their local characteristics, the two are significantly different. Shenzhen is a city of young migrants, so it is relatively less burdened than Guangzhou in terms of institutional transformation and individual families; while Guangzhou is a city of local residents, where the well-known "Punti–Hakka Clan Wars" took place. Certainly, the two cities also differ from each other greatly in urban planning. In fact, the two cities do not differ that much in terms of singular building space, but the different is great in terms of building relations or community layouts. And this is caused by different local characteristics under different unspoken rules.

Doreen: What specifically are these unspoken rules?
Jun: They are space-related, not the architectural spaces specified in the drawings but the unspecified, or the specified that are not implemented or improperly implemented. They reflect a collective mentality, that is, mutual understanding of client and designer. This is the difference between the two cities.

Doreen: These unspoken rules seem very interesting and I would like to go some further. So does this mean, even if the same drawings and plans are provided to cities in the north and the south, they may produce different results?
Jun: Probably very different.

Doreen: When comparing Zhujiang New Town in Guangzhou with Shennan Avenue CBD in Shenzhen, I still see some similarities.
Jun: That's because, given the condition of China's governance system, local governments at all levels share similar development strategies and behavior patterns, which may lead to similar urban spaces. Differences, however, mostly exist in some bottom-up spaces, such as some villages in Dongguan, where certain industrial chains are maintained as a tacit understanding between the indigenous villages, or some unspoken rules are observed by different clans in history. They work together in making shoes, mobile phones, and things that are beyond the traditional urban spaces, that are not planned by planners, and that are produced by the locals themselves. These things exist but do not represent the mainstream in Shenzhen.

Doreen: Huaqiangbei in Shenzhen is a very interesting example, and it is the most active market for electronic products in China. It seems that there are certain rules followed by people and logistics in this area, which however seems quite different from other PRD cities.
Jun: I think Huaqiangbei is a typical example of self-upgrading by learning from Hong Kong. The self-upgrading here refers to industrial upgrading, while the learning is primarily about space. How to densify the limited space in Shenzhen? I think Hong Kong has done a good job in this regard and we should learn from it. Huaqiangbei is home to a number of well-known high-tech enterprises, but competing in a relatively low-end may lead to unhealthy industrial environment. Now through the spatial densification, the whole industry can be re-organized through a not completely natural but somewhat artificial process of selection to promote healthy competition among more capable enterprises. I fully understand the situations in Huaqiangbei, though I haven't yet seen the results of the design competition.

Doreen: The design competition for Huaqiangbei Project is intended merely to tackle something formal, so there is not much room left to discuss the competition itself. But how we look at the project is more than important. The competition is about the design of multi-level streets to temporarily solve some current problems like traffic flow, pedestrian and vehicle circulations, but actually, many participating design firms, including NODE, found that the problems of Huaqiangbei could not be simply resolved through something formal. For example, the conflict between pedestrian and vehicular circulations should be addressed from something more fundamental, such as the backstreets and other logistics areas, and the whole industry should be studied to see how the business format is formed and operated. Only after understanding all these issues can we return to the design of urban spaces. The case of Huaqiangbei actually reflects a current mentality towards solving existing problems, that is, there is no time to explore their causes, to study how they originate and evolve. It's not that we don't care about these problems, but that when things get urgent, the responsibilities can be naturally and easily shifted onto the architect, who is expected to solve the pressing problems in the most straightforward and visible way. Form may bring about superficial changes, but it can never fundamentally eradicate or solve problems.
Jun: Indeed, theses are very common problems. Government-led plannings are usually intended for spatial rather than regulatory purposes, while, as a matter of fact, planning should be a means of spatial regulation, aimed at macro control over urban economic and industrial structure, reformulating or updating the overall urban strategy, and deciding which strategic direction to prioritize. Strategy should always be decided first, before resource allocation, industry organization, and industry chain integration, and followed by space, project development in new space, and project management. However, the urban planning nowadays is far from that comprehensive, as it

relies too much on a preconceived spatial planning, and fails to provide a proper understanding of the industry from a professional perspective. Sometimes such understanding could even be a bit arbitrary. Moreover, the implementation does not always mobilize the thorough cooperation across the whole society. I think this is a typical planning process in many Chinese cities. But my knowledge about the urban planning process in Shenzhen is quite limited. As far as I could recall, the urban planning officials of Shenzhen are very competent.

Doreen: Undoubtedly, Shenzhen's Urban Planning Bureau is one of the best in China, well reputed for its standardized and rational practices. Now let's go back to the common problems with planning in the entire PRD region, especially in the second- and third-tier cities, including Guangzhou. As for Guangzhou, a city that no one can really precisely describe it, or its development, there must be some new forms or new things to demonstrate its achievement in planning, and in this regard, architecture naturally plays a very important role. Just as Koolhaas said, now there are many objects on the earth, which are in fact not related to each other, and cannot form an organism. There should be some other dynamics that make these objects into a subject and a city. Isn't this what we need to think about right now? But I don't think we are clear about it, anyway. In addition, due to the discontinuity of policy implementation, it is impossible to go deeper into these intangible issues. Still, physical buildings and forms must be put in the first place. In the long run, this may adversely affect urban development and community growth. Shenzhen, as you said, has very limited space for development, so it must rely on spatial densification to further promote urban development. Guangzhou, on the contrary, has expanded from more than 1 000 km^2 to 7 000 km^2 and suddenly had much land available for development. In this case, spatial densification is no longer something important to it, as the city still keeps expanding. But I believe that, such unlimited urbanization can bring great harm to our future generations, because natural lands are irreversible. I am not sure how helpful our thoughts would be for the city.

Jun: Our proactive thoughts, I think, actually exert less impact on urbanization than the passive changes in the industrial chain. Dongguan, for example, also tried to promote its industrial transformation through the so-called high-tech industrial parks when "Made in China" was in its heyday. But a few years after the parks were completed, they basically turned out to be some empty shells. Nowadays, given the relatively singular industrial structure, it is not realistic for Dongguan to promote industrial upgrading through one single project. In this round of decline with export-oriented economy, the low-end industries are being phased out of the market; and it is the independent enterprises that will shape the future of Dongguan.

Doreen: Now I am quite interested that, as you said, 30 years later, cities will be packed with buildings, many of which are in fact vacant, and maybe even the land will be left idle. Therefore, there will be a big problem with the idle land, and this may be the result of the industrial upgrading. For example, the eastern part of Nansha New Area, after years of development, still has a lot of lands undeveloped. These lands are left idle primarily because the developers have no clue as to what projects can be placed there to drive the development of the area. Now that everyone is talking about improving land use efficiency and returns, the government is also pushing ahead with corresponding measures. But still it takes time before permanent projects can be implemented and completed, so I wonder if there is any intermediate planning, or rather, any flexible strategies such as temporary planning and temporary buildings to fit in this gap time and adapt to the unpredictability of the current urbanization process, in a way that even their complete removal wouldn't be a problem in the future.

Jun: There is a marginal effect between input costs and economic benefits. Some regions, or some projects in early stages may lack the capacity, the money, or even the patience to wait for the corporatization to happen. If they occupy the land at a earlier time, it will more and more become a burden later, because it is difficult to destroy the built spaces. In fact, these projects will physically restrain the development of the whole industry, and, with the old spaces, hinder the generation of new vitality. Maybe the Nansha New Area can be counted as one of the few examples that urban pattern is created by integrating industry chains through long-term planning and large-scale investment.

Doreen: Nansha New Area, in my opinion, is a special case, because it was developed by a foreign developer without any prior experience. The east part of Nansha is 22 km^2, about the size of Macau's main island. Regarding the new city development, I think the developer did not really have a comprehensive or well-devised concept about it, but instead, oversimplified things with a utopian fantasy. Their understanding of new city development was still based on creation of architectural forms. So when the development kicked off without a clearly defined philosophy, it had to turned to the solution of attracting people's attention through varied architectural forms. This is also quite common in many other areas. The early development of Nansha was based merely on a master plan, which was worked out by a famous Spanish architect of the post-modern architecture period together with his assistants. As for the implementation, it involved basically the modern planning plus some postmodern architecture. So the final result was just a skin with collages of a plan and various architectural forms. Such a pure architectural approach of design and implementation failed to attract people to Nansha nor enabled a mechanism that can well promote the natural community growth. However, this is a problem that the architects can hardly provide a solution, both ten years ago and now. Speaking of the community growth mechanism in new cities, I think our discussion will be helpful in some meaningful ways. If we take Nansha as an example, we can see its development has been quite slow, while such a slow pace actually did not really cause much harm, or form too sharp contrasts of conflicts. But interestingly, the University Town (also known as Guangzhou Higher Education Mega Center, GZHEMC), which is 18 km^2 and of the similar size of the eastern part of Nansha (22 km^2), was built into a "city" of millions of square meters of floor areas within 18 months and brought tens of thousands of students to the "city". Yet despite of the massive built spaces and a small population there, it's still technically not a normal community. As the saying goes, "Rome was not built in a day." Why? The residential communities in Panyu were built within a very short time, as the the land cost and housing prices were low there and the development met the market needs. Over the years, these communities developed gradually in a relatively healthy manner and based on that, the community upgrading is considered. I wonder if, many years later, the development of new city models like the University Town will follow the footsteps of the sleeping city in Panyu, or otherwise. What do you think?

Jun: I think there are some differences between the three cases. In Guangzhou, most people work in the downtown, while Panyu is partially a "sleeping city". The two are connected by good public transportation. Many people in Guangzhou make money at home without going to work every day. They can collect rents of their apartment(s) in downtown and buy a house in the countryside. Many of them are the elderly people who frequent tea restaurants. Their children mostly live overseas, while these elderly people have their own stable income sources. I don't think this is quite the same case in other cities. Aging in other cities will cause crisis, but this is not that serious in Guangzhou, partly because of its export-oriented economy, where people may support themselves by doing some small businesses through certain trade channels, so retirement for them would not be a big problem. I think they form an important source for the vitality of the community. Due to the low land cost, the housing prices in Panyu were quite reasonable at that time, so people lived a less stressful life there. As for the University Town, it appears to have single function and serves just as a "city for education", where the migrant population has been constantly renewed and a relatively stable consumer group formed. Students do not need to go downtown at all. They can simply spend their time reading in the library and playing balls in the basketball court. Besides, universities offer opportunities for mutual exchanges, and students can attend classes in other universities. In fact, this urban structure is very simple, where the main body, i.e., the students, have very clear goals, relatively stable mobility, and are renewed every year. They also support several urban villages in the University Town as these villages can provide services that the universities cannot. The problem with Nansha, I think, primarily lies in transportation at present, as the planned one-hour economic circle has not been fully realized. If the economic circle of one hour or a shorter time can be set up, the population inflow is still expected in Nansha. Besides, the proposed settlements of enterprises in Nansha have not been completed, and the completed ones have not really realized large-scale production. So the migrants cannot immediately find jobs here, nor those who already have jobs constitute the main population of Nansha. All these issues need an incubation process, as Nansha is a relatively independent new city.

Doreen: Interestingly, speaking of the one-hour economic circle, what is Nansha supposed to be if it is to serve as the geometric center of a one-hour life circle? I think this depends on our understanding of everyday life. I am one hour away from Shenzhen, Guangzhou, and Hong Kong, and I go to these cities for different purposes. Usually I go to Shenzhen for business but I don't live there; instead, I live in Hong Kong, but our office is based in Nansha. Currently we have no project in Nansha nor live here, so I think Nansha is just an imaginary center, dispensable and in lack of important urban functions. But to go to Guangzhou from Shenzhen, you must pass Humen Bridge and pass by Nansha without necessarily staying there. So there is still a long way to go to turn Nansha from a geometric and imaginary center into an indispensable and practical living center. Then what kind of city should it be?

Jun: The main population of Nansha in the future will be composed of the main workforce brought by the currently planned industrial structure and supporting industries. Industries should serve as a link between the traditional and emerging industries. The former includes the entreport trade and export processing in the PRD region, while the latter means the relatively independent manufacturing and processing industries. These industries rely on the favorable location at the one-hour economic circle to handle the logistics, and their corresponding services can also be organized centering around the economic circle.

Doreen: As you mentioned right now about the industry and the one-hour economic circle, I think it is the best to place industrial logistics in Nansha, for its shortest possible transportation distance. But if we consider it as a living circle, another possibility arises. If Nansha is considered as a sleeping city, maybe you can live in Nansha, and work in Shenzhen, Guangzhou, Hong Kong or Zhuhai; or vice versa, work in Nansha while living in

Shenzhen, Guangzhou and Hong Kong. Anyway, our life is basically about living and working, and how would you spend that one hour? You can imagine the center as a sleeping city, and that you work outside the one-hour economic circle. It's a matter of space allocation. There might also be a third possibility, that is, Guangzhou, as well as Shenzhen or Zhuhai, has their own work and life circle, so no one really needs Nansha. Actually, this is another scenario, and now things are happening following the second scenario. So Nansha may end up as a logistics center or transfer center, rather than a living center.

Jun: Anyway, it takes time to develop a life style, which also needs certain number of residents. If Nansha is merely a place to work, it would lose vitality at night. In view of its scale, Nansha has to be a mixed-used and relatively independent satellite city, where the spotlight should be on its tertiary sector, though its secondary industry may have already been well developed but not particularly attractive, as it is merely a means of production. The attractive tertiary industry, however, can only be guided and cultivated instead of being planned. It can create quality community environment and public spaces, so that people will think Nansha as a place worth staying, living and working in. Anyway, it certainly takes time.

Doreen: Yes, I think it takes at least three or four years from now. Now people are talking about differentiated development, which means, Guangzhou and Shenzhen will follow different development paths, and so will Macao and Hong Kong. Shenzhen and Hong Kong will follow integrated development, and it is the same with Guangzhou and Foshan. This makes Nansha virtually marginalized. Even if there is a mechanism that slowly cultivates a community, the identity of such community is vague. So now indeed, what kind of city should Nansha be? People are talking about Shenzhen and Guangzhou. But to go to these cities, you have to pass Nansha. Still, it continues to be marginalized. Spatially the positioning of Nansha is still unclear. Like you said just now, maybe the most effective way is to promote the growth of a living community through an industry. Actually, there is no need to think too much about what exactly it will be.

Jun: If Guangdong Province really wants to make Guangzhou-Nansha an important axis that is distinguished from the Guangzhou-Shenzhen-Hong Kong Axis or the Guangzhou-Zhuhai-Macao Axis, what it needs to do is to integrate these two axes with the Hong Kong-Macao axis underway now. When the three sides of the PRD are complete with clear relations and functional division, the importance of Nansha will immediately show up. In the past few years, the PRD region has been fragmented, with a lot of overlapping construction. But in recent years, complementary advantages, differentiated competition and coordinated development are much encouraged. Guangzhou and Dongguan started to work in coordination, Guangzhou and Foshan began to realize integration, Shenzhen and Hong Kong jointly strengthened cooperation, Guangzhou and Hong Kong gradually established a sound relation; positioning of Guangzhou-Foshan, and Shenzhen-Hong Kong, the two eastern metropolitan circles of the PRD, gradually became clear. When industrial division and urban positioning along the chain are all clear, Nansha's role will also become clear. Another axis is from Guangzhou-Foshan to Zhuhai-Macao, which is also being integrated. After Hong Kong-Zhuhai-Macau Bridge opens to traffic, this axis will gradually gain its importance. After the urban rim around Nansha takes shape, the role of Nansha will become prominent. I think this is exactly what Henry Fok sees. He sees a geometric space established on the completed urban rim around Nansha, before it can truly serve as the geometric center of the one-hour economic circle and play a role in allocating surrounding resources. Passing by Nansha, you know exactly what kind of intermediary and facilitator role you can play for people passing by. Industries that are intended to deploy resources across the entire urban rim can stay in Nansha. Now the east side is coming into shape, and it will not be long before the west and south sides take shape.

Doreen: This urban integration in the PRD region has basically concluded by 2011 with the completion of the express railway, and this PRD model might has something quite different as compared to the YRD region and BER. Honestly, I have no idea about the latter two, so what would you say about their differences?

Jun: Very significant differences, mainly in respect of administration and geography. Geographically, BER does not have much export-oriented economy as it is dominated by endogenous economy, while the YRD region is relatively similar to the PRD. BER, as a newly emerging economic circle, is completely different in administration. Where administration is concerned, the PRD region is both simple and complex, simple because of less provinces in the region, and complex due to two SARs; the YRD region involves several provinces but has a municipality directly under the central government as the leader; BER has two municipalities directly under the central government and several major provinces. Comparing the three, administration in the YRD region should be easier, with one municipality of higher level enforcing execution and coordinating two provinces. The situation in the PRD region is quite the other way round, where Dongguan is not necessarily subordinate to Guangzhou, nor is Guangzhou to Hong Kong, and nor is Shenzhen as a SEZ to Guangzhou. This is the root cause of fragmentation in the region. But slowly, after some painful lessons, a consensus has been reached. In BER, technically Beijing possesses the central power of control over everything with the presence of the central government, who will decide how far the country will go for BER, as far as transferring water from the south to the north and natural gas from the west to the east, as far as coordinating several provinces in the large northern area, which is much larger than the YRD region, and as far as dividing interests with neighboring powers such as Russia, South Korea, and Japan. Currently, the positioning of its internal cities has not been finalized. For example, Beijing enjoys the omnipotent positioning as a political, economic and cultural center; Tianjin, which seems to be clearly positioned at present, has overlapped with Tangshan in industry and port. I think these are all risks in positioning. Beijing's role lies in its authority in administrative planning to co-ordinate who will do what first and who will do what next, such as where to relocate Shougang, where to export coals and iron ores, which part of a lake to dug first, and where to pilot the circular economy. These are all macro-control measures. Beijing needs to exert its central power to balance the relation between different regions.

Doreen: Now let's get back to the PRD region and talk about "post generic city". Actually this term comes from my recent project of the riverfront factory compound renovation in Shunde. Since Koolhaas has defined the generic city, what are the "post generic cities" in the PRD region like? Are they generic cities after industrial upgrading, or differentiated cities to form a more interesting and dynamic urban agglomeration or both?

Jun: I think there must be some differentiation. In the past, there were both differentiation and blind competition. The competition was homogeneous at the beginning. Gradually it evolved into differentiated competition, and then dislocation competition though collaboration of differential factors. The win-win status as result of such collaboration, in turn, may intensify the differentiation. Therefore, greater differentiation can make a city more competitive.

Doreen: What would this difference bring to the urban spaces? As architects, we always think about how to work on the urban design and architectural design when we take over these projects after three years. But I don't really think such difference have brought much straightforward change to the urban spaces.

Jun: Well, I do see some changes. For example, Hong Kong. I think there is no other PRD cities can compete with Hong Kong. Admittedly, as the central city of South China, Guangzhou siphons most of the resources. For Shenzhen, it surely should join hands with Hong Kong, and provide cultural and economic value to the latter; meanwhile, and brings in Hong Kong's administrative, financial, and other international practices. Very different from Guangzhou or Hong Kong, Shenzhen is more creative with numerous northern cultural elements. Such creativity may make up for the cultural monotony in Hong Kong. Actually it is quite fun to explore the urban spaces in Hong Kong, where the creativity is prized over the content inside. With the identity of special administrative region as its core competence, Hong Kong attracts numerous elites from Northern China. If Dongguan still takes the path of manufacturing in the future, it will still be a world factory; so it must quickly start the self-transformation. I believe that Dongguan will be a manufacturing city for a long time.

Doreen: As you just mentioned Hong Kong, I think it would be interesting to take a look at its convention and exhibition function. Hong Kong brings together the Eastern and Western cultures. Compared with cities of the Chinese mainland, it has different governance system and open mechanism that automatically trigger off certain vitality of the spaces. For example, the infrastructure spaces of the airport can be and have been fully expanded to drive the growth of other social functions and tourism. As new urban spaces attached to the infrastructure, these ancillary functions, together with a flexible system, enable diversified uses of the convention and exhibition center in Hong Kong. In contrast, the convention and exhibition centers in Shenzhen and Guangzhou, such as Baiyun Convention Center and Pazhou Convention and Exhibition Center, are still designed as an isolated and single "island". The competition focuses on building "size" and number of five-star hotels. Shenzhen has not obviously differentiated itself from Guangzhou in terms of convention and exhibition function. The two still compete for the same resource, which leads to similarity in urban spaces. In the long run, I think what you call differentiation is the overall competitiveness derived from the understanding and expression of the differentiated additional functions in the competition for the same resources. In the future, the PRD region should seek differentiation through overall competitiveness, rather than the difference of single function.

Jun: The three economic centers we mentioned just now still have their own overall competitiveness, such as the Canton Fair in Guangzhou, the China Hi-Tech Fair in Shenzhen, which is also a major high-tech event in Southern China, and various trade fairs in Hong Kong. Trade fairs in Hong Kong are generally smaller than Canton Fair and China Hi-Tech Fair, so they are unlikely to replace certain functions of the two in the short run, and must focus on the tertiary industry. In this way, each city maintains its competitiveness and core positioning. Of course, Hong Kong, after years of development, shows a more prominent overall competitiveness with well-established infrastructure and more refined practices in many aspects compared to inland cities. Regarding "post generic city", I think Koolhaas's view may not fit the situations of some Asian countries. In China, it's untenable for some cities to be generic as Chinese culture is unlikely to be assimilated easily amid the globalization. Actually, what happened in the space outweighs the space itself in a city that refuses to be assimilated, since the space can be energized in use. In fat, culture has a resisting force against the globalization. It is localized during the globalization process. In the future, the city that is more likely to globalize will be more localized, as it has to differentiate from other globalized and generic cities for globalization. The acquisition of identity is closely connected with the local culture.

Doreen: If we see architecture as a symbol, a city can be localized by effectively combining the symbol's globalization with the local culture.
Jun: I call it the symbolization of architecture.

Doreen: I don't like the word "symbol" as it sounds superficial. The globalization in architecture also leads to homogeneous projects with same volume, size, material and form. They are also symbols, the rigid index of globalization.
Jun: Facilities that form part of the globalized functions, such as convention and exhibition centers, terminals and airports, are often globalized to a limited extent. Unable to complete the full process of globalization, most of them update and improve on their own. I think the future culture must be localized before revitalization. When I was in Mongolia, I found that it was because Mongolian music was on the verge of extinction at that time that Mongolian musicians were able to tour around for performance and found the way out, while those imitating European and American bands may already disappear.

Doreen: I think the way you define the culture may reflect the acceptance and use of public spaces. The urban spaces defined by functions, such as airports, terminals, and convention and exhibition centers, have their own functional definitions. These defined functional spaces share common purpose and formal vocabulary, and even the same decoration... such as McDonald's. The only difference today is that such facilities are Ritz Carlton Hotel, Guggenheim Museum, opera house designed by Zaha Hadid or airport designed by Norman Foster. It seems that only other public spaces than those spaces or symbols subject to global context can be localized o present a local lifestyle.

Jun: In China, many efforts are in vain. But eventually, the fact is that there are many public spaces for people to sing and dance. This is unimaginable for those who do not know China well.

Doreen: Yes. The spontaneous creation of Chinese people always work faster and better than any elaborately planned, sophisticated and visionary planning. The planning may be arbitrarily revised, finally backfiring the city managers but delighting the people. As we know, Chinese people are good at and like spontaneously deciding how to use these public spaces. That is why they seem to easily accept globalization, but never stopping pursue a lifestyle they feel comfortable from their inner hearts. I think such randomness and flexibility are the basis to preserve the local culture and to renew the localization and individualization of urban spaces. Understanding these local needs is key to the future urban planning and development trend in China. Therefore, what Chinese-style or local planning need is more straightforward and well-structured game rules. I think we can try temporary planning, buildings or development strategies, and make them a design experiment at this stage. Maybe, such experiment can bring us another PRD that is more carefree, more dynamic and more globally visible than the one in the past three decades.

Jun Jiang, architect, critic, former cheif editor of URBAN CHINA.

BALANCE IS MORE

平衡即是多

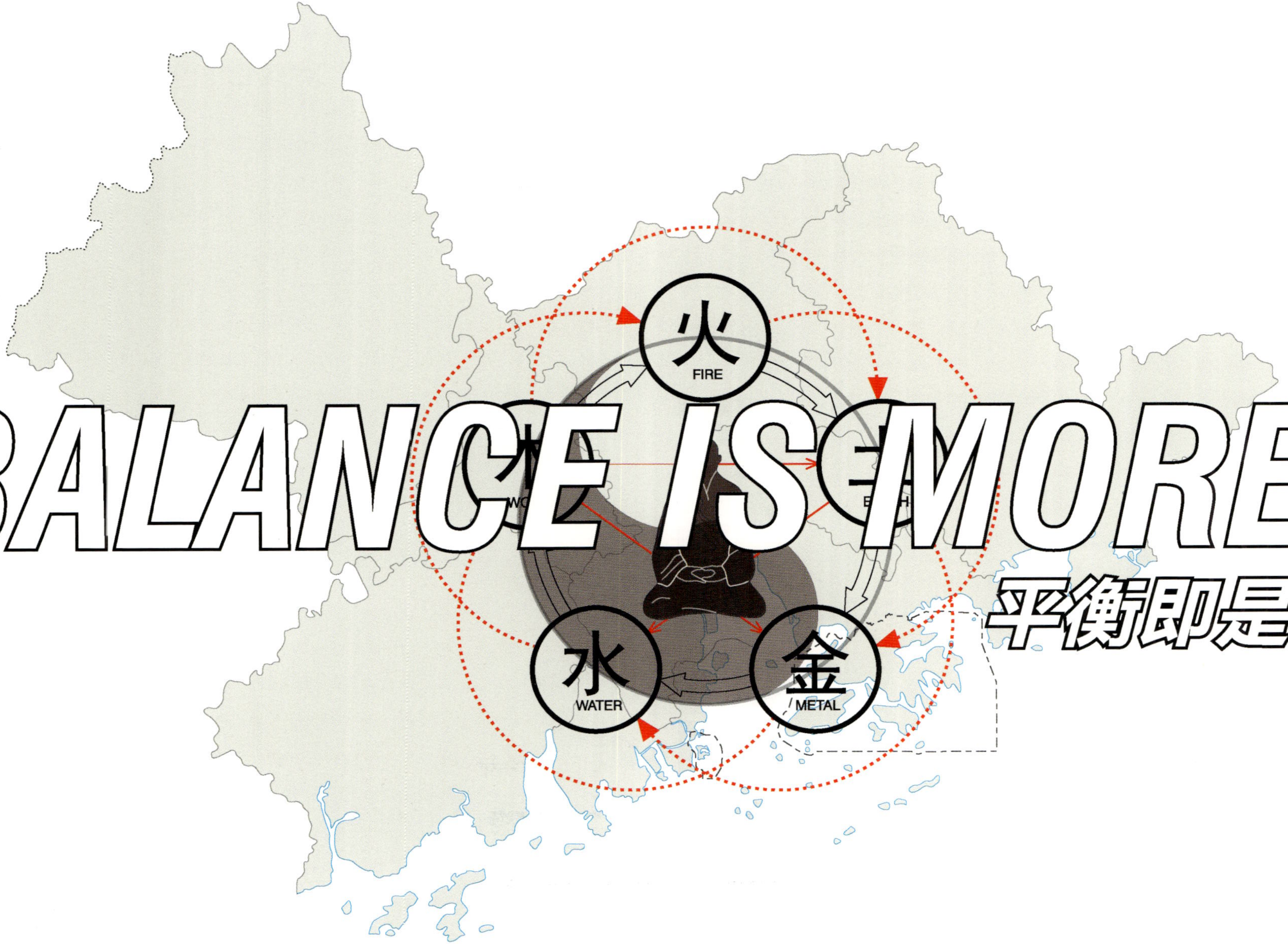

DESIGN

设计篇

N

戈们尝试把给深圳带来极高效率的城市道路进行重新解读，拆分并建构，一方面，让它与城市
约物流系统相整合，共同形成一个全新的物品空间界面（道路+物流混合层），这个新的隐性的
物品空间界面"将错就错"地与现有技术条件及城市建设的程序相结合，因而具有了未来的可
实施性；另一方面，将现有城市建筑空间（地面与建筑）和信息系统相整合，共同形成一个全
新的显性的生活空间界面（建筑+信息混合层）。这个"显性"生活空间界面和"隐形"物品空
间界面同时组合在一起，共同形成未来城市的基础设施支撑系统。

通过这套新型支撑系统的建立，可以将城市的流动性进行分离，从而使可见的城市生活空间真
正转化为"体验和休闲"的生活空间，而非被机动性和物流系统所控制、分隔、异化的空间。
这个转变过程同时也会释放出大量的空间资源，提供给未来城市农业、果园、游戏、动物、淡
水等与人和自然相关的要素，从而给生活界面带来更多的空间和时间，更多的内容和体验，让
社会和自然有了全新的视野和环境，使得经济、社会与生态这三者最终得以在动态的界面上平
衡发展。

On the one hand, we try to reinterpret, redistribute and reconstruct the urban roads that bring about high efficiency to Shenzhen so that they can be integrated with the urban logistics system and form a brand new object spatial interface (hybrid layers of roads + logistics). Following the apparent mistakes made, this brand new implicit object spatial interface is perfectly integrated with the existing technical conditions as well as the urban construction procedures, creating the futuristic feasibility. On the other hand, we would also integrate the existing urban architectural space (ground and buildings) with the information system to form a brand new explicit living spatial interface (hybrid layers of architecture + information). This "explicit" living spatial interface is grouped together with the "implicit" object spatial interface to provide full support for the infrastructure of the futuristic city.

With the establishment of this new support system, we can truly separate the mobility of the city such that the visible urban living space is truly transformed into a living space full of "experience and leisure" instead of having a space being controlled, separated and differentiated by the mechanical and logistics systems. This transformation process would also release a large amount of spatial resources catered to the futuristic urban agriculture, orchards, games, animals, freshwater reservoirs and other elements related to mankind and nature. By doing this, it creates more space and time, more contents and experiences to the living interface, granting a new vision and environment for the society and nature so that the economic, social and ecological aspects can

SHENZHEN

This is a story about the
future of a city.
A city which always
involves contradiction and balance of
[life, space and boundary] during the process
of development. It is a new story that is often told.

这是关于一个城市的未来的故事。
这个城市的发展过程总是涉及生活、空间和边界的矛盾和平衡。
这是一个新的故事，却时常被人讲述。

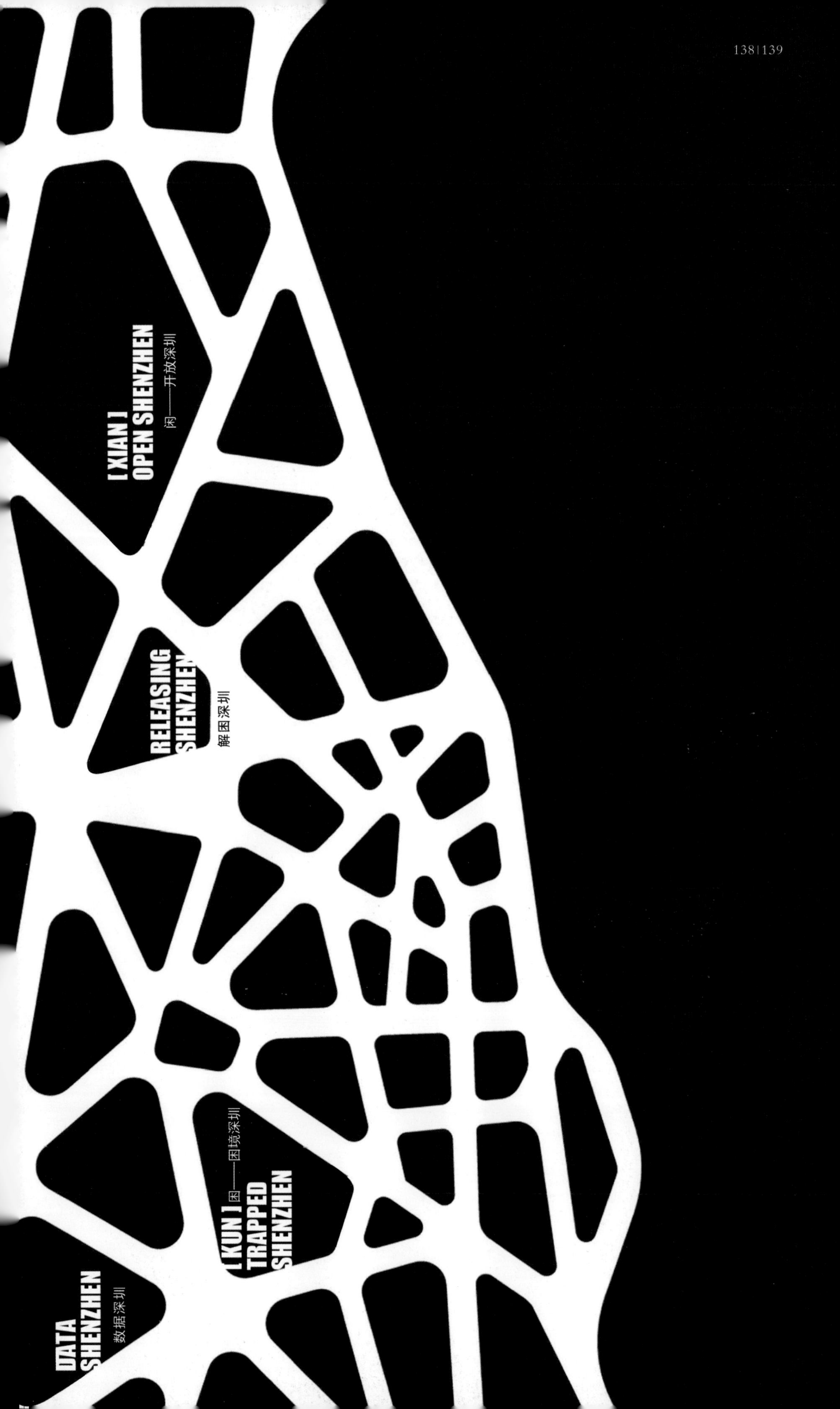

[XIAN]
OPEN SHENZHEN
闲——开放深圳
RELEASING
SHENZHEN
解困深圳
[KUN] 困——困境深圳
TRAPPED
SHENZHEN
DATA
SHENZHEN
数据深圳

DATA SHENZHEN
数据深圳

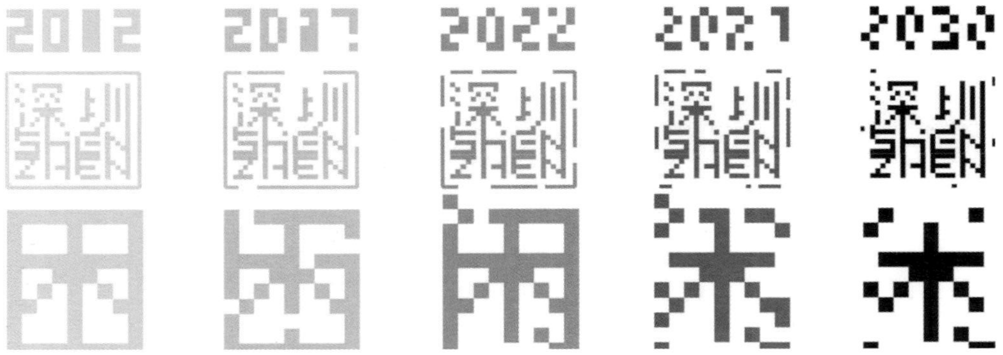

如今，我们的世界正在经历着多元和深刻的变革，城市化的速度也在加快，用地不足、能源短缺、气候变化、人口暴增、可持续发展等成为了全球共同关注的问题。虽然中国在经历一个世纪的停滞后才开始奋起追赶，捉住了城市化加速的最后机会，但还是面临着发展的瓶颈，以及继续加速发展还是放慢脚步的两难境地。作为中国城市化快速发展过程中的试点城市，深圳正处于选择的交叉路口。

Today when the world is undergoing diverse and profound changes as well as accelerated urbanization, issues such as lack of available land, energy shortages, climate change, population explosion and sustainable development have become the common concerns worldwide. Though China has woken up after a century of stagnation and taken advantage of the last opportunity of accelerated urbanization, nevertheless it also confronts development bottlenecks and the dilemma of whether to continue such acceleration or slowdown. Shenzhen, a pilot city for China's rapid urbanization process now stands at the crossroads.

《建筑设计》新城市化中国专辑，2008年9月/10月，第78期

追随珠三角
——立足现实的观点

刘珩

1996年，雷姆·库哈斯联合哈佛大学设计研究生院在珠江三角洲地区进行实地考察，后据此于2001年出版《大跃进：哈佛大学设计学院的城市项目》一书，影响深远。该书介绍了中国的快速城市化转型，以及随之而来的城市混乱如何影响世界。最重要的是，库哈斯在书中倡导“一种新的城市共存形式”。他还创造了“一些受版权保护的术语”来向世人描述和分析这种全新的现象。这种城市共存新形式到底是什么，是与他提及的西方百年城市化进程，还是中国的“一百年不动摇”有关？当处于不同历史时期的城市状态突然融合，并同时影响西方时，其冲击力堪比“彗星陨落”。由于中国过去长期远离世界舞台，也由于西方对于国内的了解还普遍处于“无知之云”的笼罩之中，有关珠三角城市的信息输出及其快速传播对西方产生了更大的影响。

受邓小平“致富光荣”和“不管黑猫白猫，能捉老鼠的就是好猫”的激励，20世纪70年代末，珠三角地区以前所未有的速度“创建全新城市”，以满足该地区对制造业生产的大量迫切需求。同时，受国际化大都市香港的影响，珠三角地区快速发展起来，大量外来务工人员涌入珠三角城镇和市中心周边的工厂。早期，香港曾是主要的劳动密集型制造业所在地，以“香港制造”而闻名。当时香港至少有700万名劳务人员，后将制造基地转移到内地。到了20世纪80年代初，六七十年代的“香港制造”最终变成了“中国制造—香港转手”。由于珠三角地区劳动力成本低廉，自然资源丰富，这一生产中心得以制作出物美价廉的产品，逐步提高了全球知名度。

随着“中国制造”标签影响力的扩大，珠三角地区已成为中国最大的制造业出口地区和全球重要的生产中心。正如萨拉·邦吉奥尼在其书《离开中国制造的一年：一个美国家庭的生活历险》中所述，“中国制造”已经成为世界主要的经济现象，对其他国家/地区人们的日常生活产生了前所未有的影响。萨拉·邦吉奥尼和家人花了一年时间试图避免在美国购买任何带有“中国制造”标签的商品。然而，这谈何容易。她总结道，今天的“中国制造”，就像70年代的中国“台湾制造”和中国“香港制造”，以及20世纪初的“日本制造”和“韩国制造”一样，完全无法摆脱。

珠三角地区进入“中国制造”阶段之时，城市主义应运而生，这可以理解为一种新型城市状态，道路基础设施和“普通城市”蓬勃发展。正如雷姆·库哈斯所说，“普通城市不过是当前需求和能力的反映。这种城市没有历史，对每个人来说都足够大。它易于管理，无需维护。如果规模太小，它会扩张。如果变老变旧，它还会自我迭代和更新。每一处地方既令人激动，亦令人扫兴。它可以“在每周一早晨产生一个新身份”。短短数年内，珠三角地区已在随机和有序的混沌中发展成为一座拥有4000万人口的超级“普通城市”。

然而，应了中国的一句老话，“三十年河东，三十年河西”，风水轮流转。如今，随着制造重心再次转移，“中国制造”进程正在逐步减缓，进入新一轮经济转型阶段。“中国制造”变成了“世界其他地方制造”。珠三角地区资源使用成本日益升高，导致制造业萎靡不振。珠三角地区进入了新的消费周期和经济阶段，进一步标志着劳动密集型生产时代的落幕。

随机和受控的城市化

中国经济高速发展的弊端是多年来无节制的城市扩张，造就了“脱离城市主义的世界”，一切只着眼于物

质。然而突然之间，城市景观周边冒出了无数的主题城——家具城、灯具城、时尚城、美食城、按摩城、24小时娱乐城。此前，这些区域都是由多个单一主题的展厅构成；许多同类小展厅迅速、集中、密集地组团，就形成了同质化“城市”。这些“城市”已经成为当地甚至国际闻名的商业和旅游目的地，如1989年由香港画商建立的深圳大芬油画村，现已成为重要的油画（原作、复制品）生产基地。油画作品远销北美、欧洲、澳大利亚、亚洲等世界各地。大芬村声名远扬，吸引了无数国内外游客。此外，深圳大芬村这种流行而随机的城市形态也对应了一种特殊的城市策略，即：其发展是受地方政府管控的。这些大型同质主题项目也造就了品牌城市：大学城、会展城、机场城、科学城和生态城。这种同质现象可以被直接解释为规模经济的物理形态——一种具有“中国特色”的完美经济模式。这种将城市打造成同质化超级产品的单一城市推广模式是否可以被视作“新型”城市建设？这就需要思考：中国的“普通城市”是否可以迈出国门，输出国外？

中国特色

城市大规模高速发展的同时，能源消耗也在不断增加，自然资源正被快速消耗殆尽。可持续发展的重要性日益凸显。温家宝在《2008年国务院政府工作报告》中预测，2008年将是中国“最困难的一年”。虽然困难会涉及当时国家发展的许多方面，但报告中关注了这样一个问题，即：如何在环境成本较高的条件下进行大型项目的开发，同时满足高速经济增长的需求。由此可见，当前快速、大规模“生产”的城市化阶段，只是更宏观过程或周期的一部分。早期或初期阶段，这种“生产”模式有些急于求成，囫囵吞枣。不过中国人或许有充分的理由为自己的无畏正名。从1865—1887年，拜伦·奥斯曼只用了20年的时间，就把巴黎改造成如今世人熟知的欧洲大都市，到处是宽阔的林荫大道和宏伟的城市中心。一旦对物质环境有所“重视”，哪怕是随意规划，这座城市也会在时间的流逝中逐步孕育出独有的文化。如果城市停止发展，我们可以炸毁它，然后重建。虽然这样的生命周期是短暂而快速的，但它能不断更新城市面貌，让城市鲜活而精彩。我们对目前的中国城市创造方式持乐观态度。这种对变化的渴望可以将任何消极元素转化为积极元素。时代已经发生了改变，现在，中国已经发展壮大，进入全球化阶段，这种无畏的“意识形态”可谓一种中国特色，可以输出和推广到世界各地。

输出中国

与此同时，中国的城市（设计）文化也日趋成熟，近几年来国际关注度日益提升。劳伦·帕克最近在伦敦维多利亚和阿尔伯特博物馆策划了一场“创意中国”展览，他预言，如果中国的设计文化“在未来三四年内继续蓬勃发展，中国建筑师将能融入国际设计界，而不会因为自己的中国身份而受到排挤”。由哥伦比亚大学中国实验室举行的“输出中国”研讨会则标志着结束和新的开始，是高速、大规模建筑和城市生产的结束，也是中国对世界输出新文化和知识的开始。但输出中国，甚至输出珠三角地区的城市文化，需要达到一定的广度和深度，才能对全球设计文化产生深远的影响。中国的城市化进程在“规模和速度”方面仍是中国背景造就的特色。也许珠三角模式只有经过充分发展才能成为影响世界的中国模式。只有当整体设计文化集中发展达到一定的量级，建筑才能发挥其影响力。

到目前为止，我们还处在混沌与成功之间，亟待进步。

Architectural Design, Issue of New Urban China: Sept/Oct 2008, Vol. 78

AFTER THE PEARL RIVER DELTA – A VIEW FROM THE GROUND

Doreen Heng Liu

Rem Koolhaas' 2001 book *The Great Leap Forward: Harvard Design School Project on the City*, based on fieldwork undertaken with the Harvard Graduate School of Design in the Pearl River Delta (PRD) in 1996, has proved seminal. It has defined the way in which China's rapid transformation and ensuing urban chaos has been disseminated to the world. Most significantly, in this book, Koolhaas advocated "a new form of urban co-existence". On identifying this wholly new phenomenon, Koolhaas also invented "a number of copyrighted terms" to describe and analyze it to the world. What exactly could be this new form is that he alluded to in his reference to the hundreds of years of Western urbanization or the China's "one hundred years without change"? When these very different urban conditions from very different moments of history suddenly conjoined and simultaneously confronted the West, the impact was one of "the suddenness of a comet". China's long absence from the world stage made the impact of this exported knowledge of the PRD's urban chaos and its rapid flux all the greater on the West, given the general "cloud of unknowing" .

Driven by Deng Xiaoping's famous phrases –"to get rich is glorious" and "a black cat or white cat, if it can catch mice, it's a good cat" – the high speed and urgency of "creating a completely new urban substance" in the PRD in the late 1970s was a direct result of the massive and immediate demand of manufacturing production in the region; Meanwhile, benefitted from the internationalized metropolis of Hong Kong, the region boomed rapidly, and a sea of immigrant workers from elsewhere in China flooded into the factories at the peripheries of the towns and city centres. The labour-intensive manufacturing industries were, in the first instance, mainly labelled "Made by Hong Kong". At least 7 million labourers were employed by Hong Kong, which shifted its own manufacturing base to mainland China. By the beginning of the 1980s, the "Made in Hong Kong" labels of the 1960s and 1970s had finally become "Made in China – by Hong Kong". The popularity of the PRD as a production centre for the rest of the world was borne out by the competitive prices it offered, which were themselves a direct result of cheap labour and readily available natural resources.

Simply evoked by the "Made in China" label, the PRD had become the largest manufacturing export power in China and a major global centre. "Made in China" has become a dominant economic phenomenon worldwide, as Sara Bongiorni demonstrates in her acclaimed book, *A Year without "Made in China"*. It has an entirely unprecedented impact on people's daily lives even on the other side of the world. Bongiorni's US-based family spent a year attempting to avoid anything with a "Made in China" label. However, the experience proved more difficult than anyone might have imagined. "Made in China", she concludes is as unavoidable to us today as "Made in Taiwan" and "Made in Hong Kong" were to us in the 1970s, and "Made in Japan" and "Made in Korea" earlier in the 20th century.

The urbanism that has accompanied the "Made in China" phase in the PRD can perhaps be best understood as a new form of urban condition, with its mushrooming highway-infrastructure and "generic city" (a term copyrighted by Koolhaas). As Koolhaas said, "it is nothing but a reflection of present need and present ability. It is the city without history. It is big enough for everybody. It is easy, it does not need maintenance. If it gets too small it just expands. If it gets old it just self-destructs and renews. It is equally exciting or unexciting everywhere. It can produce a new identity every Monday morning" . The PRD became a super "generic city" of 40 million inhabitants, created from randomness and organized chaos, within just a few years.

However, as the old Chinese idiom says, "thirty years river east, thirty years river west". All fortunes come in cycles. Today the process of "Made in China" is gradually winding down and undergoing a further economic transformation. As manufacturing modes shift once again, "Made in China" becomes "made in another part of the world". Increasingly expensive resources in the PRD have made the decline of manufacturing inevitable. The end of the era of labour-intensive production in the region has been further marked by the emergence of an increasing number of bourgeoisie, as China steps into another consumption cycle and a further phase in the economy.

Random and Controlled Urbanism

A side production of economic development in China has been years of unbridled urban sprawl, which has created "a world without urbanism" with only physical substance. Suddenly, however, the peripheral urban landscape has become dotted with endless theme cities – furniture city, lighting fixture city, fashion city, food city, massage city, 24-hour entertainment city. Previously, these areas were individually composed of a series of autonomous showrooms with a homogeneous theme; many smaller showrooms of the same kind collectively, intensively and instantly clustered until they eventually formed a "city" of homogeneity. These "cities" have become local, even international, business and tourist destinations, like the famous Dafen Oil Painting Village in Shenzhen, which was founded in 1989 by an oil painting businessman from Hong Kong, and has become the premier base of oil painting production – originals and reproductions alike. Paintings are exported all around the world to North America, Europe, Australia and Asia. Dafen's renown has become such that it draws in tourists from home and abroad. Furthermore, such a popular, random urban form in the region is paralleled with another kind of urban strategy: controlled development managed by local governments. This includes large-scale homogeneous theme projects also branded cities: university city, convention city, airport city, science city or eco-city. These mono-types we may consider direct interpretations of economy of scale in physical form – a perfect economic model with "Chinese characteristics". Could this urban mono-type branding of cities as homogenous supersized products be considered "new" city-making? This begs the question whether beyond China, the generic Chinese city can be re-exported.

With Chinese Characteristics

While high-speed and large-scale urban development continues, energy consumption has forever been on the increase, eating into fast-depleting natural resources. This has seen sustainability surface as a critical agenda. In Jiabao Wen's *Report on the Work of the Government of 2008*, he predicted that this year would be "the most difficult year" for China. Though this could apply to many aspects of the nation's current development, one of the concerns that emerges in the report is how to balance large-scale, but environmentally costly projects against the still high demand for rapid economic growth. It can be concluded from this that the physical "production" of this phase of urbanization – large and speedy – is only part of a greater process or cycle. An early or primary phase, it can be regarded as anxious but raw, hungry but dyspeptic. So the Chinese perhaps have enough reasons to say that they are right to be fearless. It only took Baron Haussmann twenty two years, from 1865 to 1887 to re-create Paris, transforming it into a European metropolis of grand boulevards and the magnificent city centre that we know today. Once "some importance" is attached to the physical environment, even it is rough and ready, time may play a significant role in nurturing culture. If it stops growing, we can simply explode it and rebuild it afresh. Although the life cycle is short and fast, it results in an ever-changing face of a city that could be vibrating and exciting. We are optimistic about the way we are creating Chinese cities today. Such is the hunger for change that it is possible to turn any negative into a positive. Times have changed. Since China is already growing big and globalised, this fearless "ideology" can be regarded as a unique Chinese characteristic, which can be exportable and marketable to the rest of the world.

Exporting China Now

Meanwhile, another dimension of urban (design) culture is developing in China with increasing global exposure in the past few years. Lauren Parker, who recently curated the "China Design Now" exhibition at the Victoria & Albert Museum in London, has predicted that if the rapid process of Chinese design culture "carries on in the next three and four years, Chinese architects will be seen as part of the international design community and not just singled out because they are Chinese". The "Exporting China" Symposium at Columbia University, initialized by China Lab, intentionally marked the beginning of the end – the end of massive architectural and urban production in scale and speed; and the beginning of China's new emerging cultural and intellectual influence on the world. But exporting China or even exporting the PRD in the sense of urban culture needs critical mass in breadth and depth in order to have a profound influence on global design culture. China's urbanization in terms of its "scale and speed" is still singled out as particular to the Chinese context. Maybe only a fully cultivated Pearl River Delta model can be established as an influential Chinese model for the rest of the world. Architecture can only be influential once an overall collective design culture has formed critical mass.

So far, we are still somewhere between chaos and celebration, and no further.

pearl river delta WORLD FACTORY

珠江三角洲 世界工厂

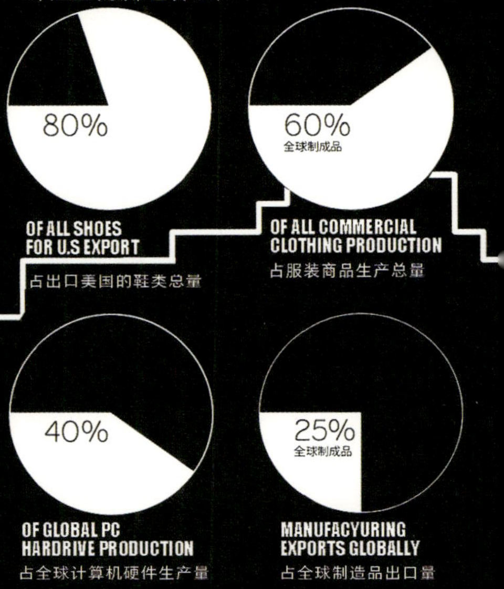

Thanks to its inherent geo-political location in the Pearl River Delta and immediate proximity to Hong Kong,

Shenzhen is actually an epitome that has witnessed the significant transformation of China. In just three decades, Shenzhen experienced the explosive growth from a small frontier town with a population of merely 30,000 to a metropolis of 14.5 million residents, a process that might have taken 150 years in the industrial revolution of the western countries.

地处珠江三角洲的核心位置、紧邻香港，深圳地缘政治位置至关重要。深圳见证了“中国速度”，在短短三十余年里完成了西方城市也许需要历经150年的发展历程，不不到3万人口的海边小镇发展成为容纳1450万人口的大都市。

1992 km²
1992平方公里
HONG KONG
香港

DATA SHENZHEN 数据深圳

POPULATION 人口

ECONOMY 经济

URBAN SPACE 城市空间

MOBILITY 交通

POPULATION 人口

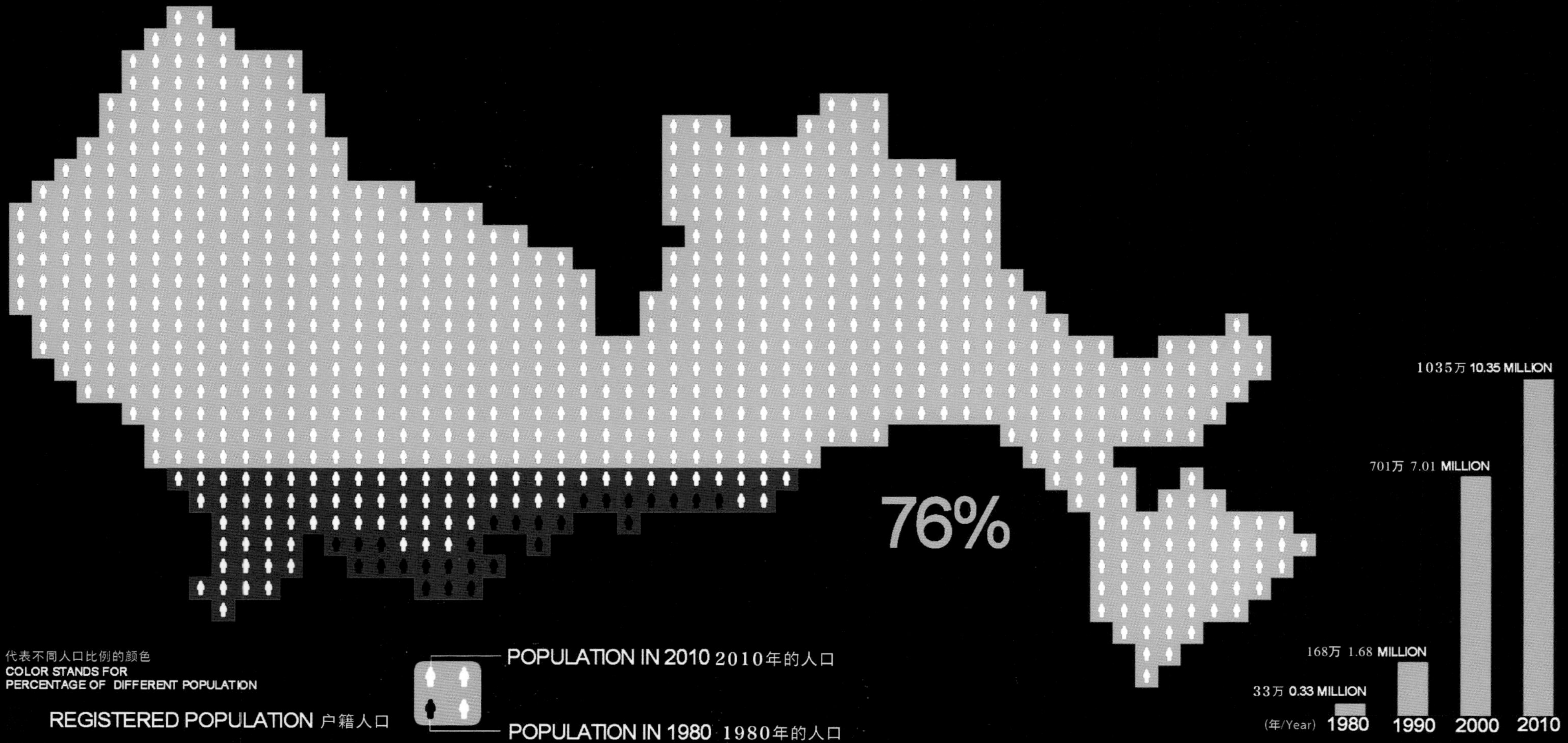

POPULATION GROWTH FROM 1980-2010

1980—2010年的人口增长情况

ECONOMY 经济

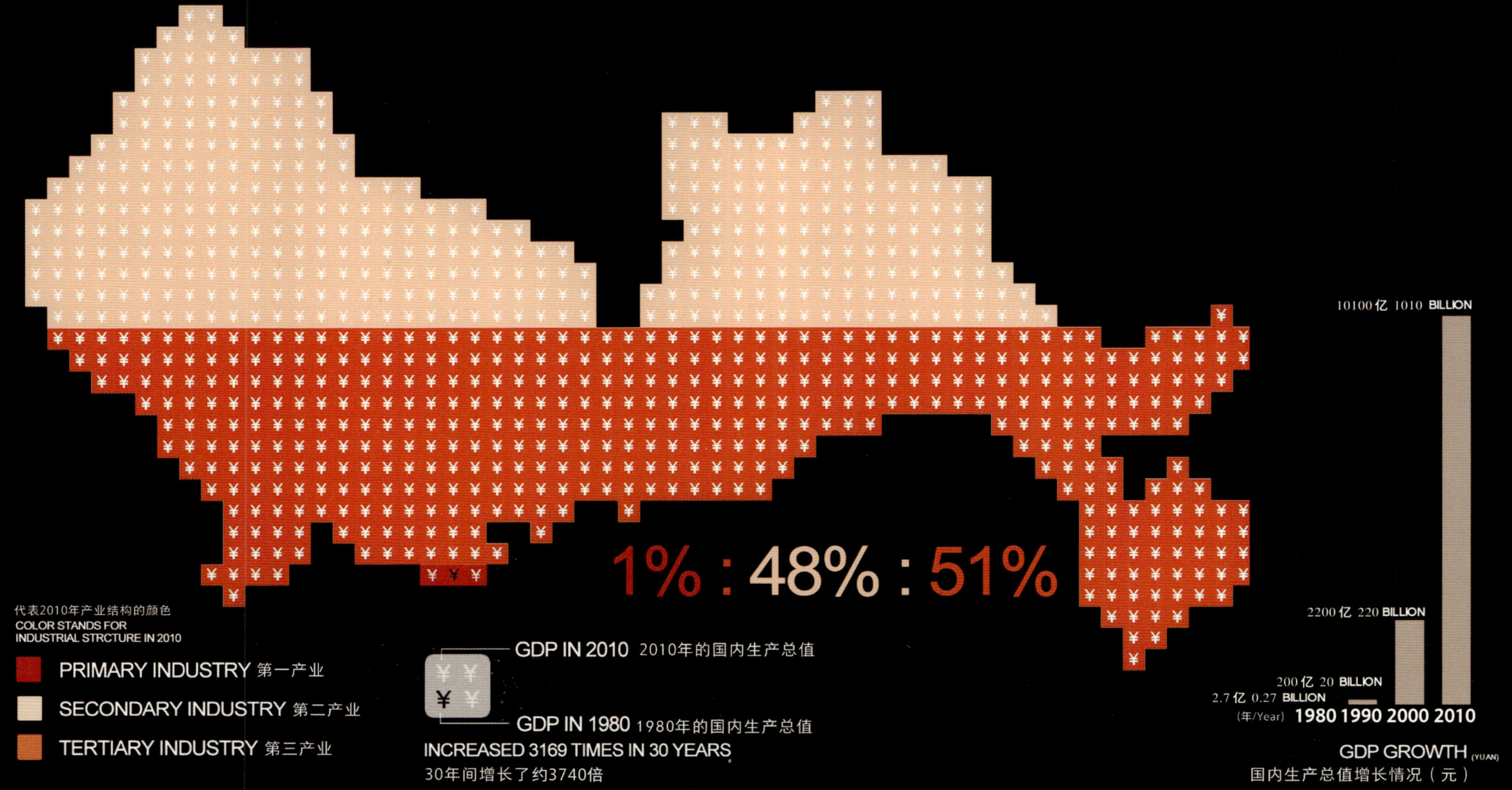

1% : 48% : 51%
代表2010年产业结构的颜色
COLOR STANDS FOR
INDUSTRIAL STRCTURE IN 2010
PRIMARY INDUSTRY 第一产业
SECONDARY INDUSTRY 第二产业
TERTIARY INDUSTRY 第三产业
GDP IN 2010 2010年的国内生产总值
GDP IN 1980 1980年的国内生产总值
INCREASED 3169 TIMES IN 30 YEARS
30年间增长了约3740倍
10100亿 1010 BILLION
2200亿 220 BILLION
200亿 20 BILLION
2.7亿 0.27 BILLION
(年/Year) 1980 1990 2000 2010
GDP GROWTH (YUAN)
国内生产总值增长情况（元）

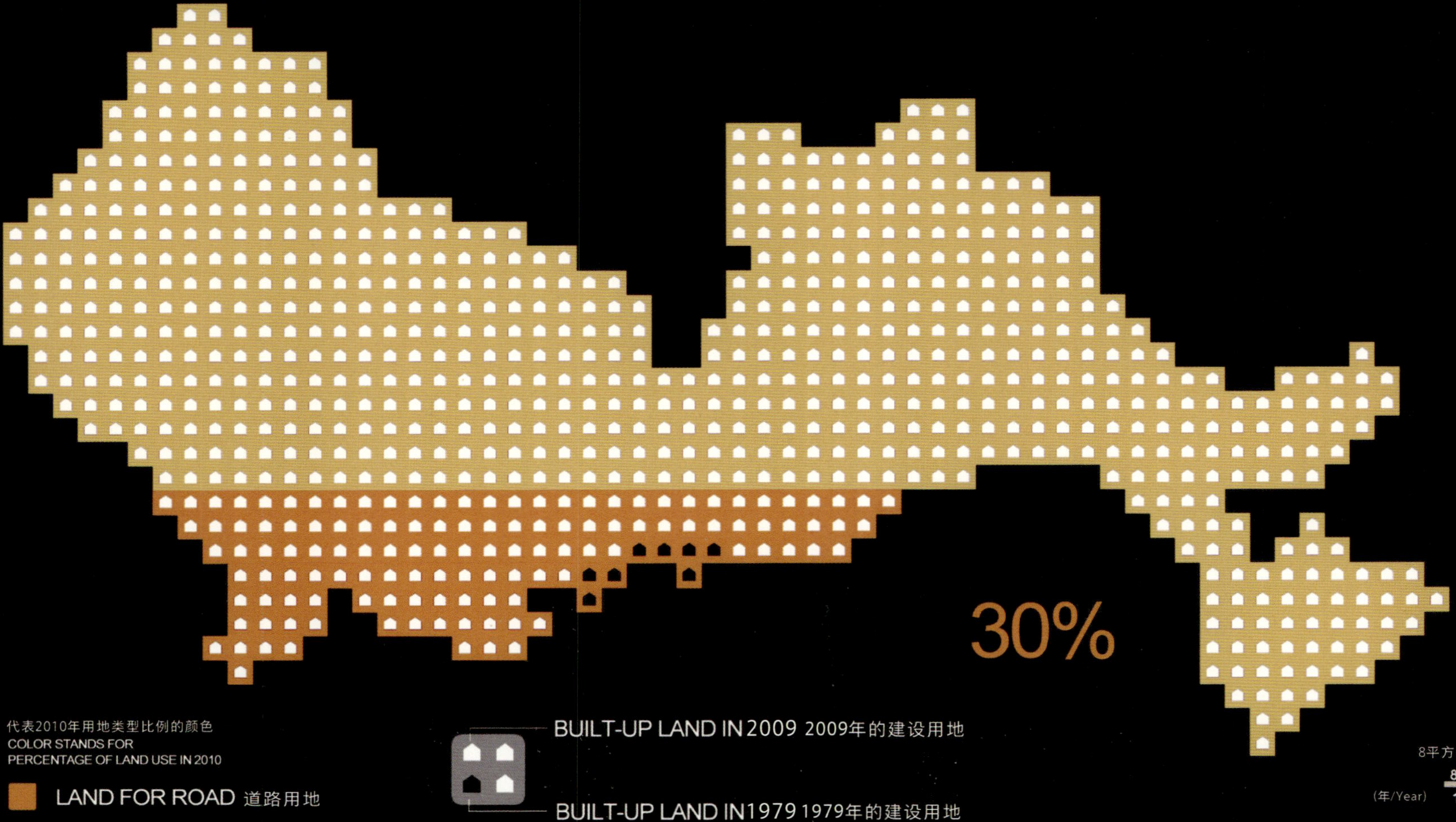

INCREASED 100 TIMES IN 30 YEARS
30年间增长了约100倍

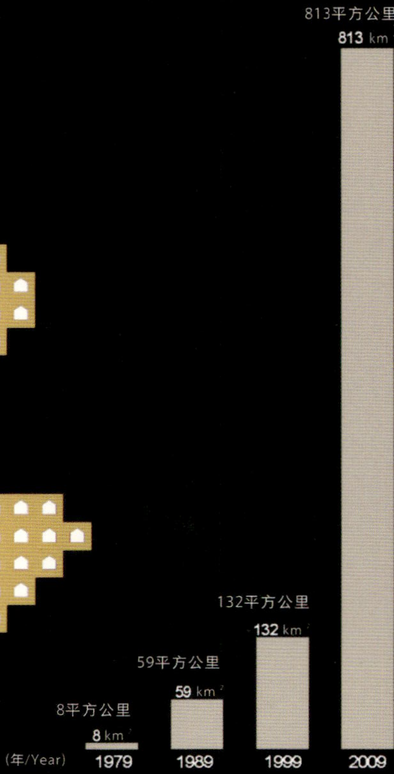

BUILT-UP LAND EXPANSION
建设用地扩张情况

MOBILITY 交通
50%
表2010年固定资产投资比例的颜色
COLOR STANDS FOR
PERCENTAGE OF FIXED ASSET INVESTMENT IN 2010
INVESTMENT IN TRANSPORTATION AND WAREHOUSE交通和仓储投资
OTHER FIXED ASSET INVESTMENT
其他固定资产投资
ROAD LENGTH IN 2006 2006年道路长度
ROAD LENGTH IN1984 1984年道路长度
INCREASED 30 TIMES IN 30 YEARS
22年间增长了约30倍
108公里
108km
209公里
209km
737公里
737km
2197公里
2179km
3313公里
3133km
(年/Year)
1984
1987
1996
2000
2006
ROAD LENGTH DEVELOPMENT
道路修建情况

Driven by the trinity of sweeping globalization, the powerful top-down rule of the Chinese government and wester-n modern planning, Shenzhen has rapidly and miraculously developed an appearance that is commonly seen in the Western cities, and become the representative of the high efficiency city where capital is the highest value.

在全球化浪潮、中国政府自上而下的有力管理，以及西方的现代规划这三种因素的联合推动下，
深圳以惊人的速度奇迹般地打造了西方国家中常见的城市面貌，成为资本至上的高效率城市的代表。

The city's existing logic of growth centering and focusing solely on the profit maximization has trapped the city.

深圳当前纯粹以利润最大化为中心、关注利润最大化的发展逻辑，困住了城市发展。

[KUN]
TRAPPED SHENZHEN

困——困境深圳

困难
DIFFICULTY
困滞
STRANDED
困乏
SLEEPY
困惑
PUZZLED
The character [kun] is made up of a tree inside a closed barrier, literally trapped inside and unable to connect with the outside.
“困”字形似一棵树“木”位于四面屏障之中，受困其中，无法与外界建立联系。

KUN 困

TRAPPED

Shenzhen, a pilot city for China's rapid urbanization over the three decades, should it continue to follow a western model of development or pursue a new urban paradigm?

作为中国三十年来城市化快速发展的试点城市，深圳应该继续采取西方的发展模式，还是追求一个新的城市范式？

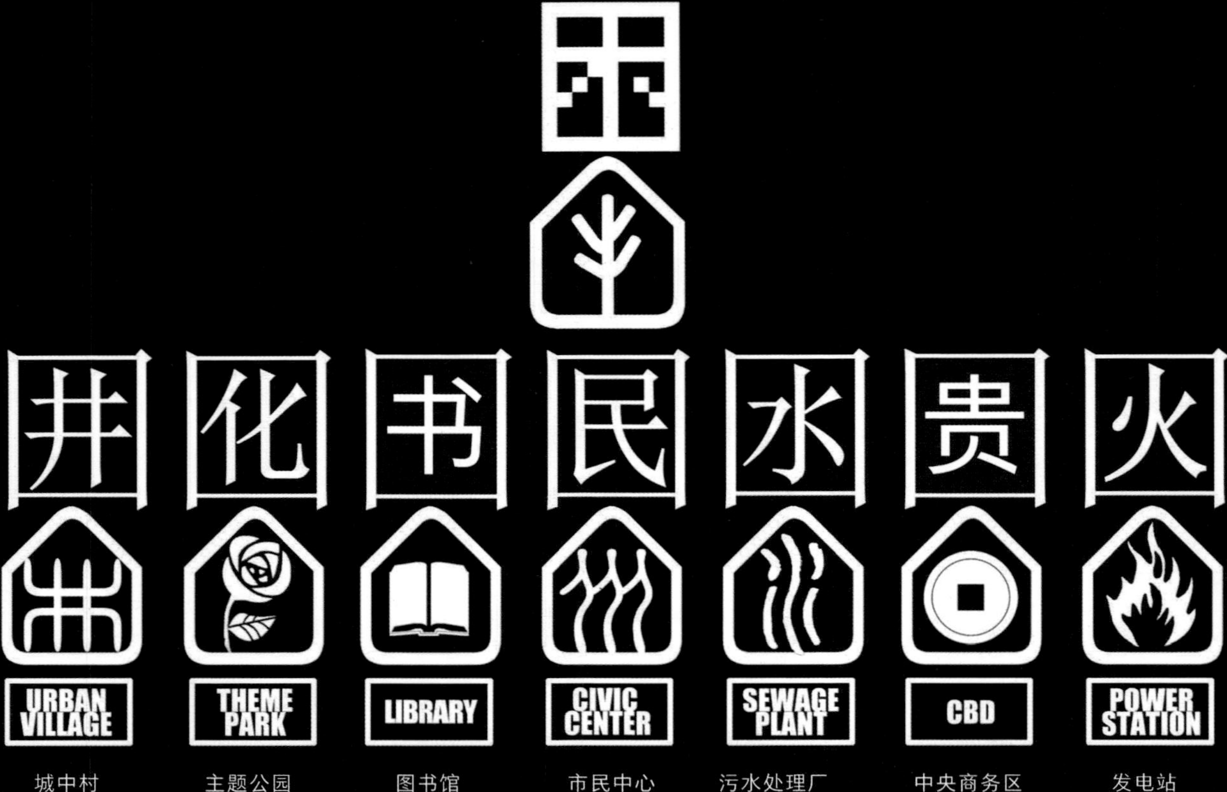

井
化
书
民
水
贵
火
URBAN VILLAGE
THEME PARK
LIBRARY
CIVIC CENTER
SEWAGE PLANT
CBD
POWER STATION
城中村
主题公园
图书馆
市民中心
污水处理厂
中央商务区
发电站

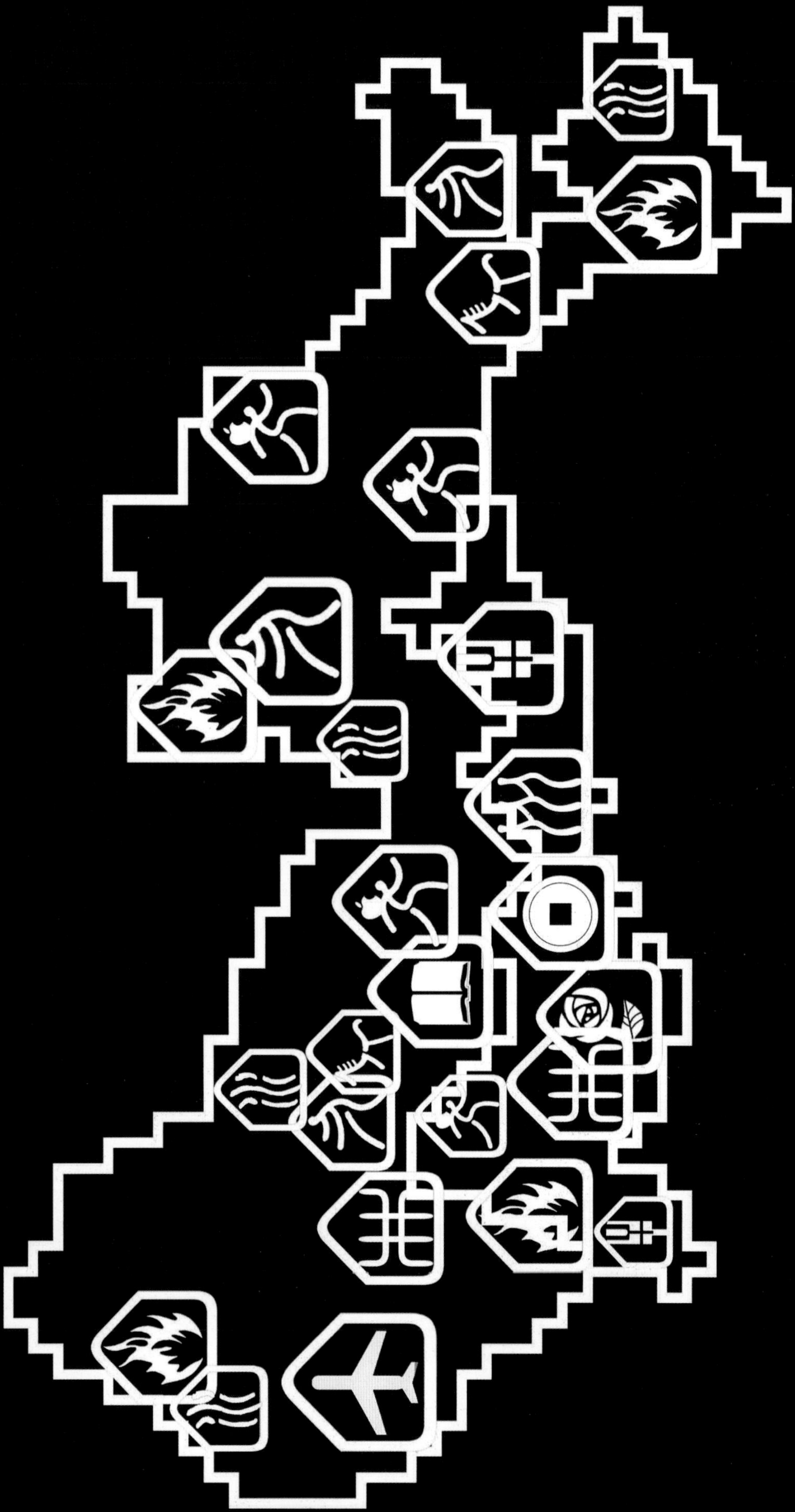

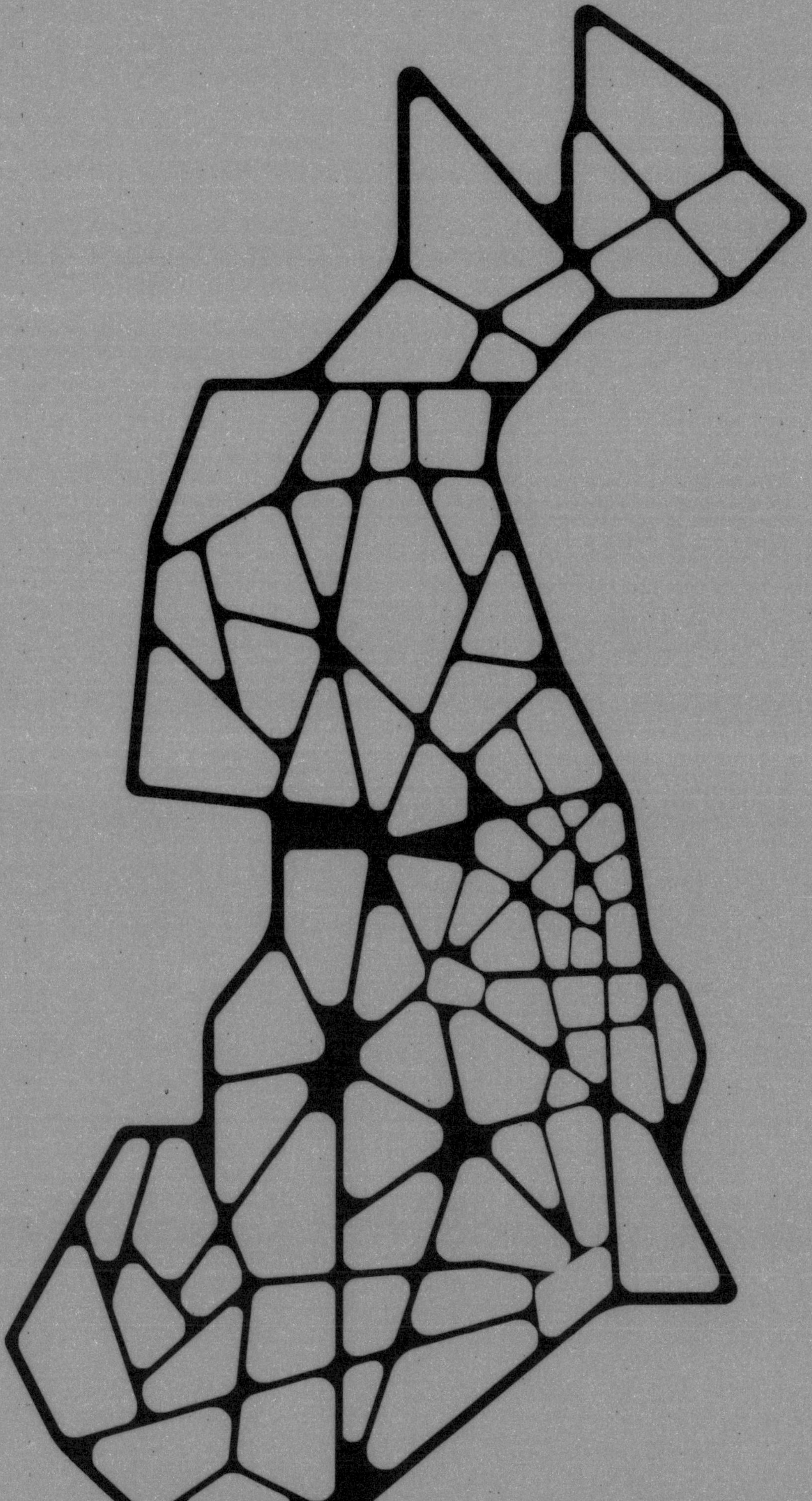

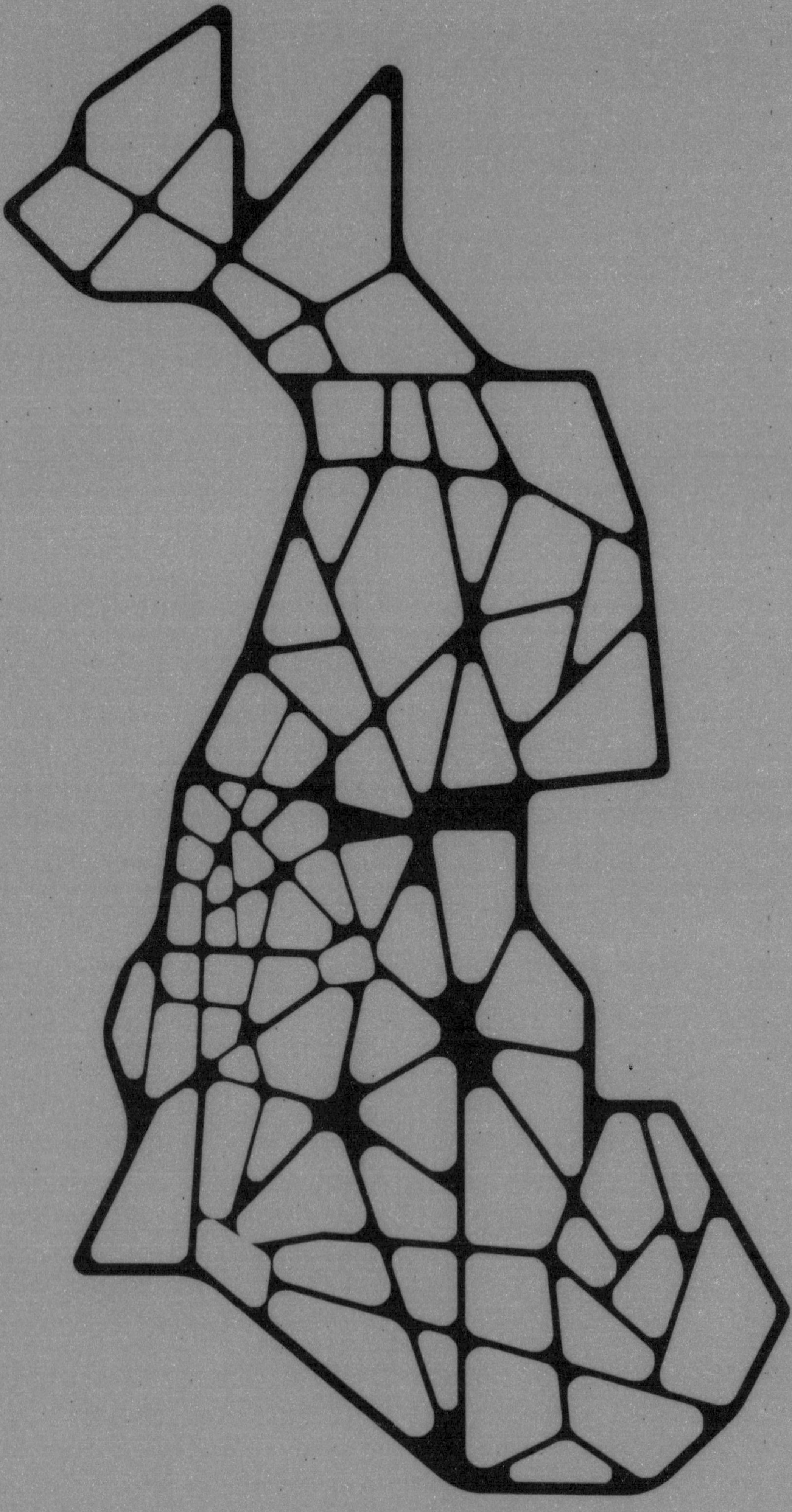

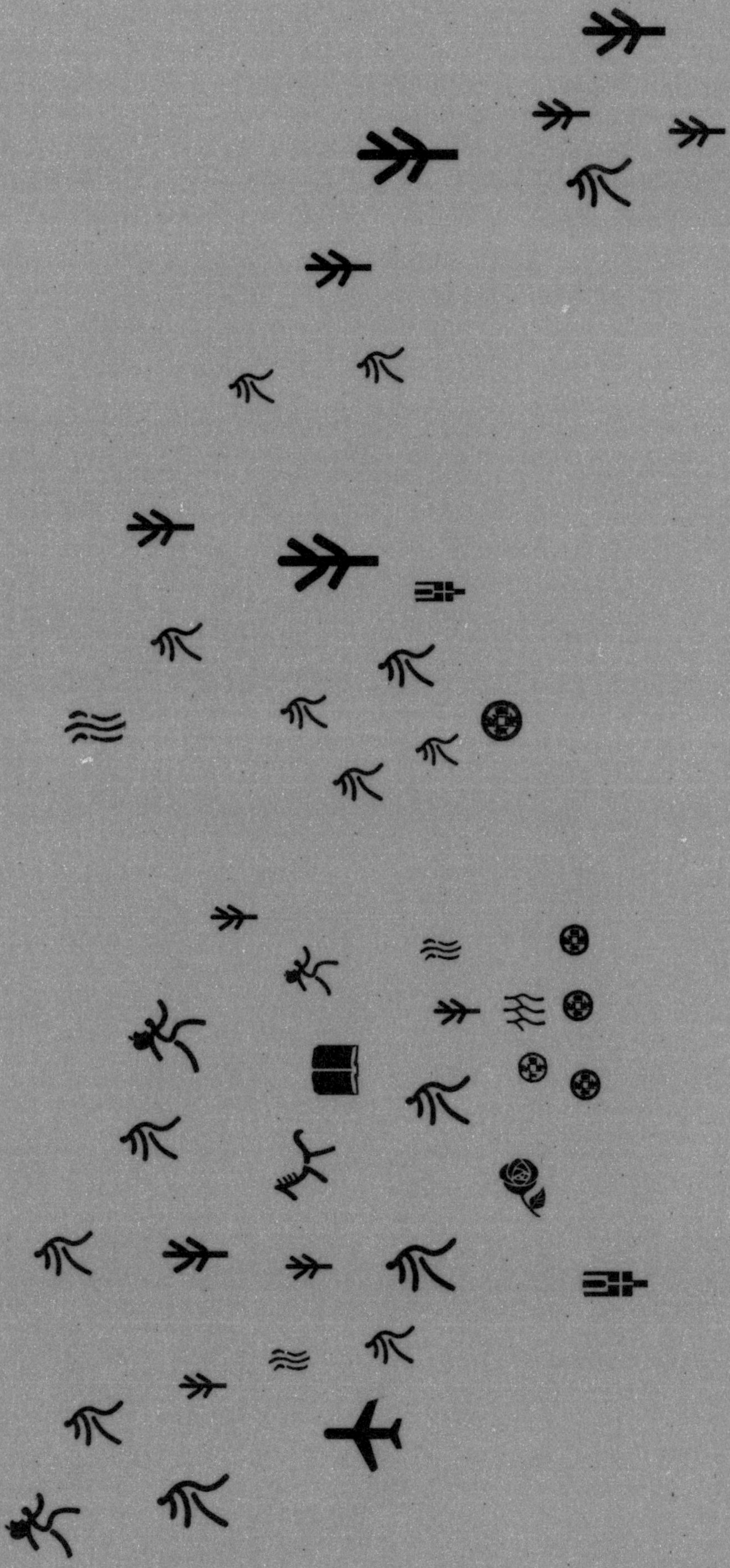

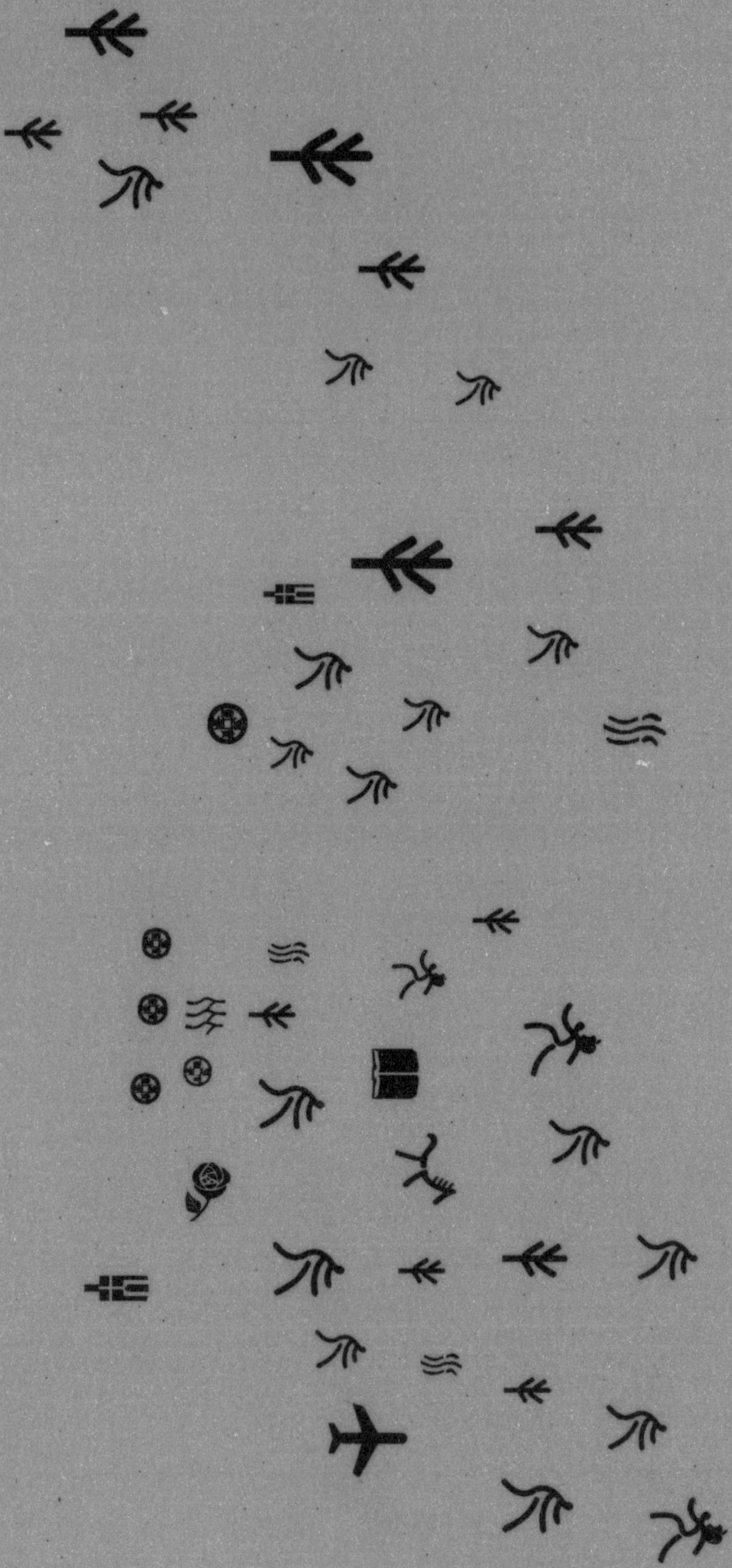

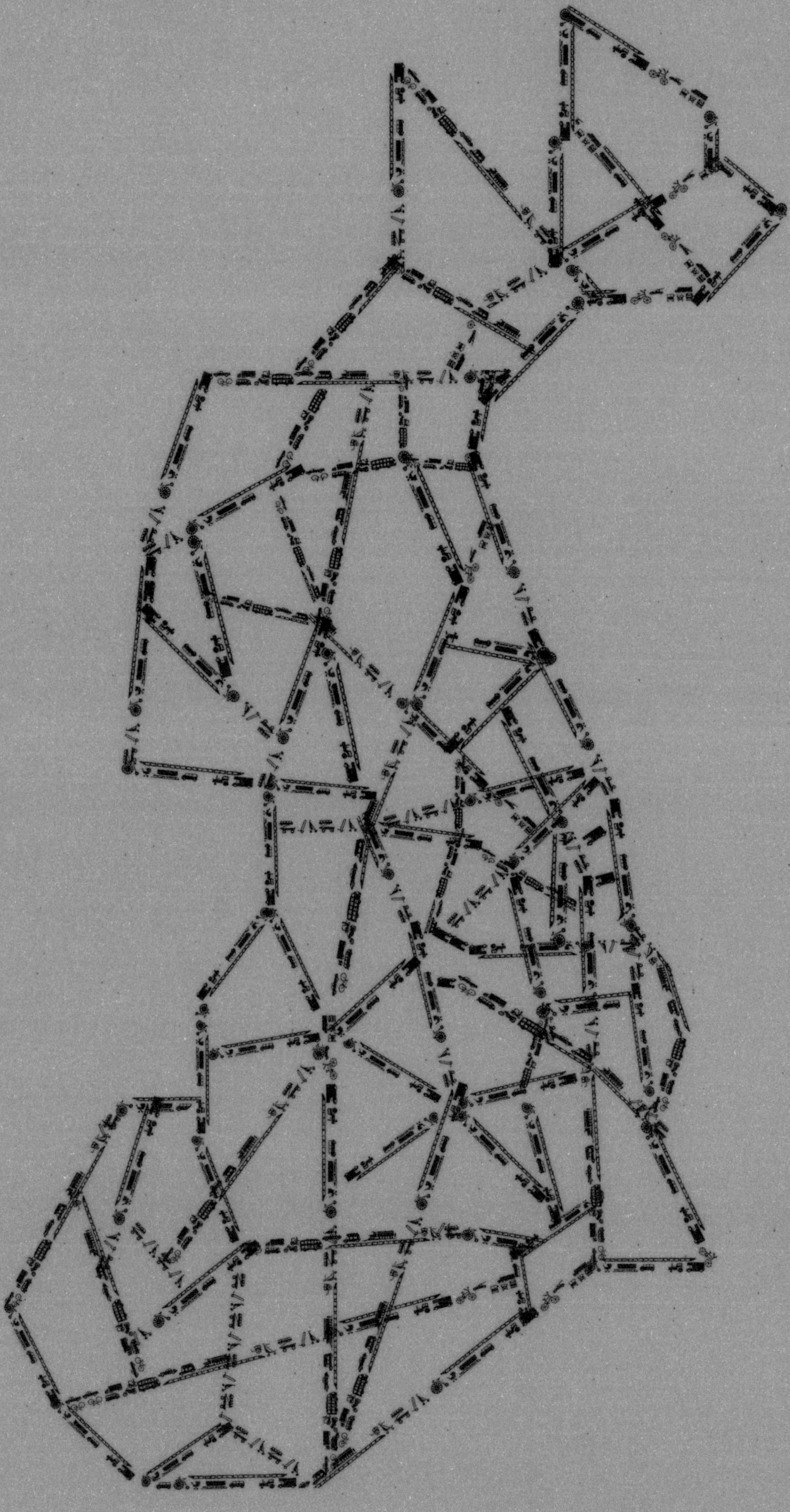

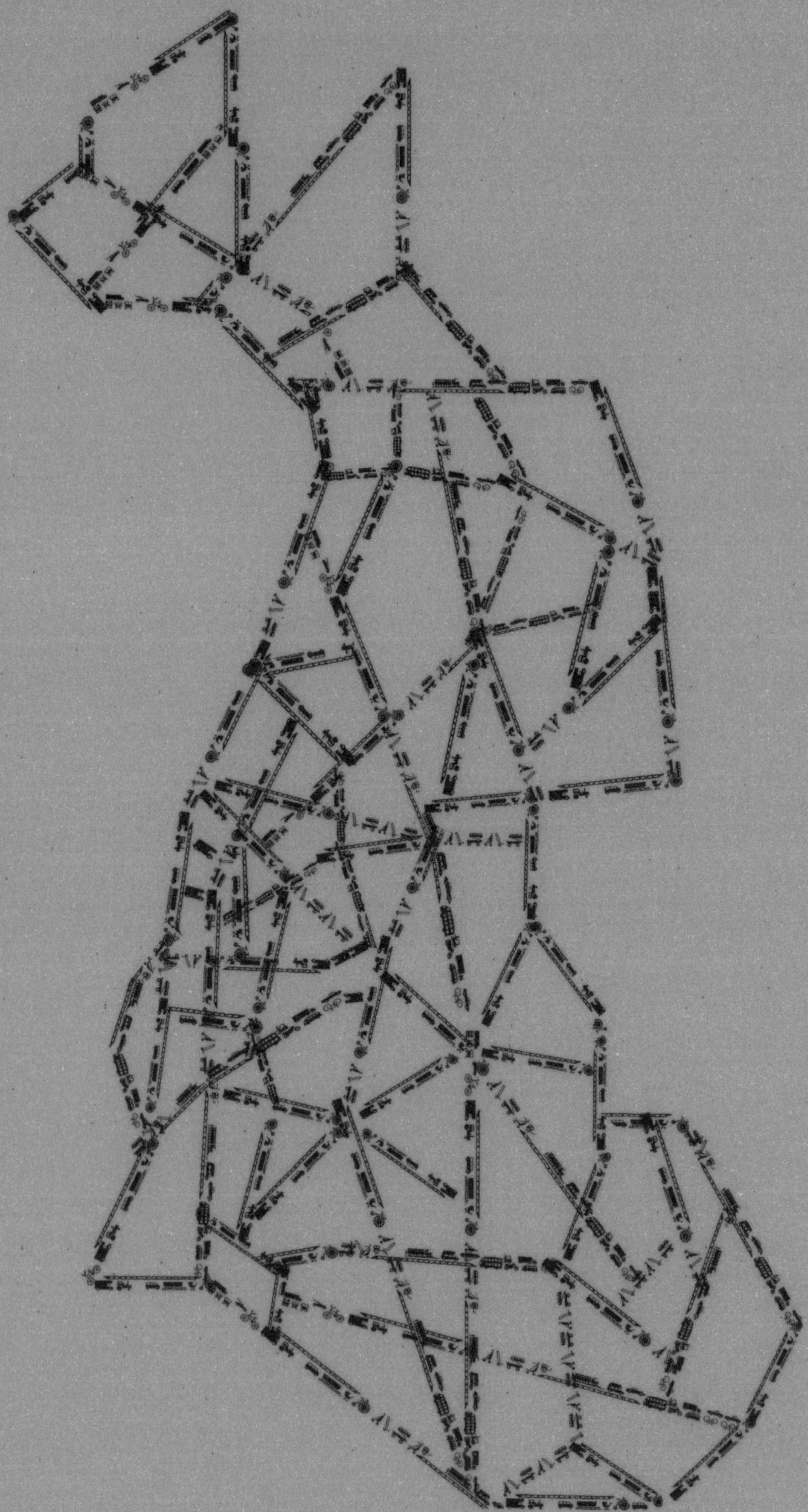

1980年
深南大道
1980
SHEN NAN
ROAD
7m

2012年
深南大道
2012
SHEN NAN
ROAD
150m

SHENZHEN 2012 KUN

Driven by a western mode of modern planning, Shenzhen has rapidly taken on the capital-driven qualities of western cities, single-use zoning and large-scale mobility infrastructure have consumed available land, divided urban spaces, isolated communities, and produced excessive reliance on imported resources. a lot of roads end up with incredible width and cover a large area of the city. The road supports flow by connectiion in one dimension, however it also creates segregation in another as consequence.

2012年深圳——困

在西方现代规划模式的推动下，深圳迅速呈现出西方城市的以资本驱动发展的特质。一次性的分区规划模式和大规模的交通基础设施消耗了现有的土地，分割了社区，形成了对进口资源的过度依赖。许多道路宽度惊人，占据城市的大片区域。道路一方面以连通的方式支持交通发展，另一方面却也造成了城市隔离。

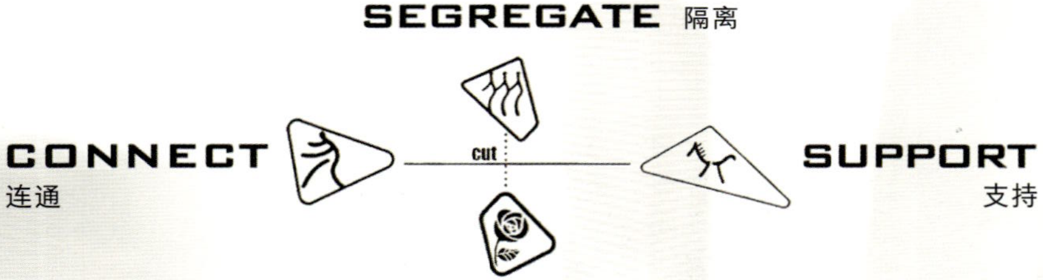

RELEASING SHENZHEN
解困深圳

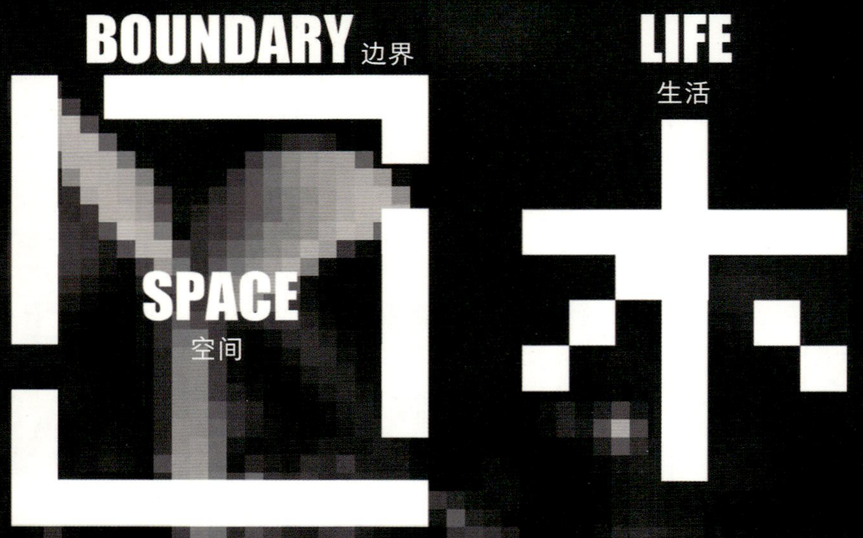

the character [KUN] also means space of chance.
the analysis of [KUN] enables us to return to the Chinese philosophy of [life, space & boundary], to reconsider the foundamental relationship of these three, and to re-define the conditions of boundary between humen beings, the life and space they live in, through means of mobility and flow, we will achieve a new and higher balance - nature and people living in harmony.

“困”字还意味着空间方面的机会。对“困”的研究能让我们重拾中国有关生活、空间和边界的哲学；重新思考这三者间的根本联系；重新定义人类与其生活和生活空间的边界情况。通过交通和流线规划，我们将会达到一种新的、更高层次的平衡——人与自然和谐共处。

EXPERIENCE EXPERIENCE EXPERIENCE EXPERIENCE EXPERIENCE EXPERIENCE EXPERIENCE EXPERIENCE EXPERIENCE 体验

rather than continue to follow a western model of development, we believe that Shenzhen should pursue a new urban paradigm. the city's existing philosophy of growth centered on the generation of capital has resulted in a state of KUN (困). our mission is to transform the city from KUN (困) to XIAN(闲), a state of open experience; to achieve balance between sorts of mobility infrastructure and a diversity of life styles.

我们认为，相比继续效仿西方的发展模式，深圳更应该探寻新的城市发展范式。深圳现在采用的发展理念以创造资本为重心，因此造成了困境。我们的任务就是要把深圳的困转变为闲，即一种开放式的体验，并且在各种交通基础设施与多元生活方式之间建立平衡。

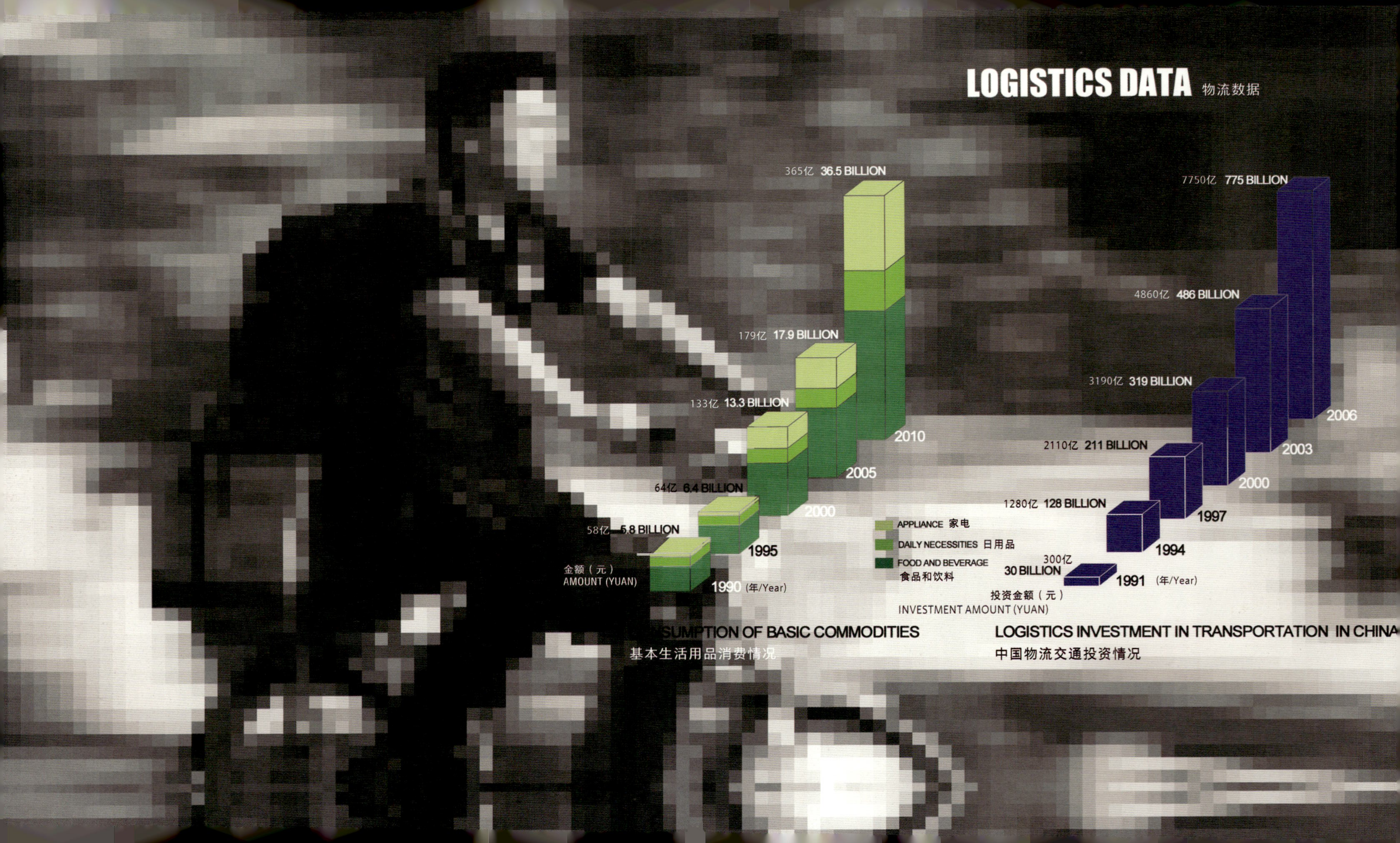
LOGISTICS DATA 物流数据
365亿 36.5 BILLION
179亿 17.9 BILLION
133亿 13.3 BILLION
64亿 6.4 BILLION
58亿 5.8 BILLION
金额（元）
AMOUNT (YUAN)
1990 1995 2000 2005 2010 (年/Year)
APPLIANCE 家电
DAILY NECESSITIES 日用品
FOOD AND BEVERAGE 食品和饮料
SUMPTION OF BASIC COMMODITIES
基本生活用品消费情况
7750亿 775 BILLION
4860亿 486 BILLION
3190亿 319 BILLION
2110亿 211 BILLION
1280亿 128 BILLION
300亿 30 BILLION
1991 1994 1997 2000 2003 2006 (年/Year)
投资金额（元）
INVESTMENT AMOUNT (YUAN)
LOGISTICS INVESTMENT IN TRANSPORTATION IN CHINA
中国物流交通投资情况

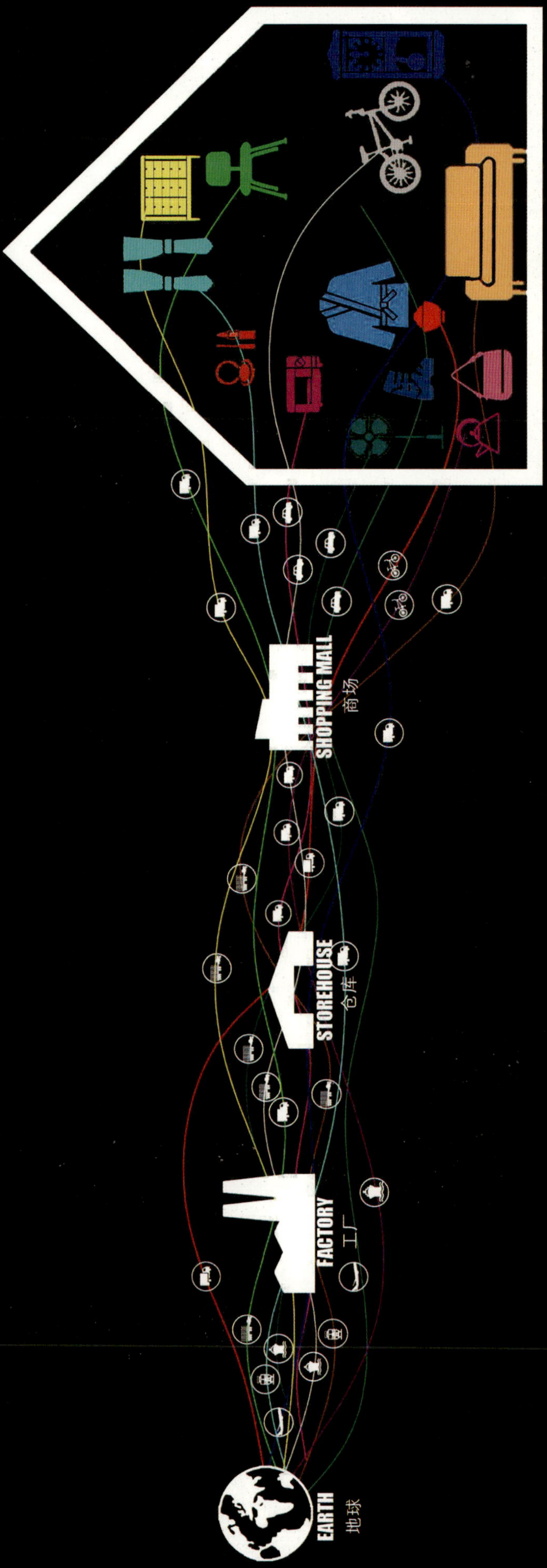
SHOPPING MALL
商场
STOREHOUSE
仓库
FACTORY
工厂
EARTH
地球

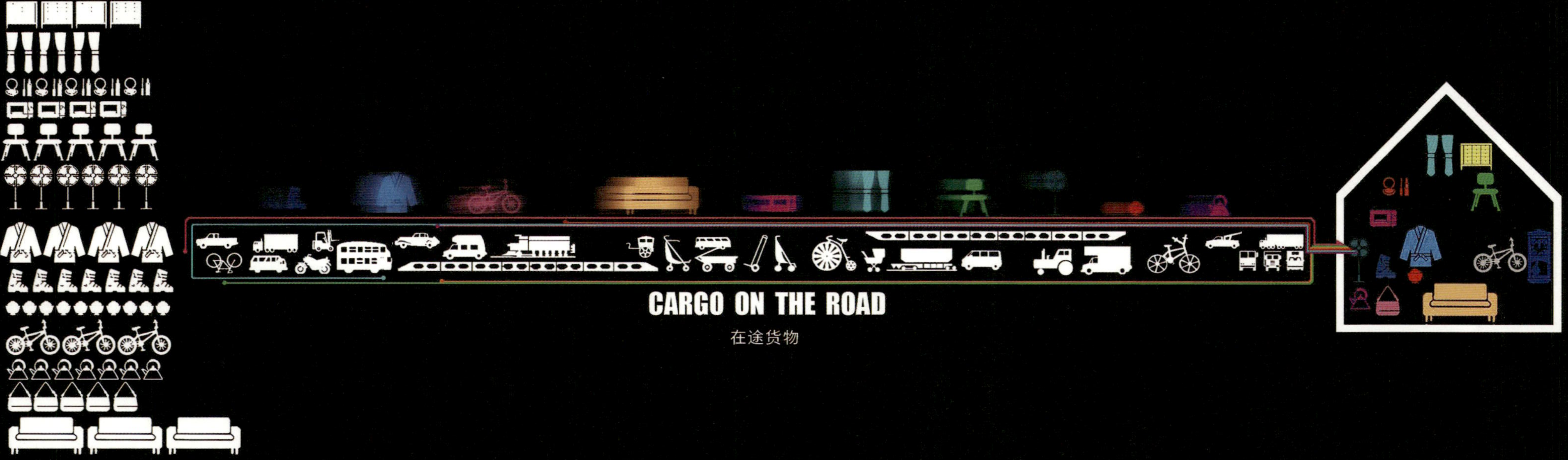

CARGO ON THE ROAD

在途货物

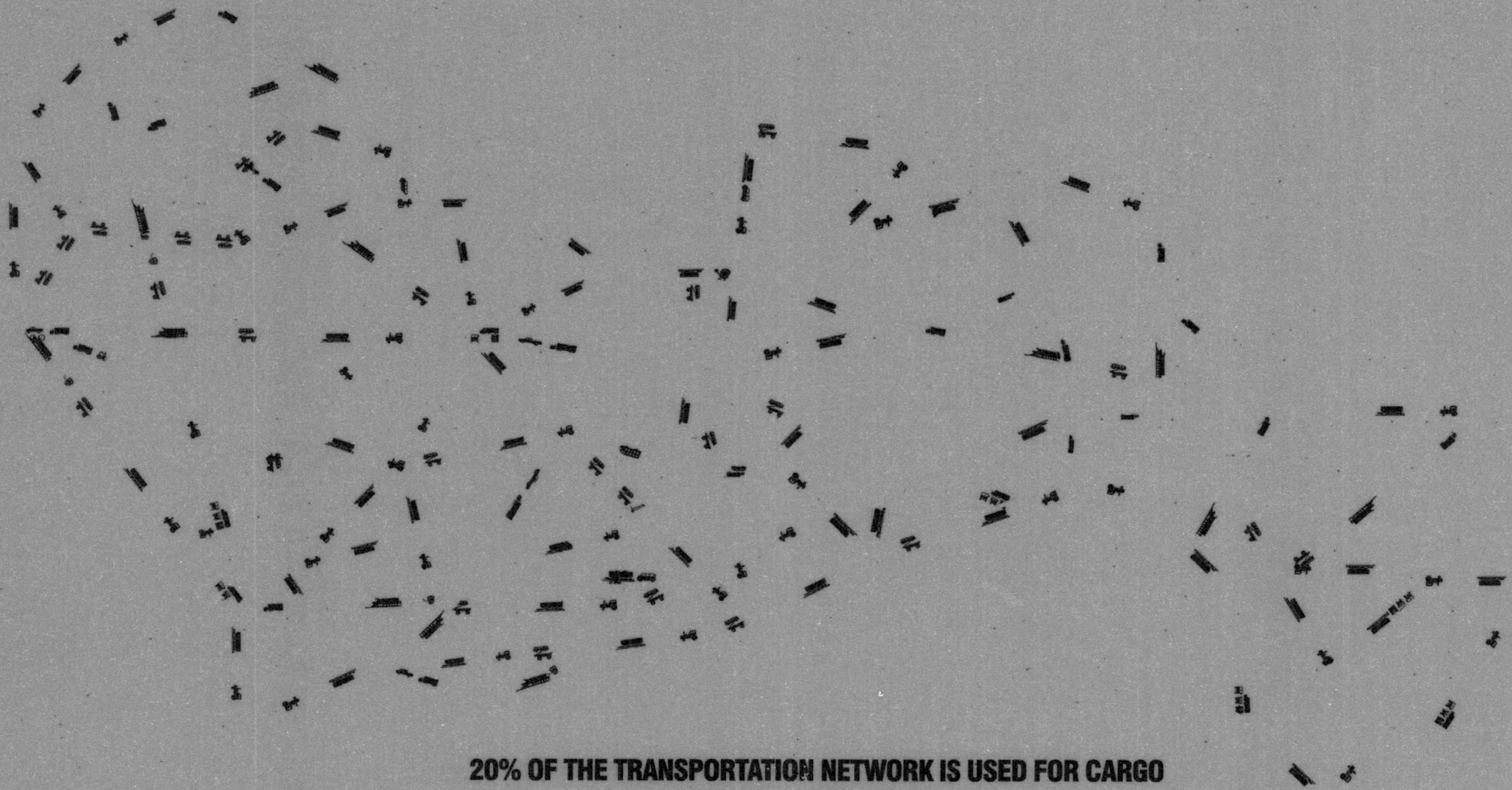

20% OF THE TRANSPORTATION NETWORK IS USED FOR CARGO

交通网络的20%被用于货物运输

20% OF THE TRANSPORTATION NETWORK IS USED FOR CARGO

交通网络的20%被用于货物运输

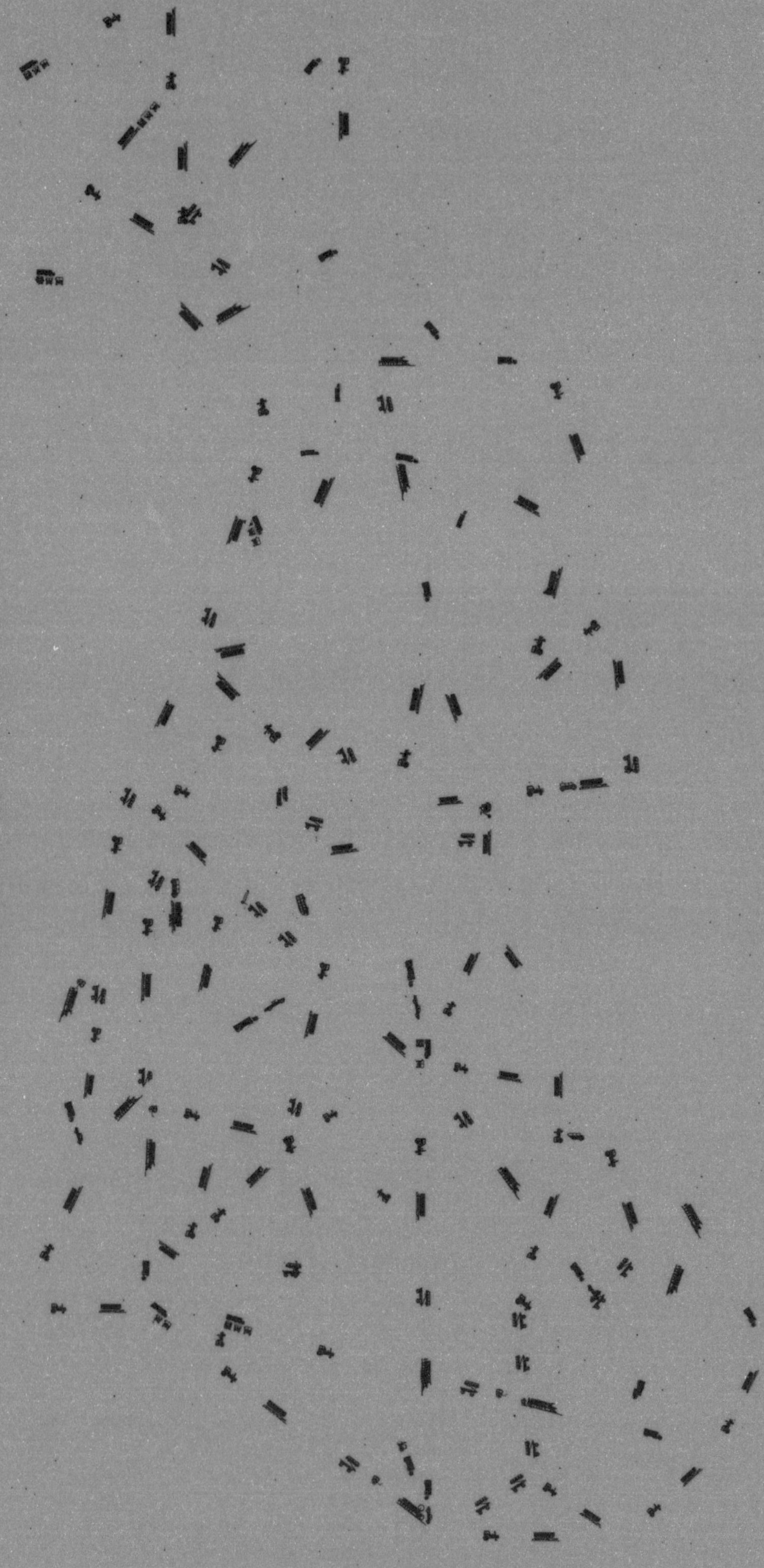

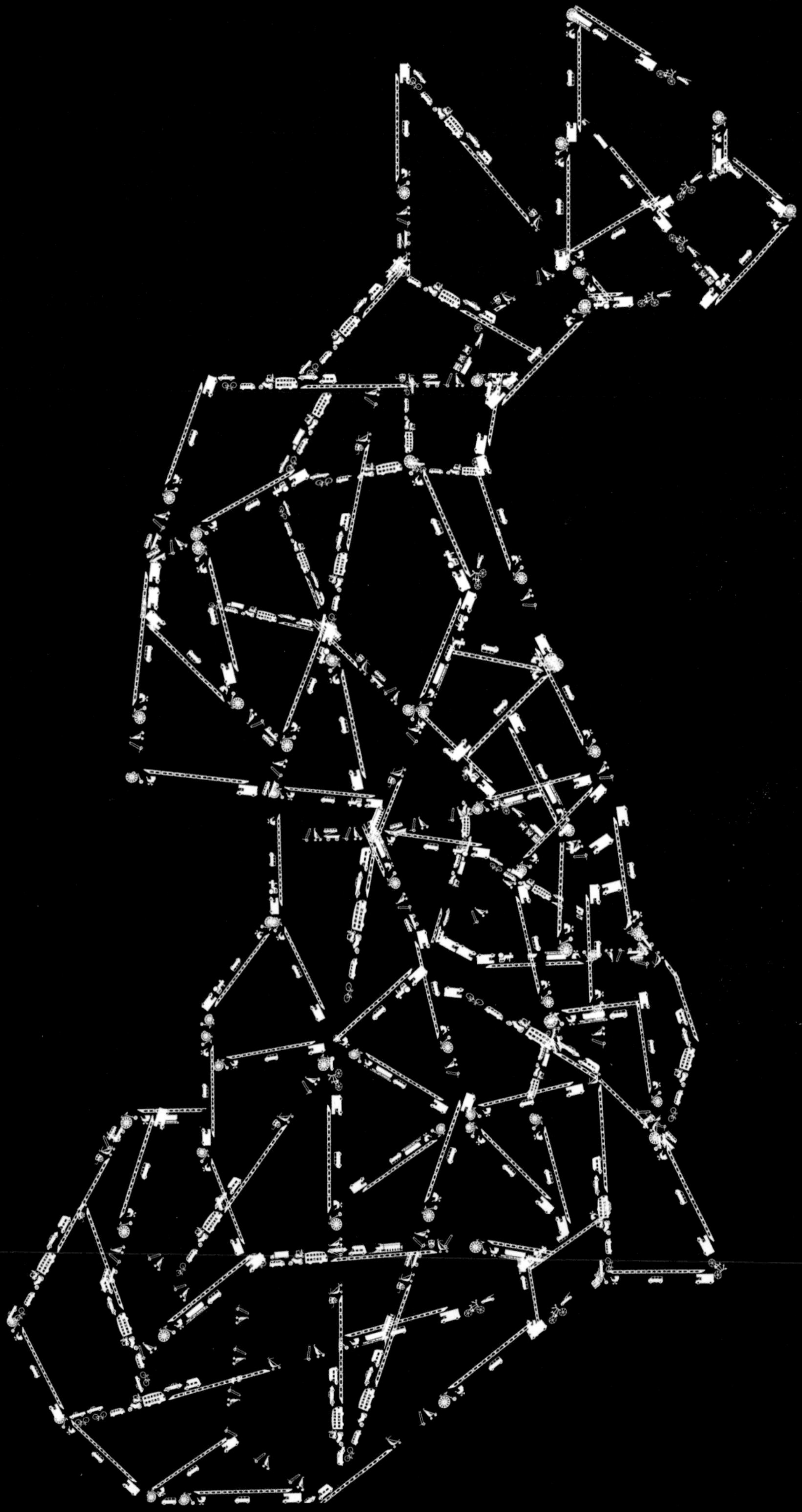

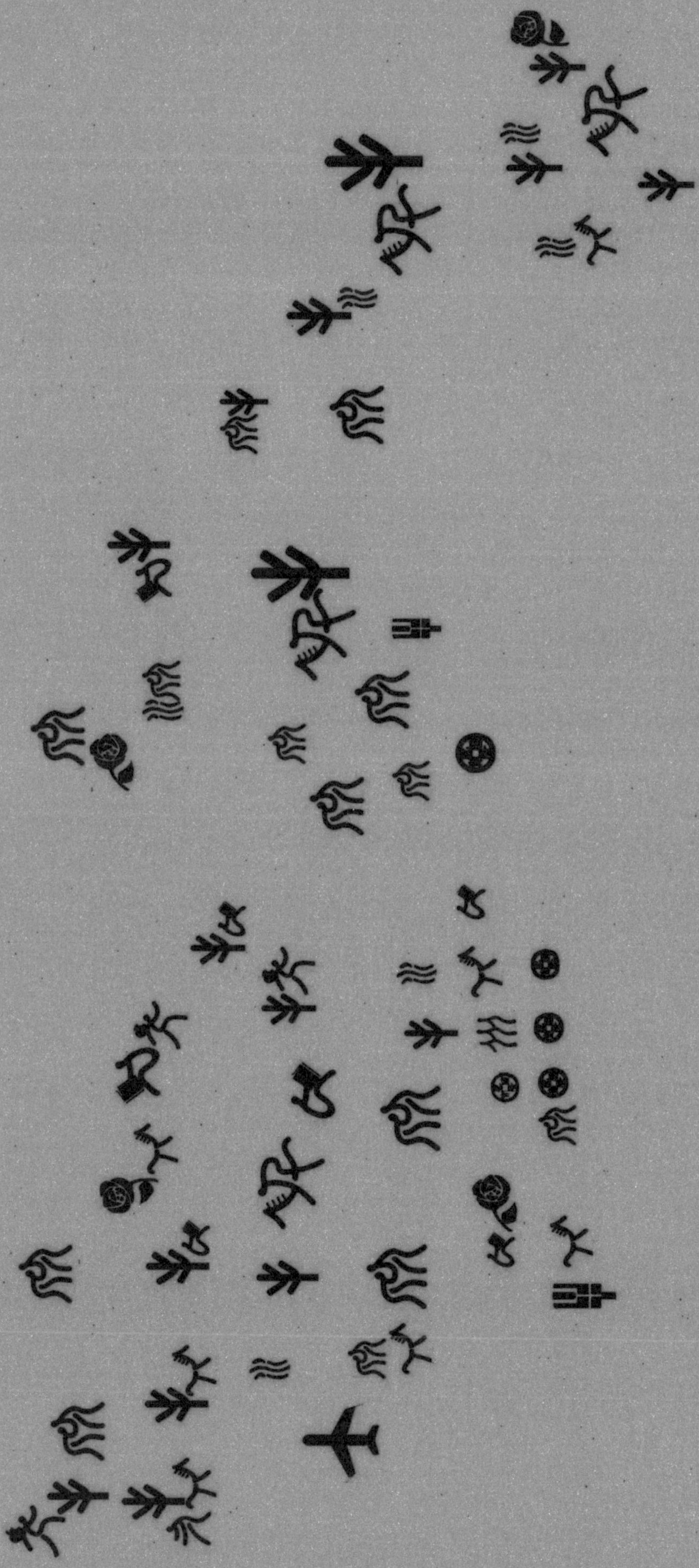

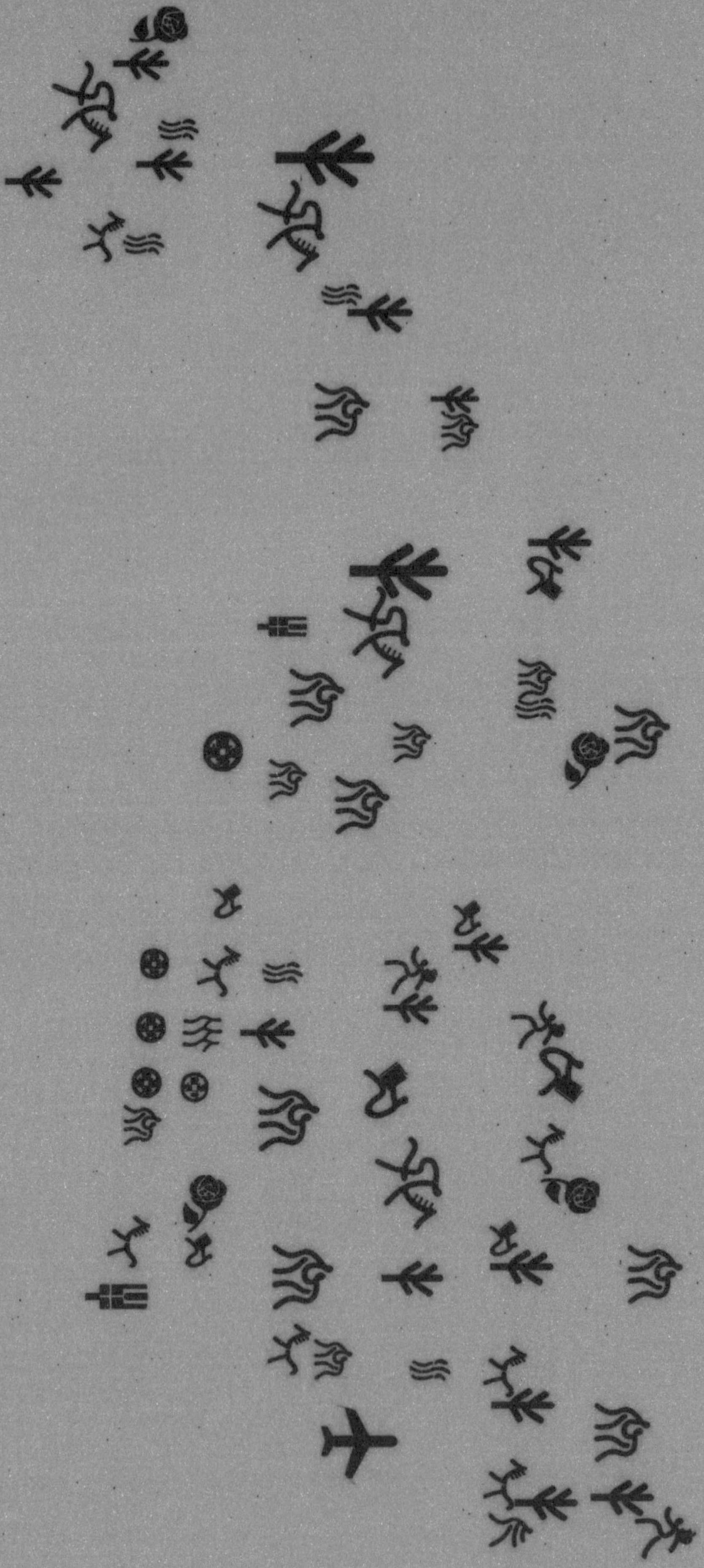

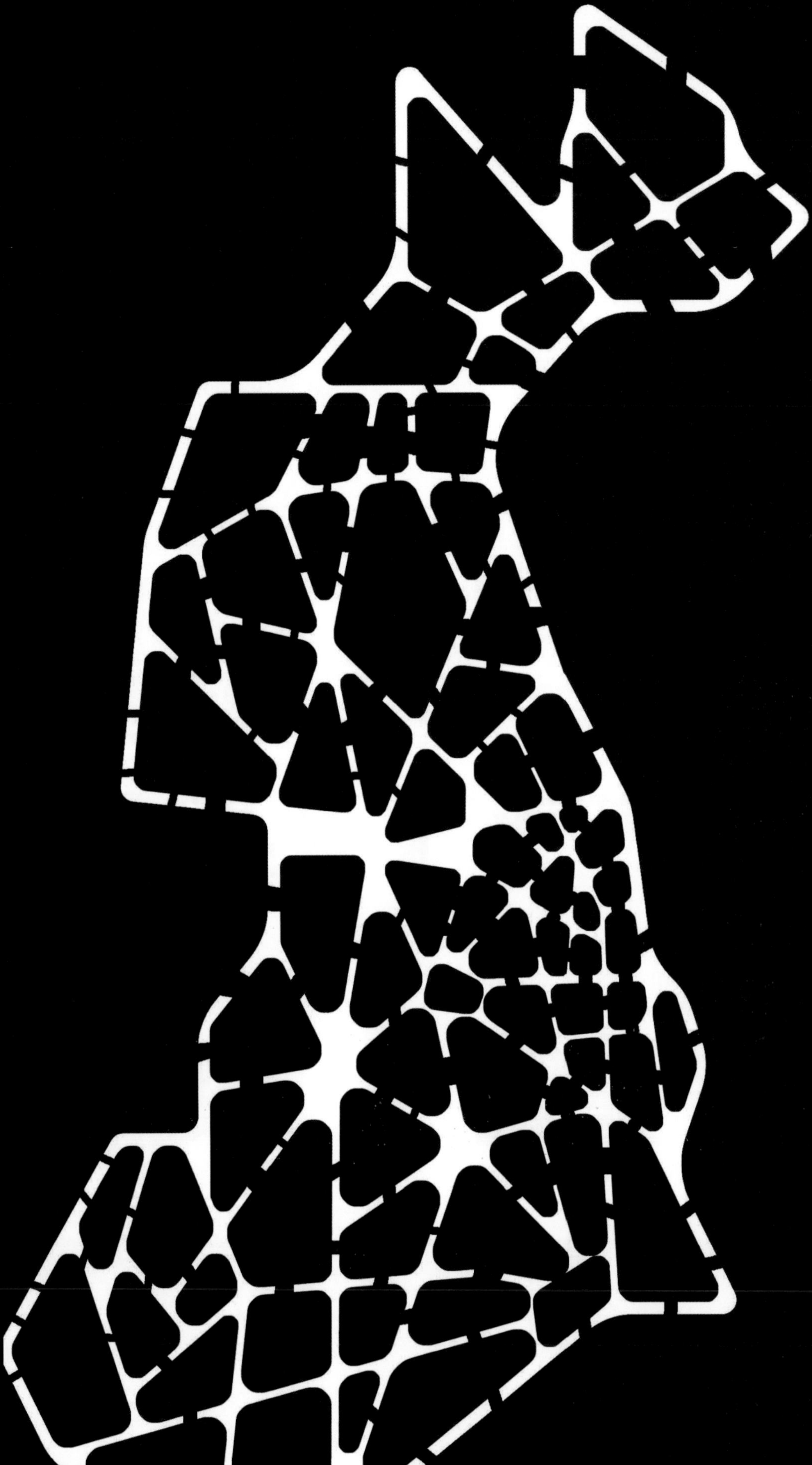

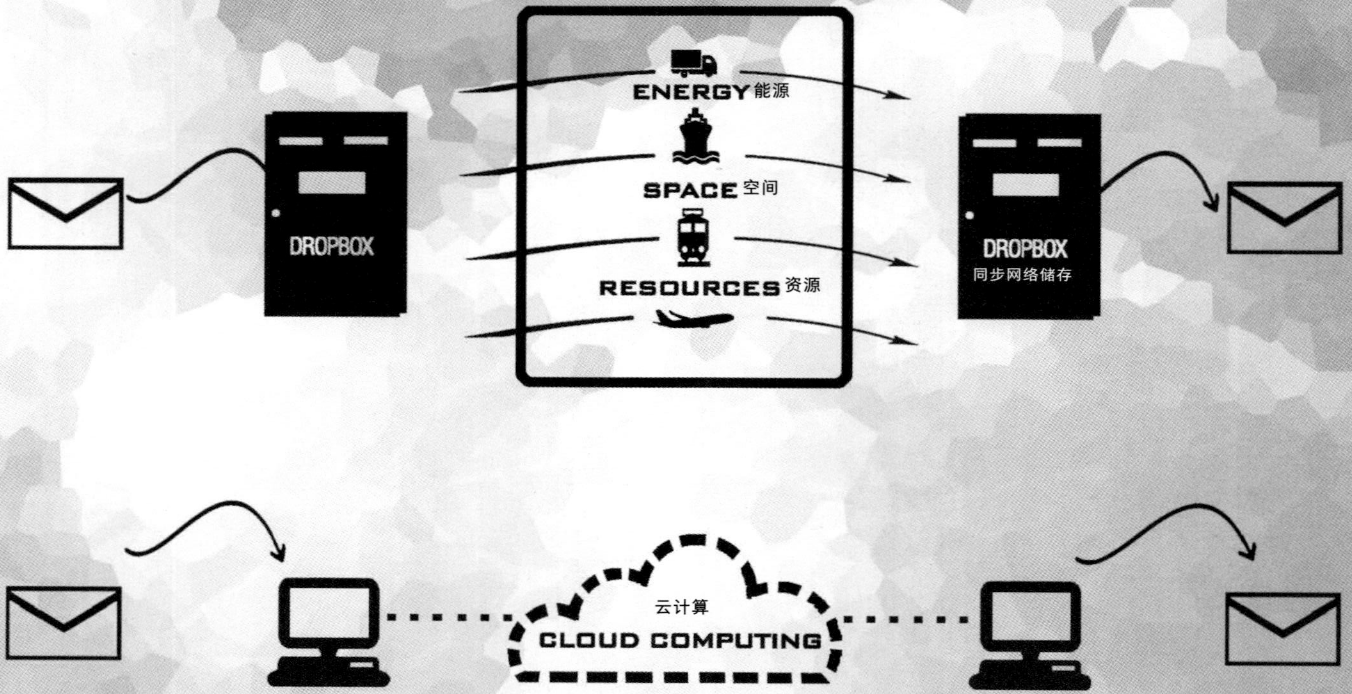

Cloud computing is a style of computing in which dynamically scalable and often virtualized resources are provided as a service over the Internet.

云计算是一种计算方式，即在网络上提供动态可扩充、普遍可视化的资源作为服务。

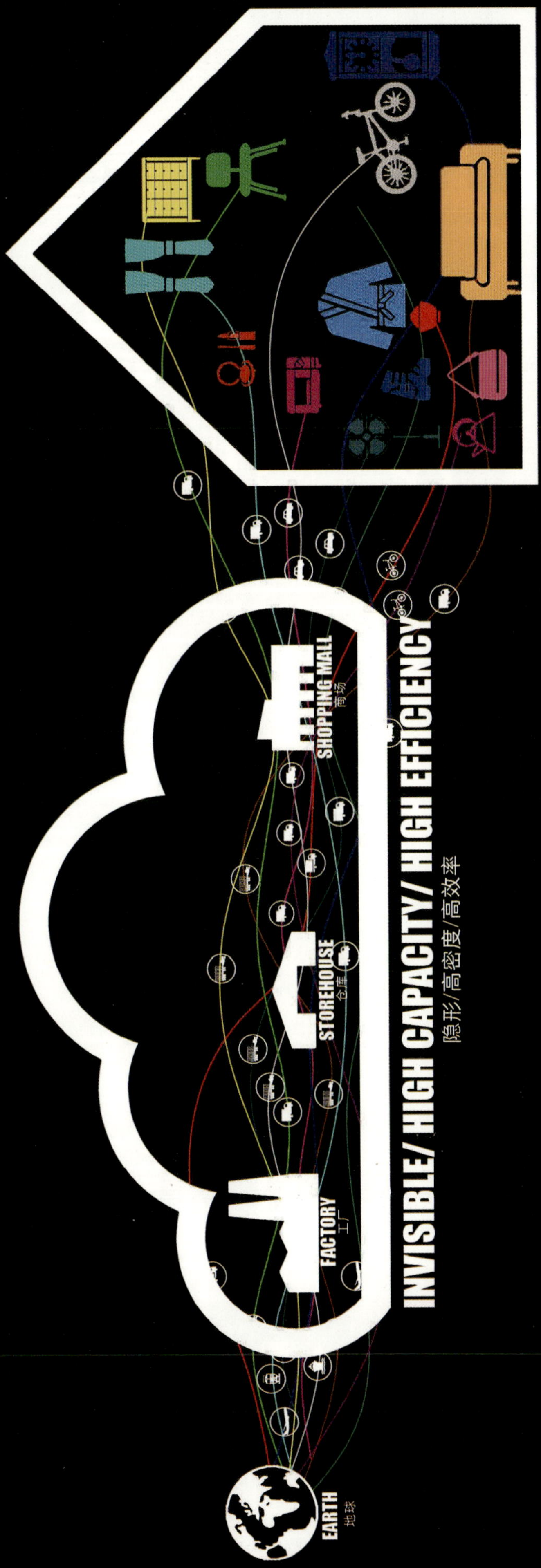
EARTH
地球
FACTORY
工厂
STOREHOUSE
仓库
SHOPPING MALL
商场
INVISIBLE/ HIGH CAPACITY/ HIGH EFFICIENCY
隐形/高密度/高效率

体验

EXPERIENCE EXPERIENCE EXPERIENCE EXPERIENCE EXPERIENCE EXPERIENCE EXPERIENCE EXPERIENCE EXPERIENCE

Modern road system aims at high efficiency of transportation, meanwhile people' experience is impaired.

现代道路系统追求高效率的交通，同时也破坏了人们的使用体验。
我们倡导更人性化和更注重体验的道路规划设计。
但要如何才能实现呢？

We proposed that the road should be more about people and experience.

How ?

cloud logistics is possible?

云物流是否可行?

EXPERIENCE
Nowadays more and more industries are paying attention to customer experience. From fixed phone to mobile phone and now the iphone, better experience is constantly being strengthened and enhanced.
如今，越来越多的行业开始关注客户体验，从固定电话到移动电话，再到现在的智能电话，提升产品体验的理念正不断得到强化和推广。

怎样做？

HOW?

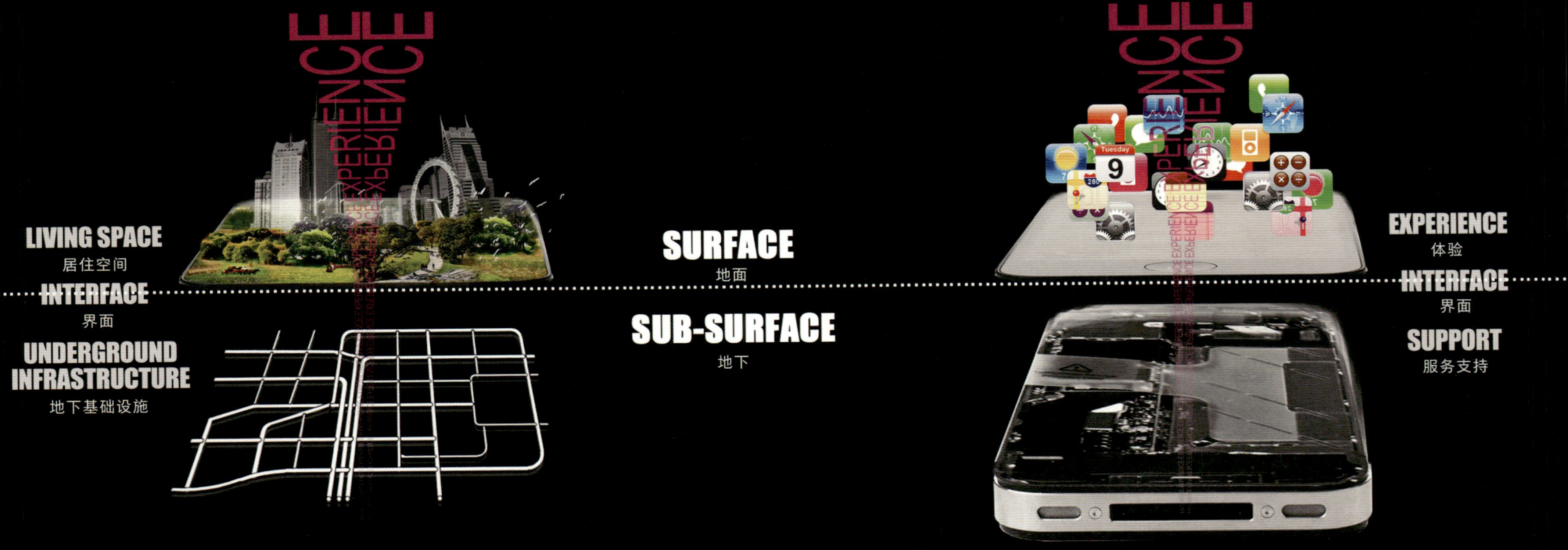
LIVING SPACE
居住空间
INTERFACE
界面
UNDERGROUND INFRASTRUCTURE
地下基础设施
SURFACE
地面
SUB-SURFACE
地下
EXPERIENCE
体验
INTERFACE
界面
SUPPORT
服务支持

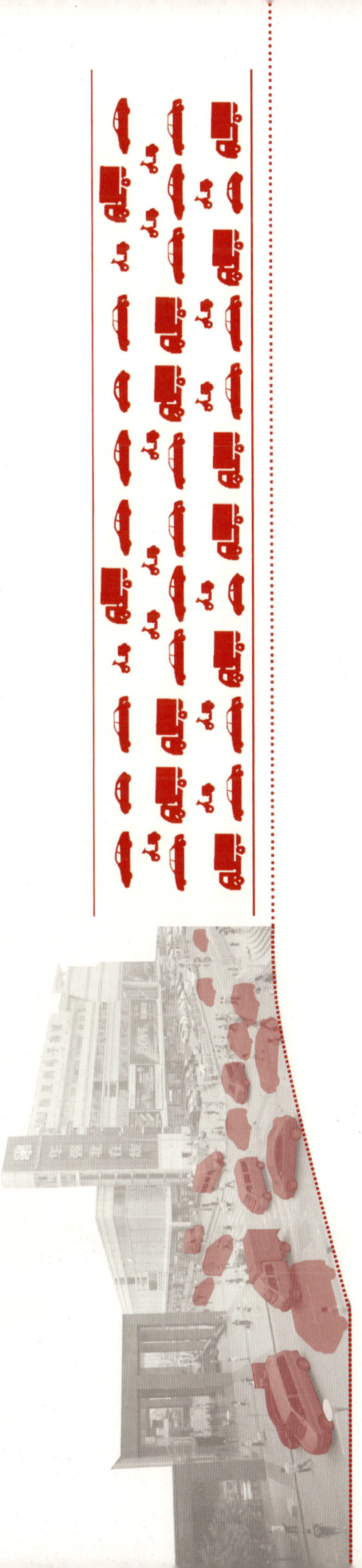

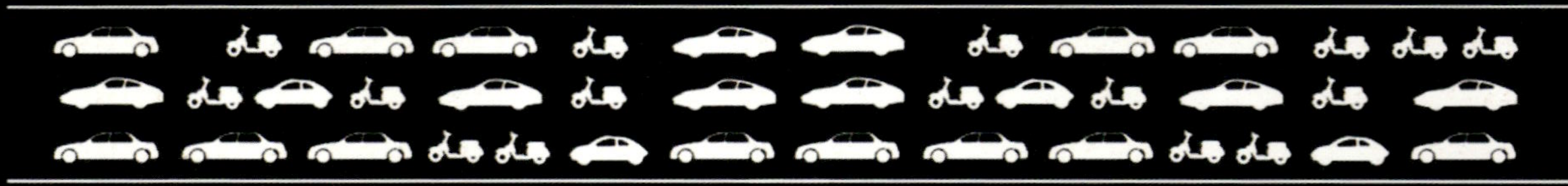

地面
SURFACE

SUB-SURFACE
地下

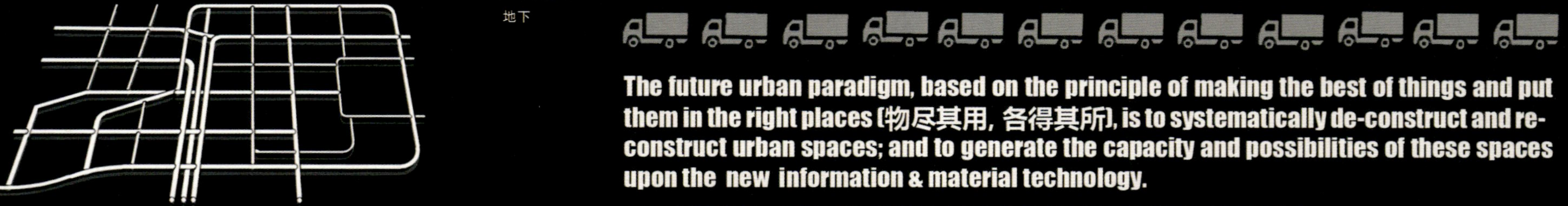

UNDERGROUND LOGISTICS SYSTEM

The future urban paradigm, based on the principle of making the best of things and put them in the right places (物尽其用，各得其所), is to systematically de-construct and re-construct urban spaces; and to generate the capacity and possibilities of these spaces upon the new information & material technology.

基于“物尽其用，各得其所”原则的未来城市范式旨在系统化地解构和重塑城市空间；并借助新的信息和材料技术，挖掘这些空间的潜力和可能性。

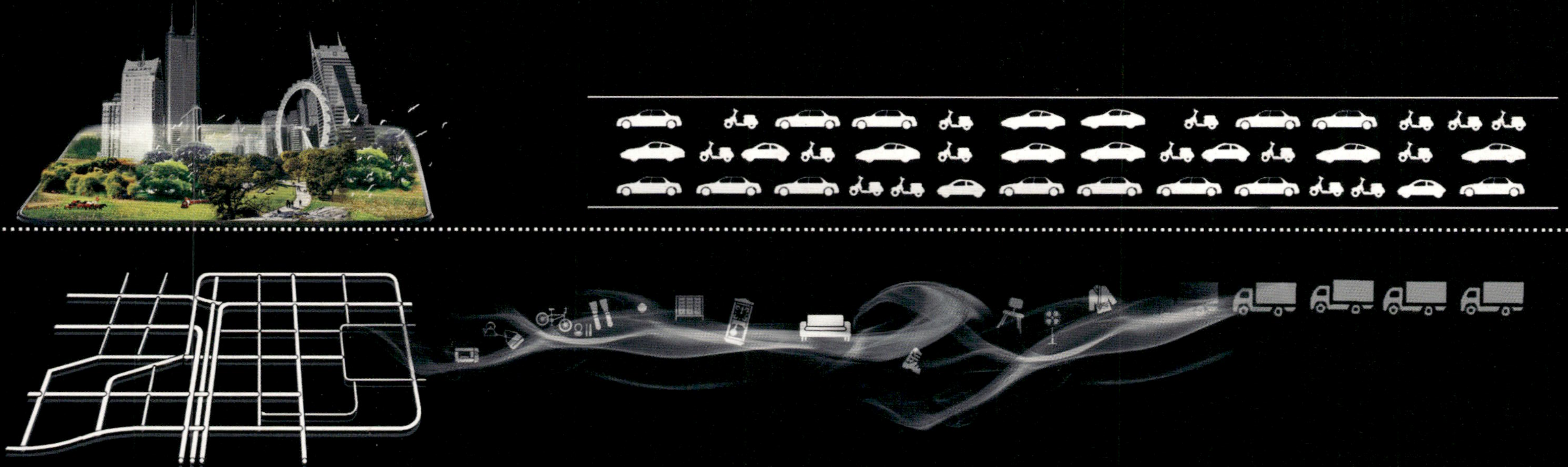

UNDERGROUND LOGISTICS SYSTEM

地下物流系统

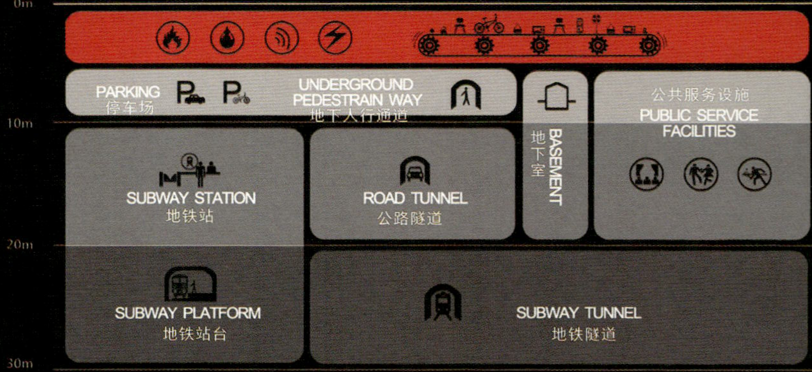

we use the wrong-doings as they are [将错就错], re-modify current mobility of infrastructure, and integrate with the future logistics system to jointly create a brand new object-space interface with a mixed layer of road - logistics. the new yet invisible interface can be well incorporated with the exising road surface, available technical conditions and negotiable planning procedures, therefore it is feasible in the intermediate future.

我们将错就错，重新调整现有的交通基础设施，结合未来的物流系统，共同打造一个拥有道路—物流混合层的全新的物体—空间界面。这种全新且隐形的界面能够很好地融入现有的道路界面、可利用的技术条件和可变动的规划程序，因而在

we also integrate existing built spaces with the information system to jointly form a brand new visible interface of living spaces with mixed layers of ground, building and information, which together with the foresaid invisible object-space interface, further establishes the supporting infrastructural system of the future city. with this new system, we could easily separate different modes of mobility, transform the urban space of overly controlled or dissimilated by mobility and logistics into a place of experience and leisure in multiple dimensions.

我们还将现有的建筑空间与信息系统结合起来，打造一个拥有土地、建筑、信息混合层的全新的、可视的生活空间界面。该界面与前面所述的隐形物体—空间界面共同促进了未来城市配套基础设施系统的建立。利用该系统，我们能够轻易地把不同的交通模式分离，将被交通和物流过度限制或分化的城市空间改造成多维的体验和休闲场所。

闲——开放深圳

[XIAN] OPEN SHENZHEN

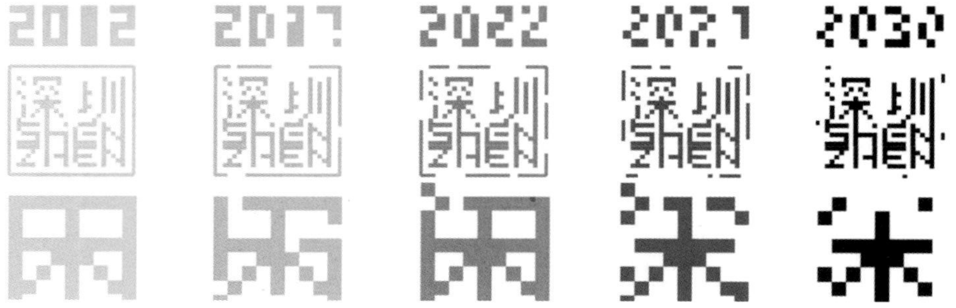

《时代建筑》，2003年2月，第70期

密度的第二性

刘珩

城市是所有事物（人口、建筑、工作、生活内容、日常经验等）的聚集地，无疑与“密度”有着很大的关系。早期对密度的见解只限于科学的计算公式，建筑面积与场地面积之比，即是建筑密度。密度在时下的概念，如同经历了从固体到液化，以至汽化的过程，成为一个看不见、摸不着，但又无时不在的物质，漫散于城市中，而且又不似这般单纯，多数情况下是几种状态的并存。就这点而言，密度其实是一个抽象、相对的概念。对密度这种不确定状态的理解和兴趣，成为我思考当代城市现象的出发点。

对于南沙的陌生客人，如果把对南沙的感性认识浓缩于一天的行程里，“密度”可以是什么？对我而言，是一天想做的事情，以及与这些事情发生的分布地点和到达这些地点的方便程度一系列的关系问题，也许我们可以称之为“经验密度”。这种密度包括了“单一经验”和“多元经验”（diversity of daily experience），在很大程度上反映了都市化的生活质量和都市的发展程度：在美国的南卡罗莱纳州希尔顿黑德岛（South Carolina Hilton Head Island）约 100 平方公里，拥有 25 个高尔夫球场，一个人每日的生活均以高尔夫球为中心而展开。在地球的另一半的香港岛，约80平方公里，以每公顷约6000人的密度，却包容了一个人一生所需要的所有东西和所有可能的经历。

这两种“经验密度”的极端，恰恰引证了雷姆·库哈斯和伯纳德·屈米对都市现象异曲同工的理解，“拥挤文化”（culture of congestion)和“事件城市”（event-city）的理论便是对一个人在一个都市里生活经验集合的关注，这种经验是通过对组成城市的建筑构架（Framework + Envelope）和构架里面发生的故事和内容反映出来的，我认为这恰恰是都市的“经验密度”问题。构架的确定性和永久性，与构架里不断变化组合的不稳定性和临时性，或者可以说，建筑密度和经验密度的动态组合塑造了一个都市活力和发展的文化整体。

密度与其作为设计终极指标，不如作为一种设计方法（method）去动态地理解一个都市的变化和发展，甚至去创造一个可塑的构架（framework）去包容一个城市的过去、现在和将来。

Time+Architecture, Feb. 2003, Vol.70

THE SECOND DENSITY

Doreen Heng Liu

As a gathering point for virtually everything (such as population, construction, work, daily life and experience), the city certainly has a close relationship with the concept of density. Initially, density was only understood as a scientific formula. For example, construction density is the ratio of constructed area to total land area. Now, however, density has evolved, like a solid turning into a liquid, or even a gas. It is now an invisible and intangible yet ever-present element that permeates cities, but even then, it is not that simple. More often, it is the coexistence of several states at once. From this perspective, the concept of density is abstract and relative. The understanding of and interest in this uncertain state of density has become the point of departure for my reflections on contemporary urban phenomena.

What does density mean to a visitor who only has a perceptual understanding of Nansha from a one-day trip? To me, density has become a series of questions about the relationship between the things one wishes to do in a day, how the locations of those things are distributed, and how convenient those locations are, which we could call the "density of experience". This idea connotes both the singularity of daily experience and the diversity of daily experience and reflects, to a great extent, the degree of urbanization and the quality of urbanized life. Take the island of Hilton Head in South Carolina of the US, for example. There are 25 golf courses scattered over an area of about 100 km^2 and the daily life of the average resident revolves around golf. On the other side of the globe, the island of Hong Kong has an area of about 80 km^2 and a population density of 6000 people per hectare, but it offers everything a person might need and every possible experience a person might want.

These two extremes of densities of experience corroborate the similar understandings of urban phenomena offered by Rem Koolhaas and Bernard Tschumi. Their theories of the "culture of congestion" and "event-cities" are concerned about the collection of life experiences of a person in a city. These experiences are reflected in the "framework + envelope" that make up the city, and the stories and other things that emerge within that framework—this is what I mean by the "density of experience". The certainty and permanence of the framework and the uncertainty and temporariness of its changing components, or rather, the dynamic interaction between the density of construction and the density of experience, has created a vital and growing urban culture.

Rather than being seen as an ultimate index of design, density could be considered a design method that allows for the dynamic understanding of a city's changes and developments, or even for the creation of a flexible framework for a city's past, present, and future.

XIAN 闲

As the important spatial carrier for the life and experience, the city is the very first and ultimate place to release KUN (困 trapped). our mission is to work out of KUN (困 trapped), moreover, to realize the transformation from the trapped (困) to the leisurely (闲), and from the efficiency of capital to the experience of life.

With the multi-dimensional readings of urban space and re-design of the boundaries and mobility that affect the living experience, the goal of an ideal city, where balance is more, can be achieved while avoiding the trap of one-dimensional development that demands more and even more resources.

作为生活和体验的重要空间载体，城市是解除发展之困的首要和最根本的场地。我们的任务是解决困境，还要化“困”为“闲”，从追求资本效率改为注重生活体验。

通过对城市空间的多维解读、对影响生活体验的边界和交通进行重新设计，我们可以成功打造以平衡促发展的理想城市，同时避免过度耗费资源的单维度发展方式。

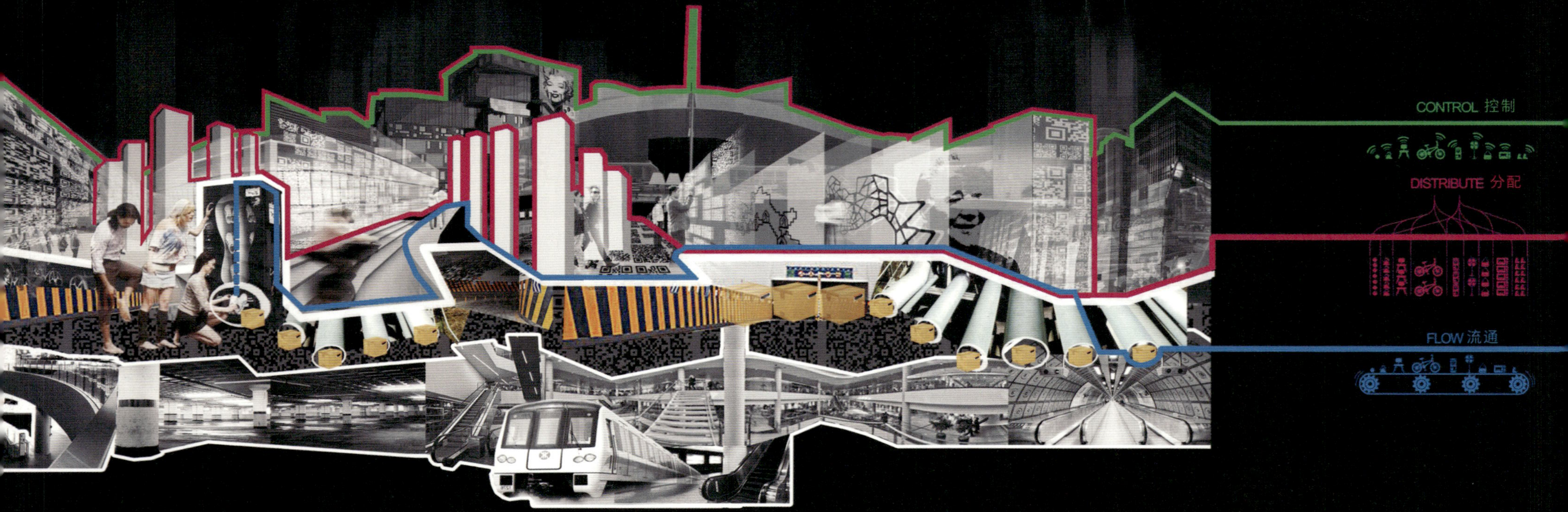
CONTROL 控制
DISTRIBUTE 分配
FLOW 流通

如何控制
HOW TO CONTROL
如何流通
HOW TO FLOW
如何分配
HOW TO DISTRIBUTE
PRONTO

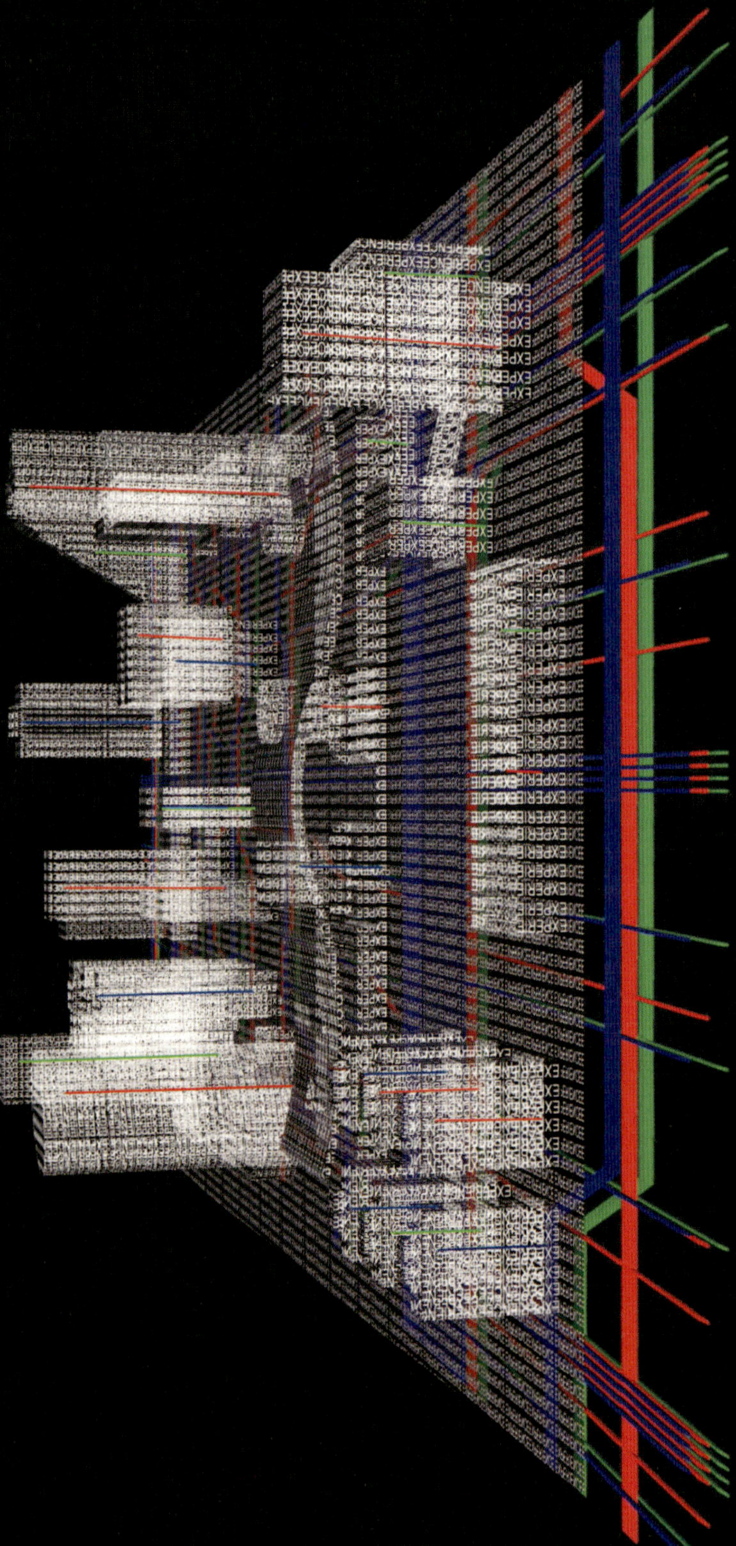

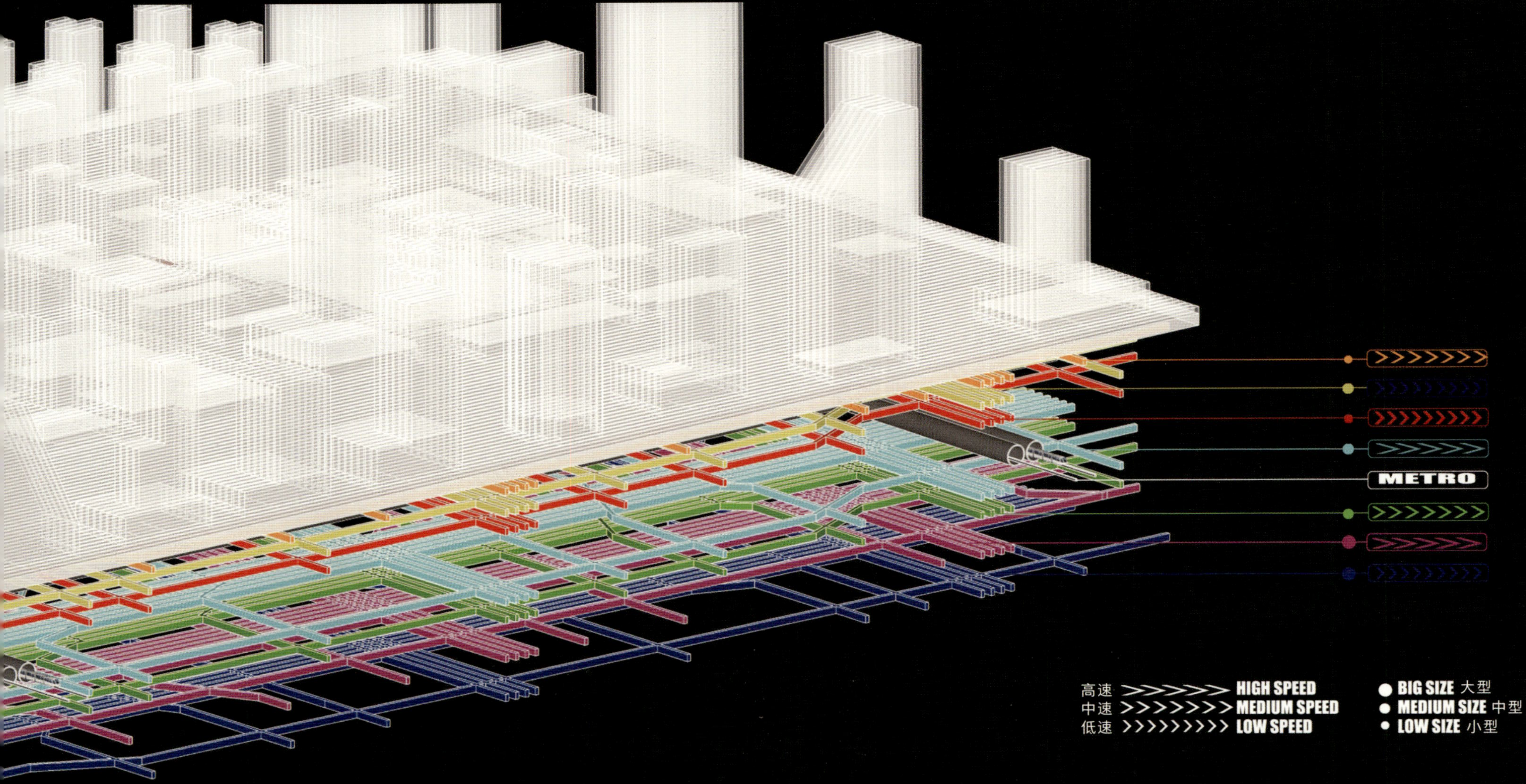
METRO
高速 >>>>>>> HIGH SPEED
中速 >>>>>>>> MEDIUM SPEED
低速 >>>>>>>>> LOW SPEED
BIG SIZE 大型
MEDIUM SIZE 中型
LOW SIZE 小型

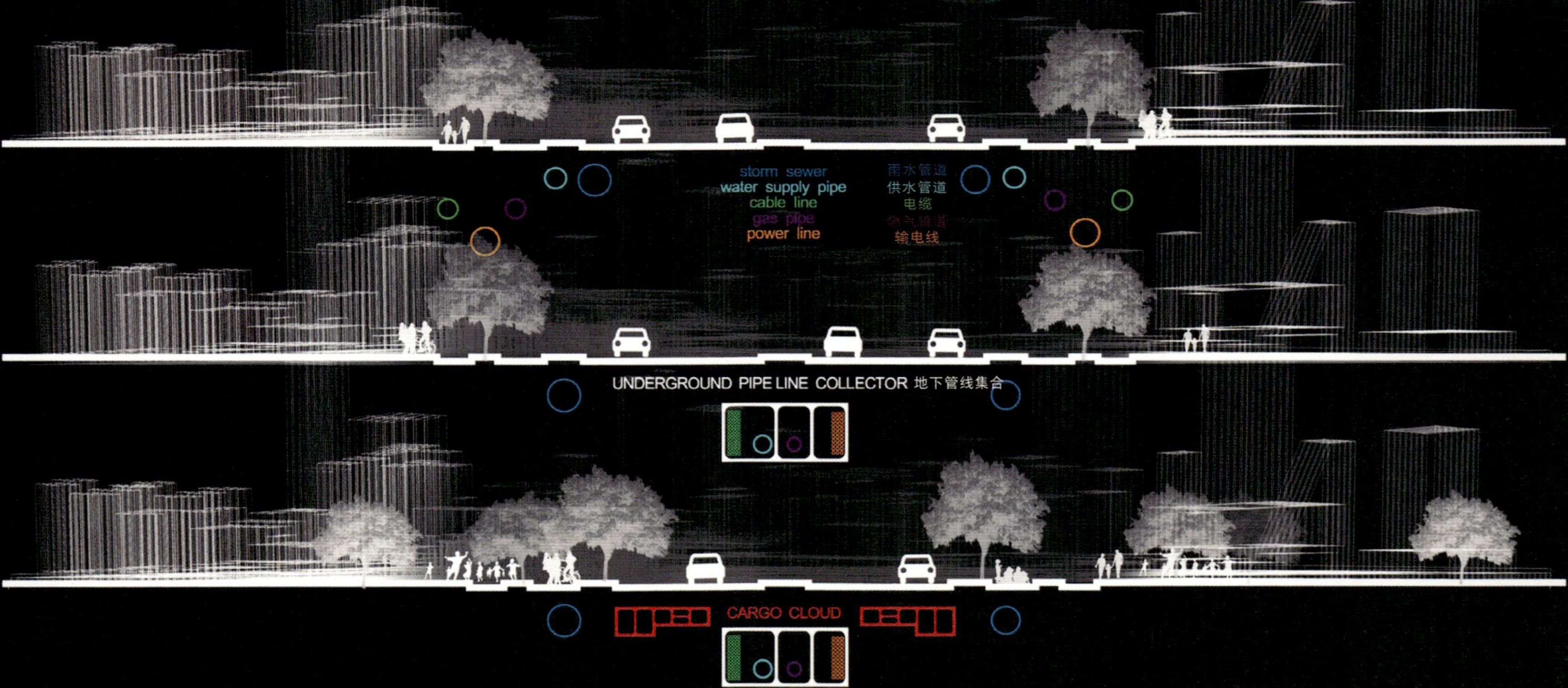

storm sewer
water supply pipe
cable line
gas pipe
power line
雨水管道
供水管道
电缆
燃气管道
输电线
UNDERGROUND PIPE LINE COLLECTOR 地下管线集合
CARGO CLOUD

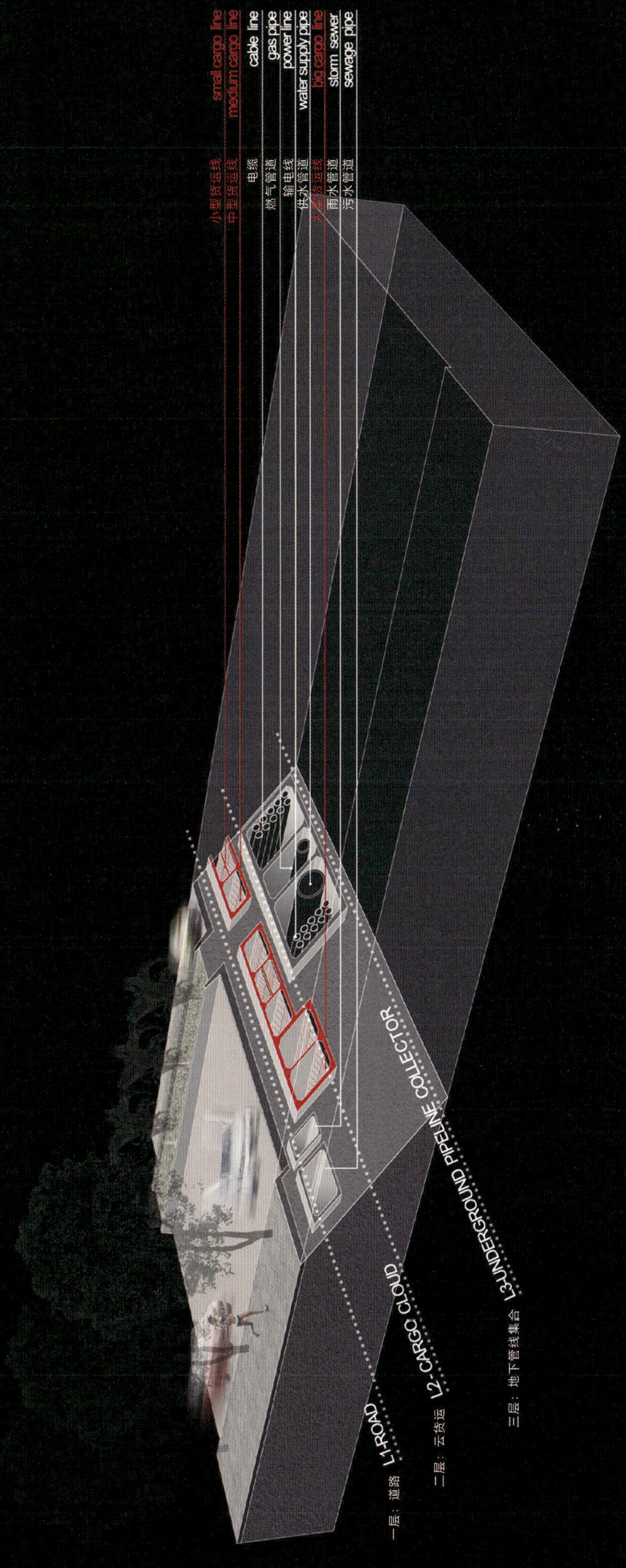

小型货运线 small cargo line
中型货运线 medium cargo line
电缆 cable line
燃气管道 gas pipe
输电线 power line
供水管道 water supply pipe
大型货运线 big cargo line
雨水管道 storm sewer
污水管道 sewage pipe
UNDERGROUND PIPELINE COLLECTOR
一层：道路 L1-ROAD
二层：云货运 L2-CARGO CLOUD
三层：地下管线集合 L3-UNDERGROUND

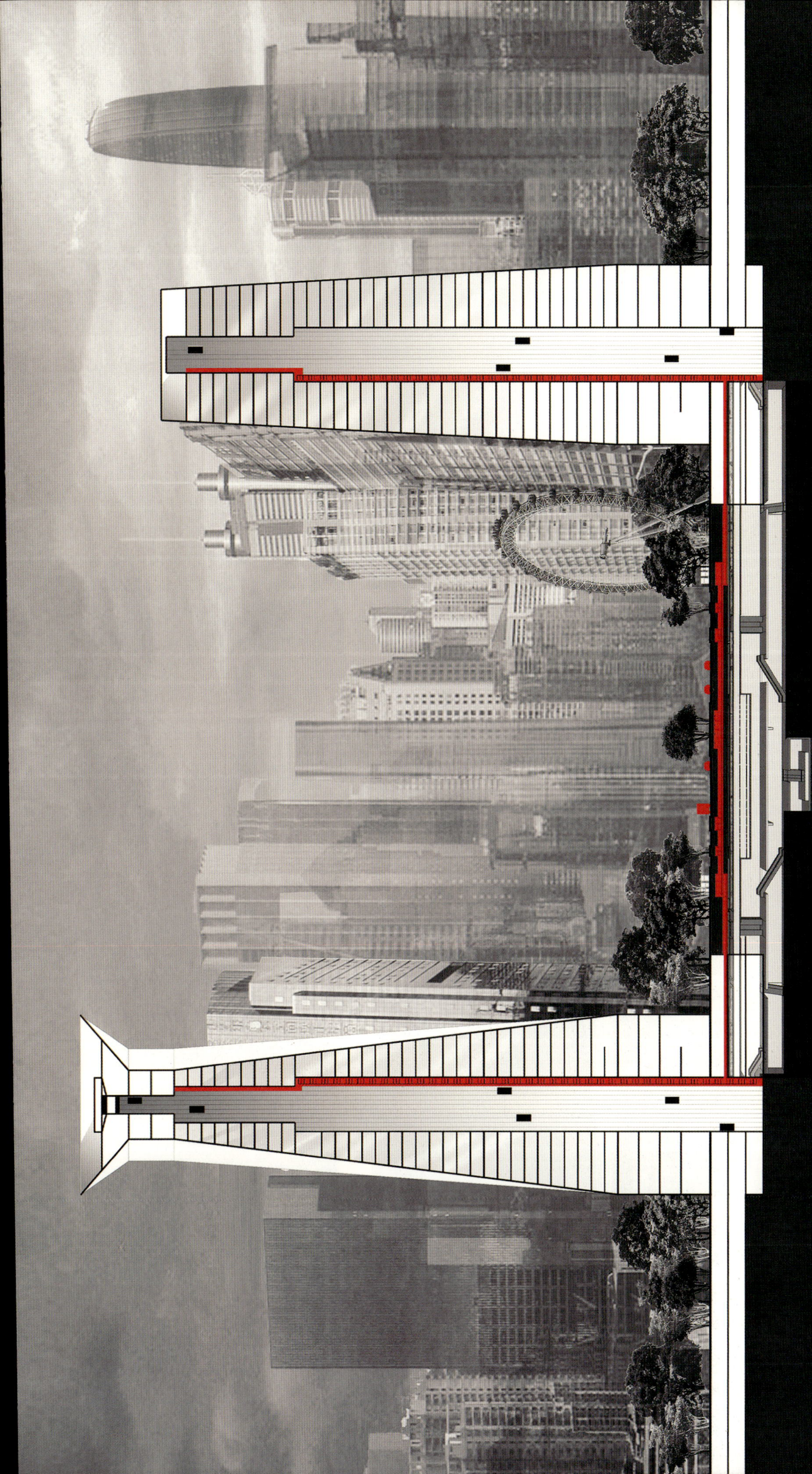

LESS SPACE FOR ROAD
MORE FOR EXPERIENCE
更少的道路空间
更多的体验空间

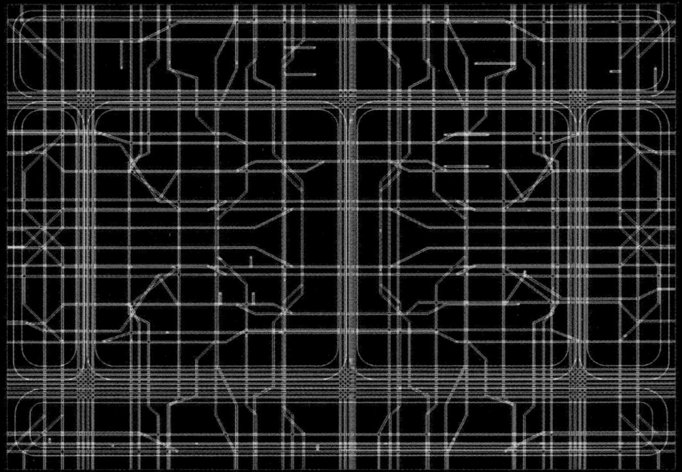

UNDERGROUND CARGO SYSTEM & PIPE SYSTEM

地下货运系统和管道系统

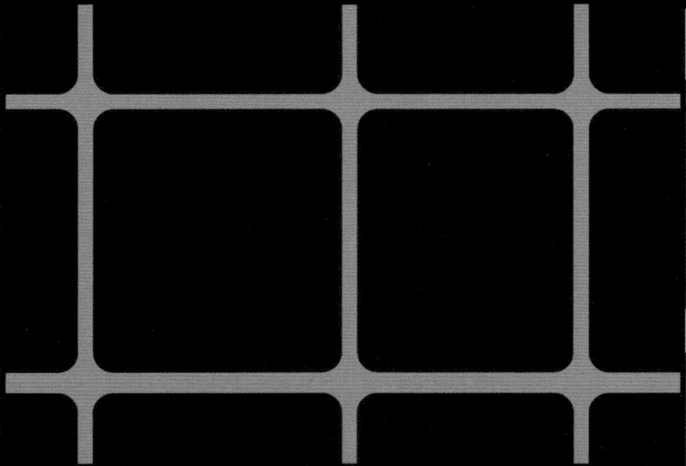

ROAD FOR VEHICLE

车行道路

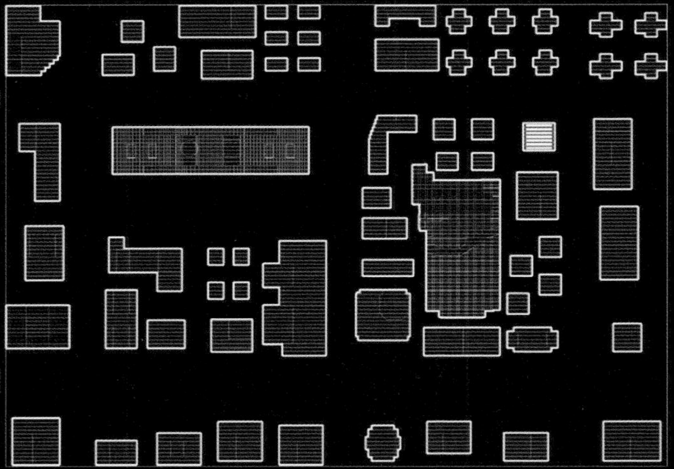

SPACE FOR EXPERIENCE

体验空间

CARGO CLOUD 云货运

地面 **SURFACE**

地下 **SUB-SURFACE**

MY CARGO
WHERE IS IT ?
ARRIVAL TIME
HOW MUCH

SHENZHEN 2030-[XIAN] 开放深圳2030——闲

During the transformation of visible and invisible interface, numerous spaces could be therefore released to provide the future city with various elements that would relate human beings with the nature, such as agriculture, orchard farming, animal, playground and fresh water. this would offer people more space and time, contents and experiences to the living interface, providing a brand new perspective and environment for both the society and the nature, and allowing for a balanced economic, social and ecological development on a highly dynamic level.

隐形和可视界面的变革过程可以释放许多空间，为未来城市提供各种人与自然的联系要素，如农业、果园种植、动物、活动场地和新鲜水源。这能够让人们在生活界面拥有更多的空间和时间、享受更丰富的内容和体验，打造全新的社会和自然视角和环境，促进经济、社会和生态的高活力平衡发展。

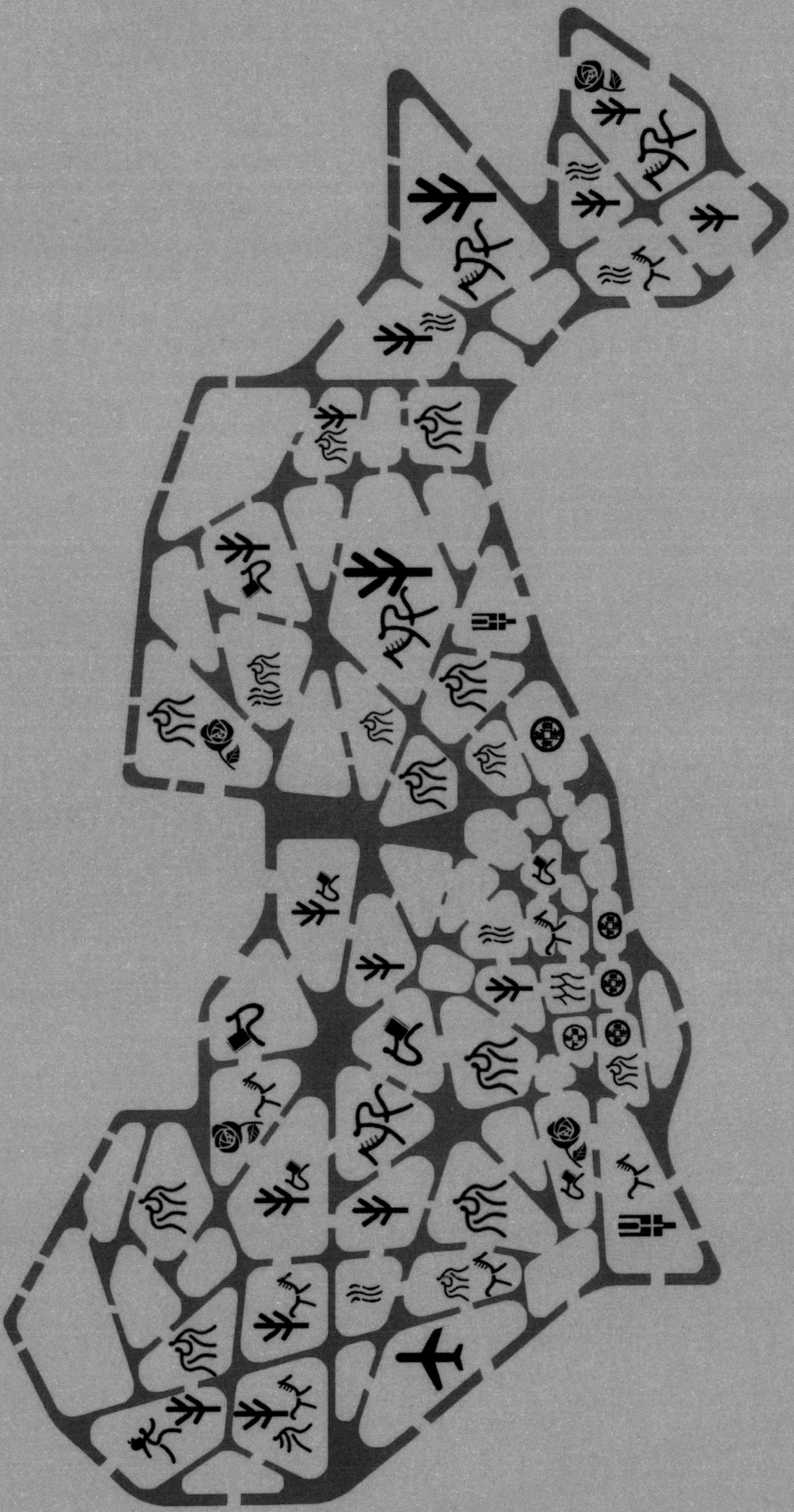

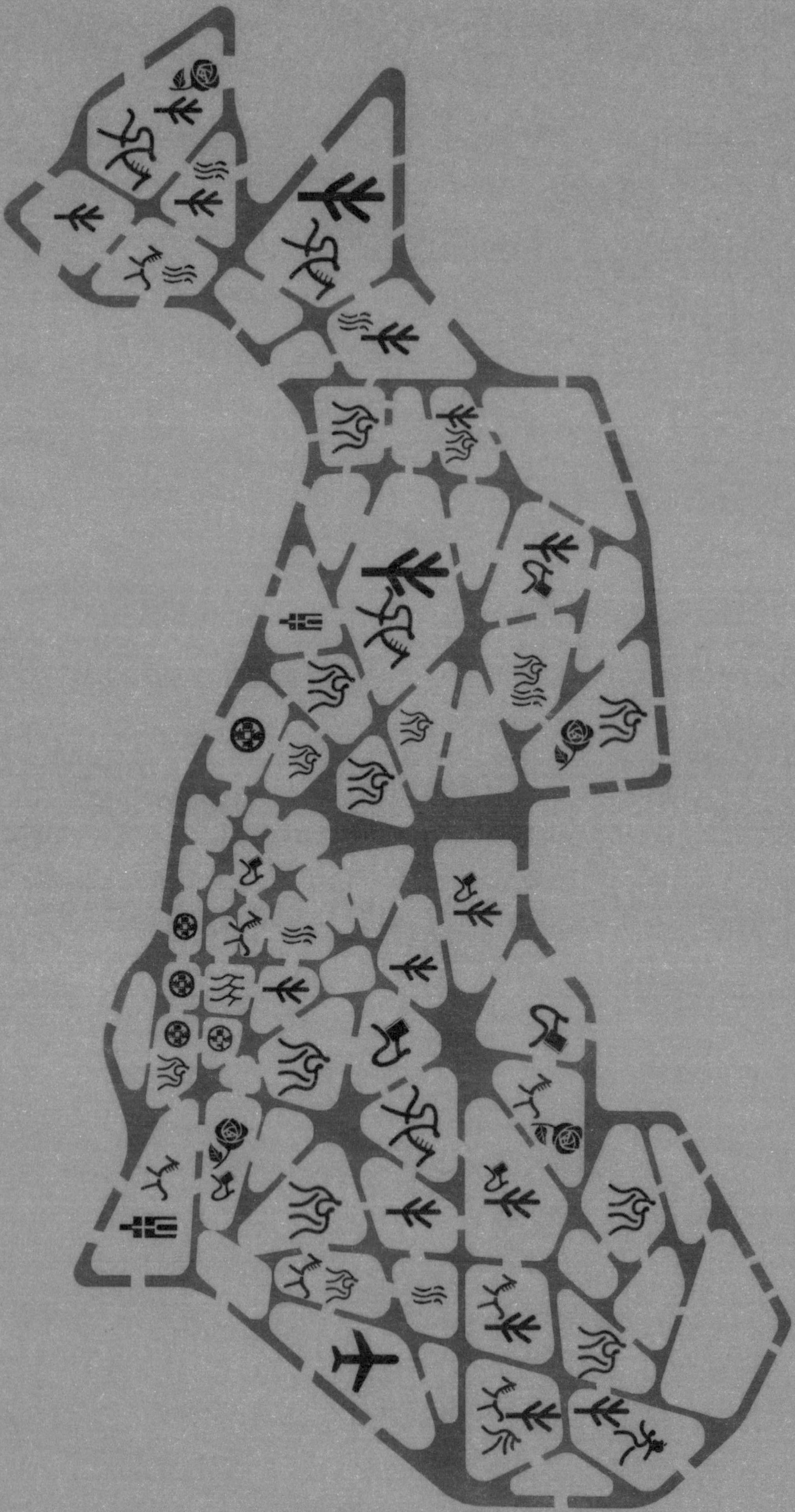

闲

开放深圳2030

OPEN SHENZHEN 2030

The future demands more, while balance is more and the multi-dimensional flow of balance gains even more. Shenzhen in 2030 is still envisioned to be a highly efficient and densely populated city, but more likely a leisure and free-minded city, a true dream city, a self-contained city, and a city full of infinite possibilities. Shenzhen's transformation from the trapped [困] to the leisurely [闲] symbolizes the city's realization and approaching to the ideal living condition advocated in Chinese philosophy, i.e. the great harmony of nature and men.

未来需要多，而平衡就是多；多维度的平衡流动甚至能实现更多。展望2030年，深圳仍会是一个高效率和人口稠密的城市，但也更有机会成为一个休闲和思想自由的城市，一个真正的理想之城、自足之城、机会之城。深圳从“困”到“闲”的转型，标志着这座城市实现和达到了中国传统哲学提倡的“天人和谐”的理想生活状态。

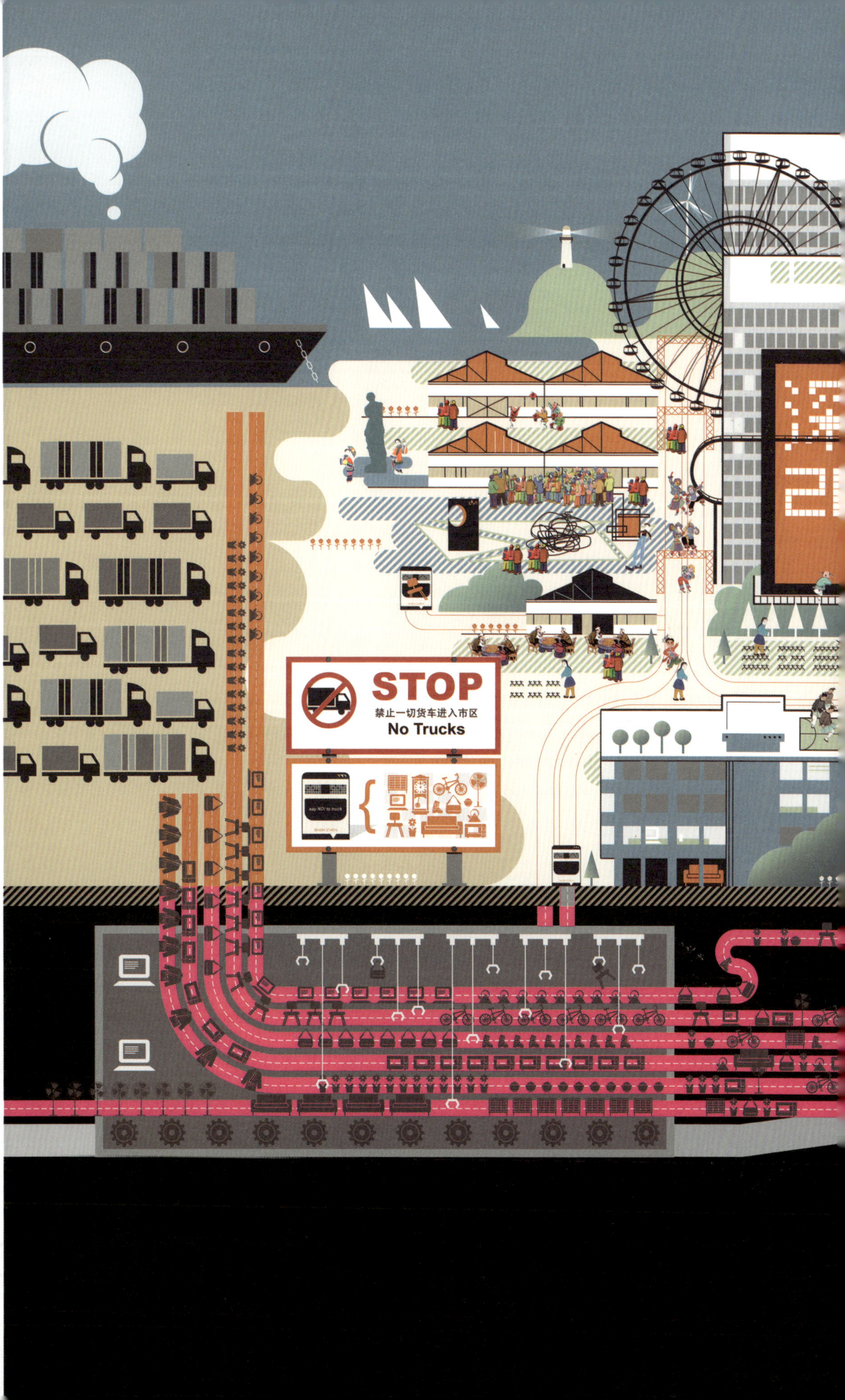
STOP
禁止一切货车进入市区
No Trucks
say NO! to truck

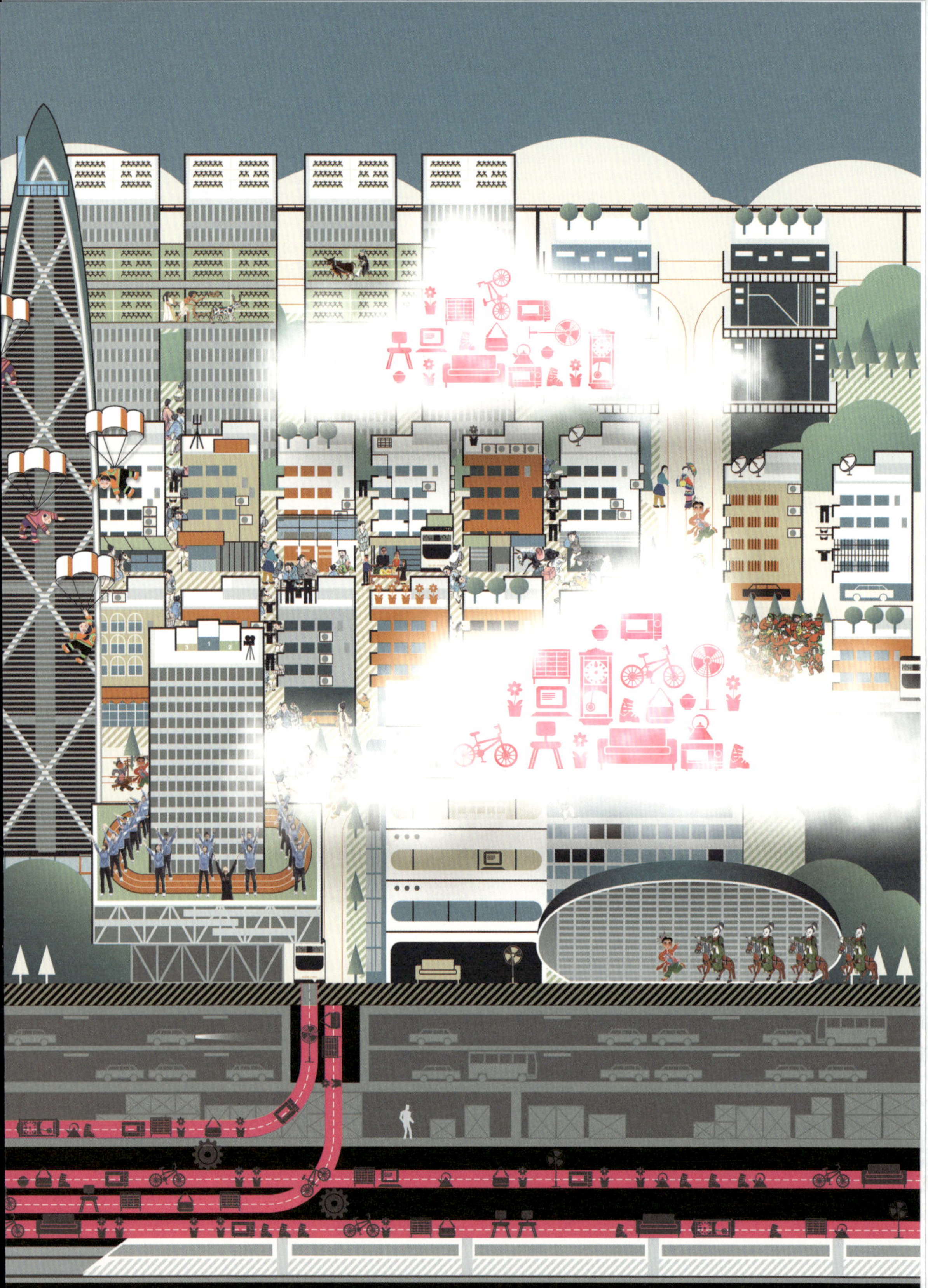

EXHIBITION

展览篇

TION

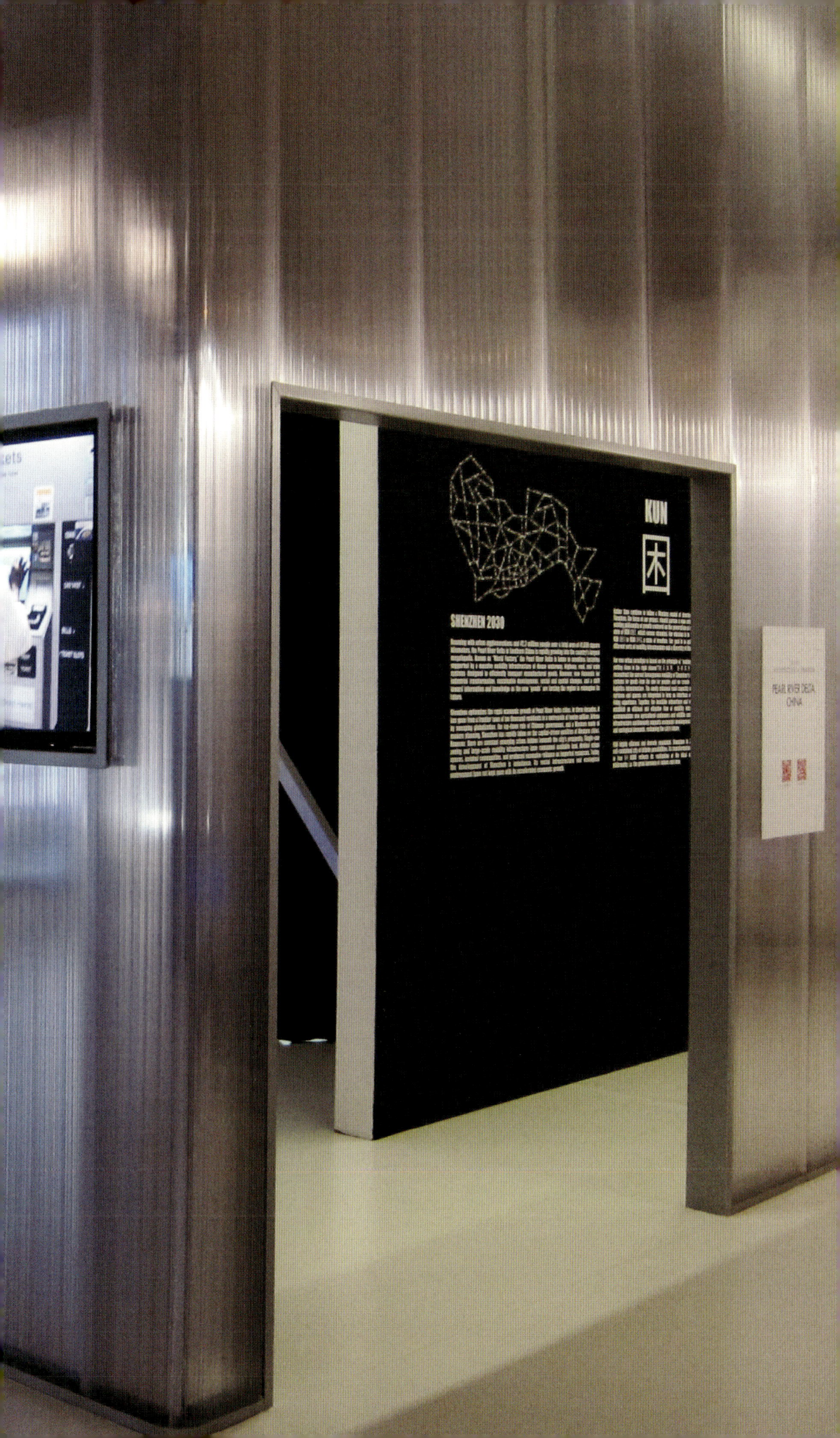
KUN
困
SHENZHEN 2030
PEARL RIVER DELTA
CHINA

KUN
XIAN
困
闲
STOP
No Trucks

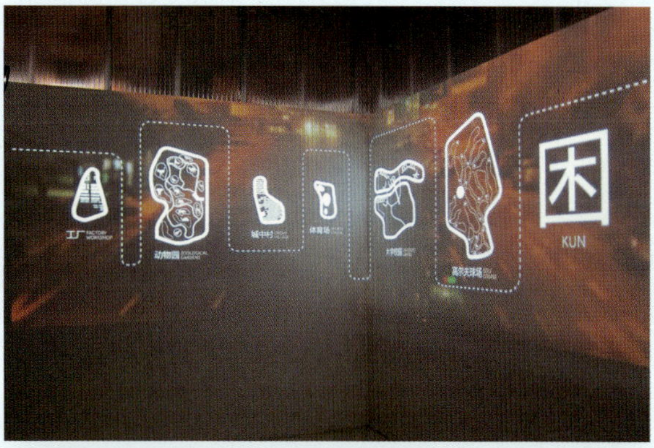
工厂
动物园
城中村
体育场
困
KUN

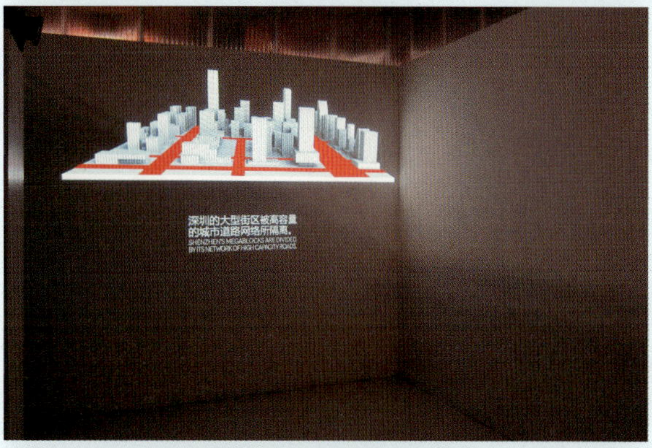
深圳的大型街区被高容量
的城市道路网络所隔离。
SHENZHEN'S MEGABLOCKS ARE DIVIDED
BY ITS NETWORK OF HIGH CAPACITY ROADS.

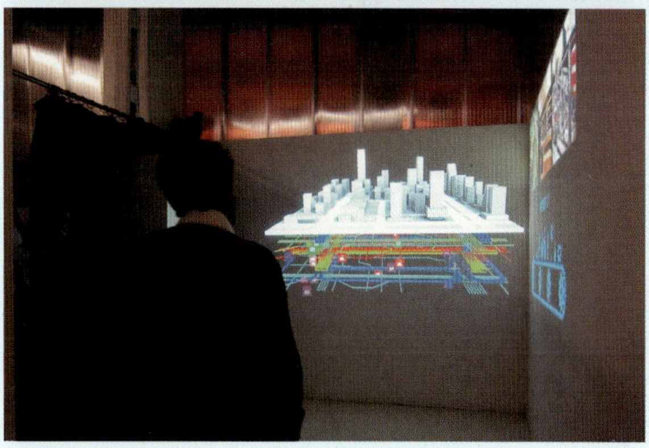

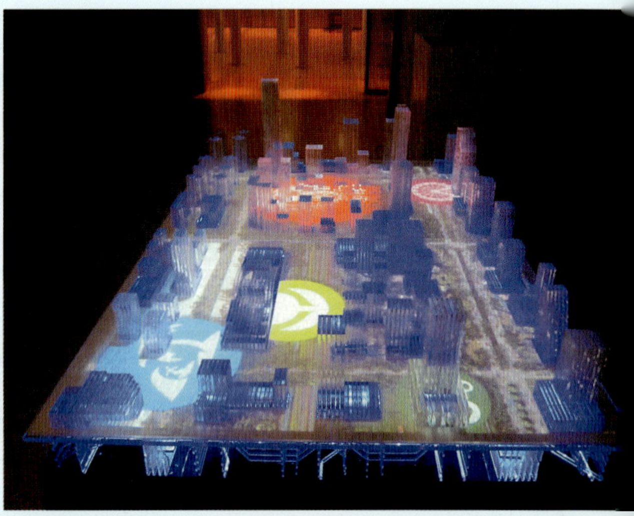

PROCESS
过程

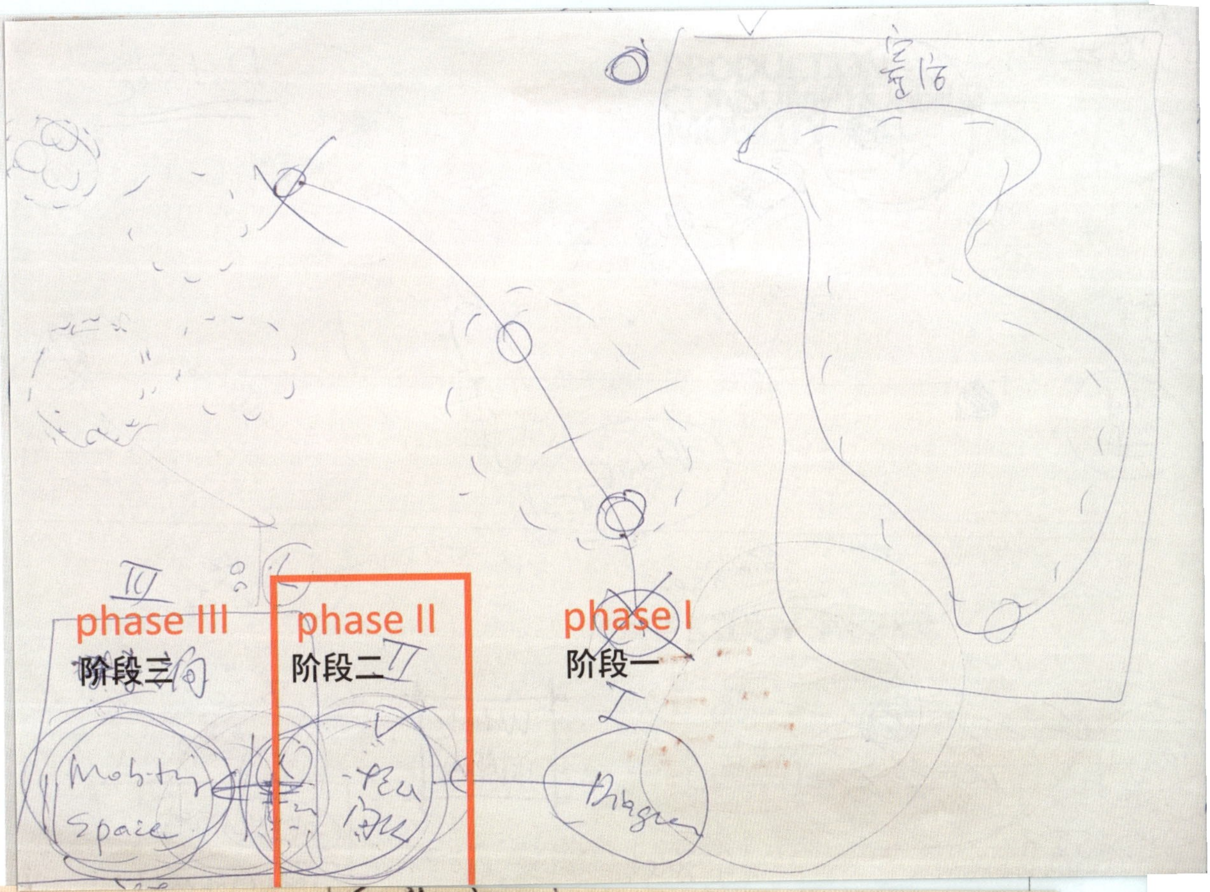
phase III
阶段三
phase II
阶段二
phase I
阶段一
Mobility
Space
Diagram

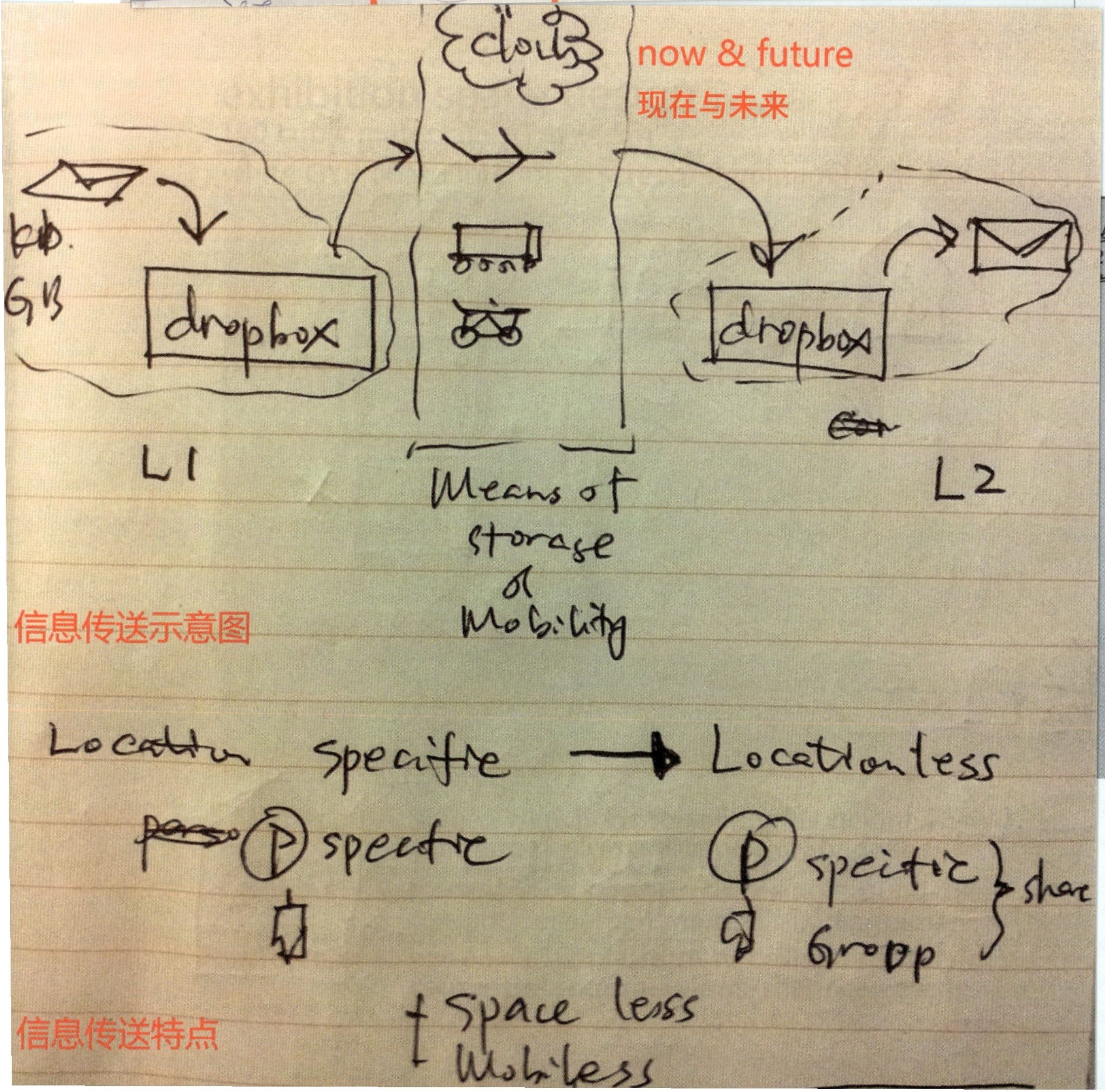
now & future
现在与未来
cloud
dropbox
dropbox
L1
L2
Means of
storage
&
Mobility
信息传送示意图
specific
Locationless
specific
specific
Group
share
Space less
Mobiless
信息传送特点

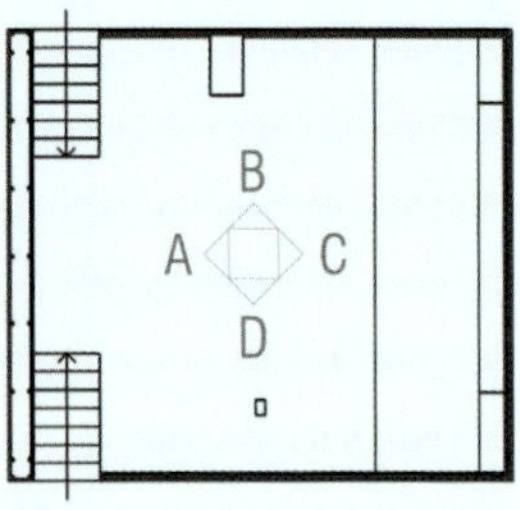

the poster海报

A

A big graphic about our concept

概念大图

B

P2: Together with P1, P3 , play linkage image

P4: 1:1 ratio people interview screen, and cooperate with earphone , broadcast the interview media files.

P2：与P1、P3共同播放联动图像
P4：比例为1:1的人物采访屏幕，
与耳机配合，播放采访视频文件

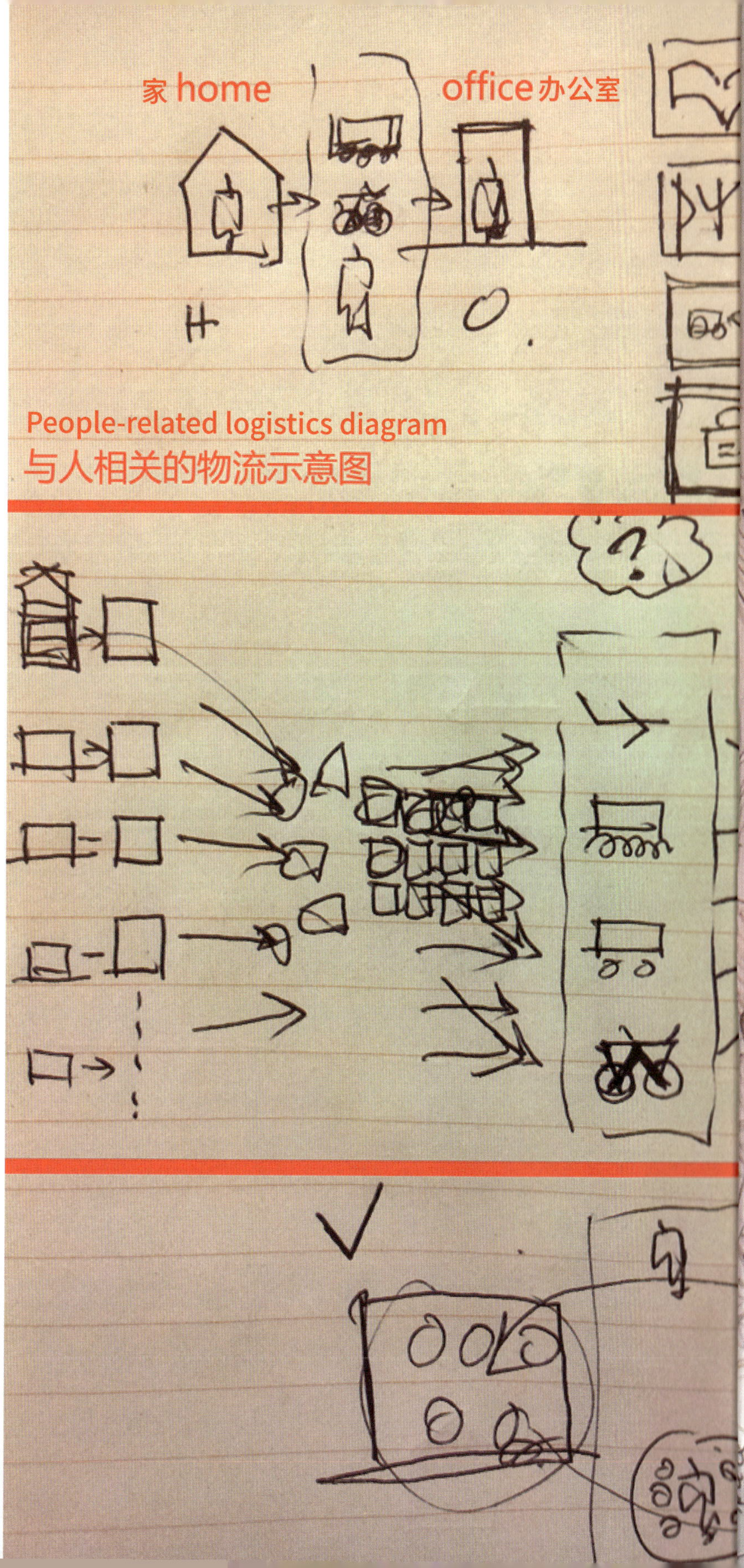
家 home
office 办公室
People-related logistics diagram
与人相关的物流示意图

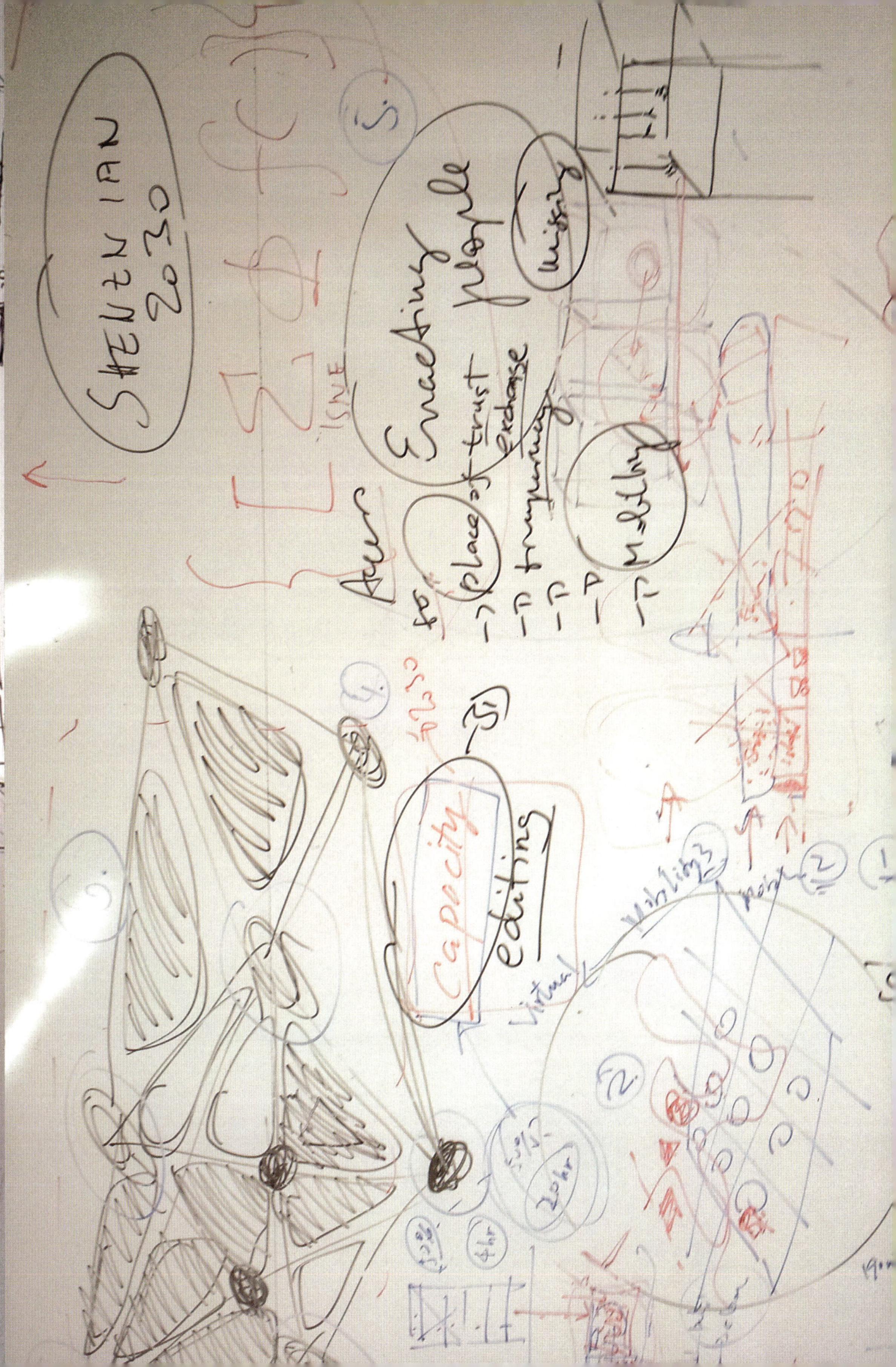

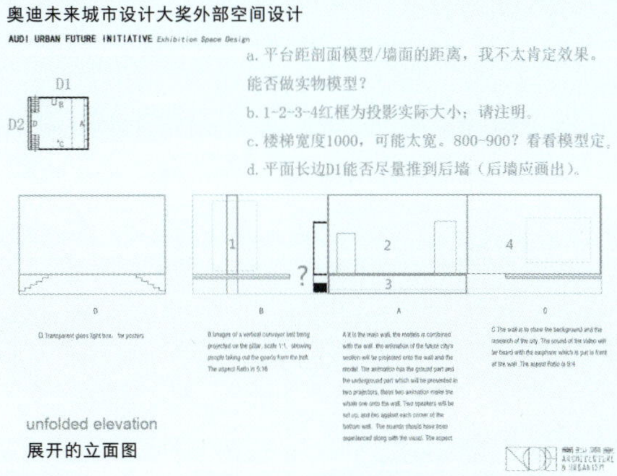

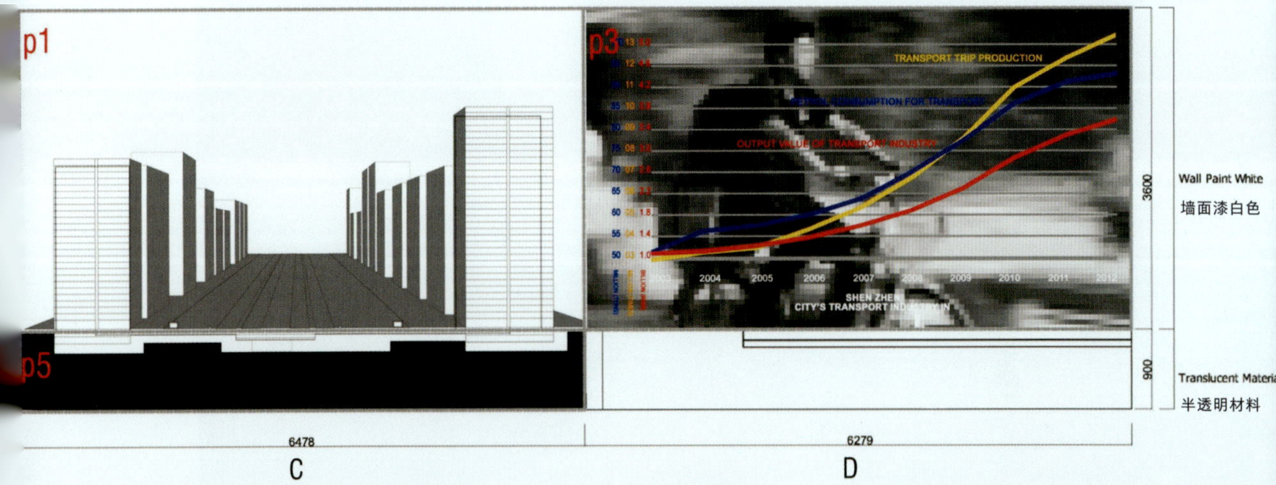

P1: The animation of Logistics system section and the future city's . Together with P2, P3, play linkage image.

P5: Backup, together with P1 play logistics system section animation image

P1：物流系统剖面和未来城市物流系统剖面的动画，与P2、P3共同播放联动图像

P5：备份，与P1共同播放物流系统剖面动画图像

P3: Together with P1, P2, play linkage image

P3：与P1、P2共同播放联动图像

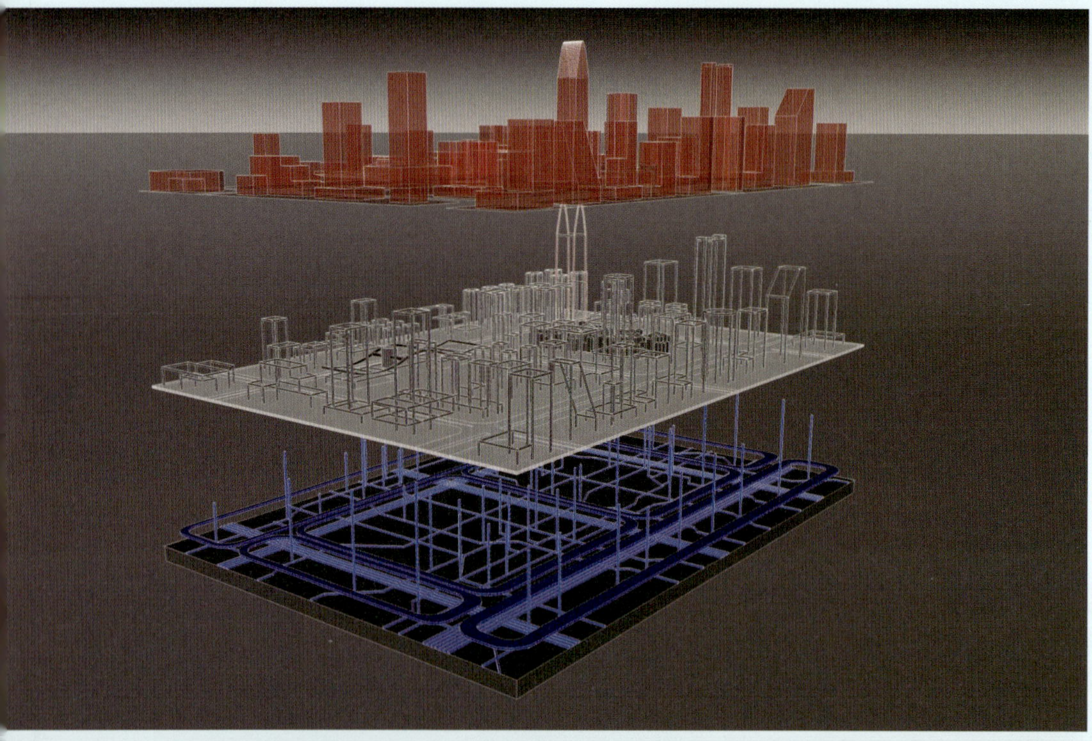

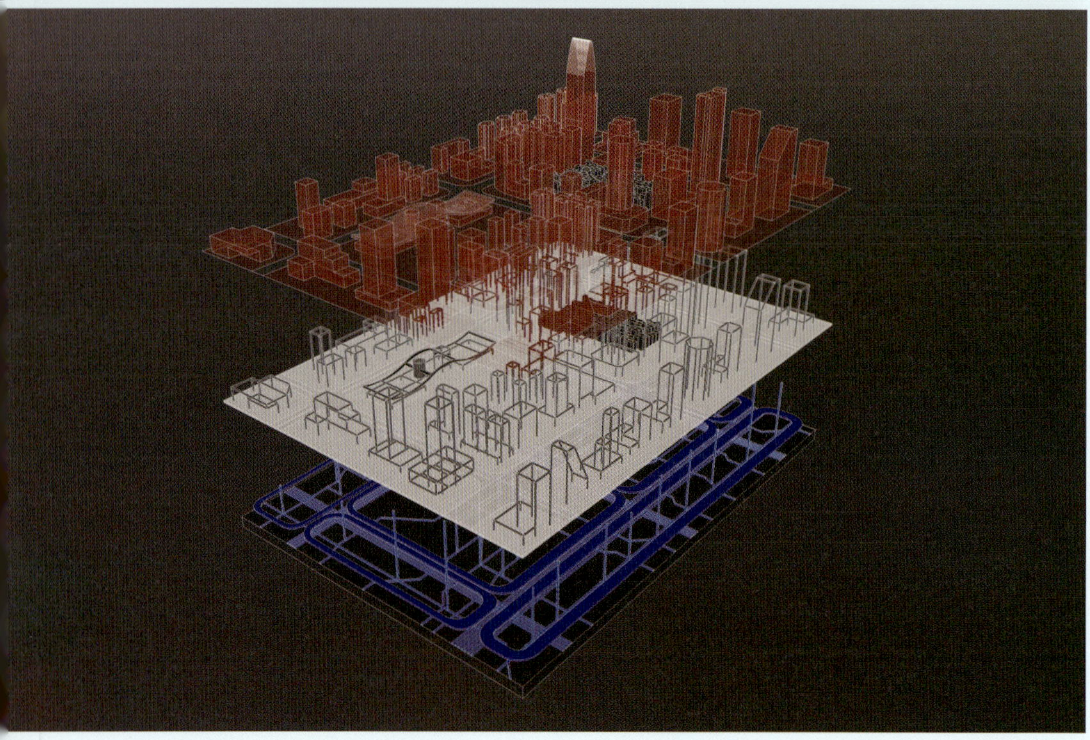

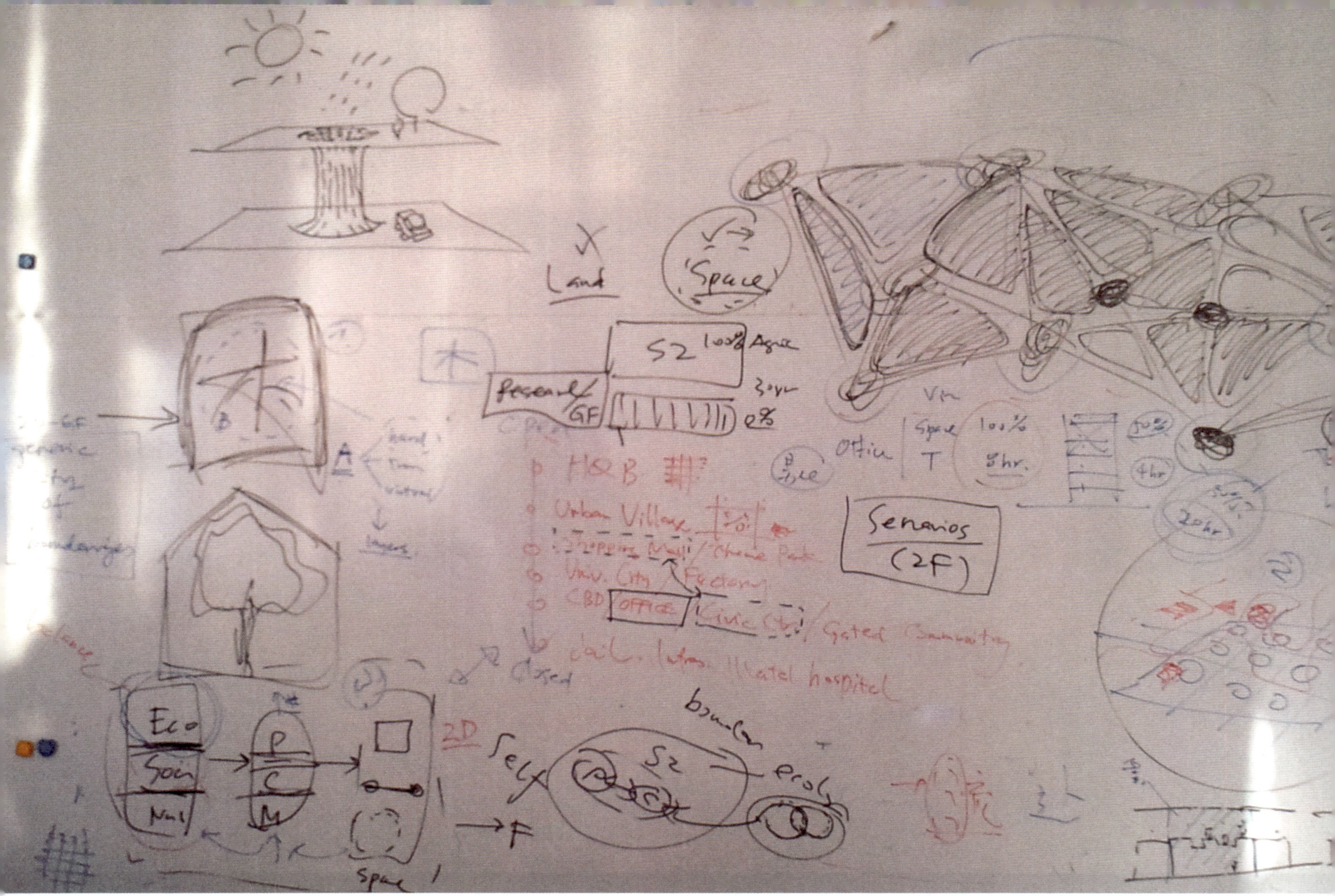
Land
Space
S2
GF
H&B
Urban Village
CBD
OFFICE
Gated Community
hospital
Senarios
(2F)
Eco
Soc
P
C
M
2D
Self
S2
F
Space

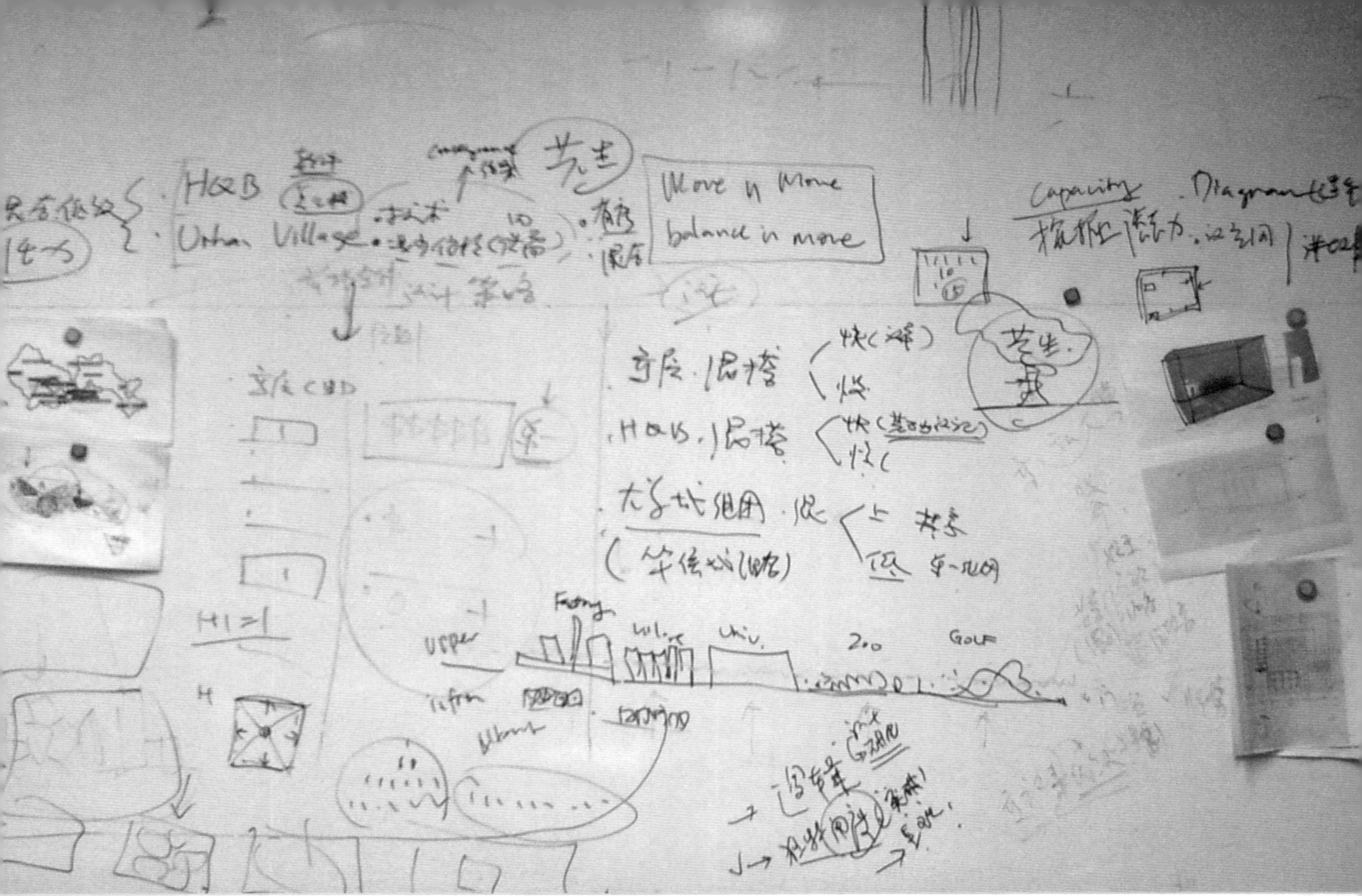

Capacity
Diagram
Move in Move
balance in move
H&B
Urban Village
CBD
H1>1
Upper
Univ.
GOLF

SHEN ZHEN
2030
STOP
No Trucks

平衡即是多
刘珩 著

奥迪未来城市大奖“深圳2030：平衡即是多”方案设计团队
主持设计师：刘珩
研究设计团队：刘珩、Ismael Martinez Merchan、刘苗、纪啸林、潘安妮
学术顾问：张宇星
设计时间：2012年4月—2012年10月

2012奥迪未来城市大奖柏林展览团队
设计团队：刘珩、黄杰斌、潘安妮、刘苗、黄锦宇、林溢晔
影像：白小刺
多媒体：Richie Gelles（访谈：四季绿洲影像工作室）

平面设计
鲁晓勇、林芸

本书专栏文章作者及对谈人
刘珩、由宓、张宇星、雷姆·库哈斯、姜珺

参编单位
深圳大学粤港澳大湾区创新设计实验室

编研团队
刘思、肖才子

图形助理团队
吴义娟、李靖、孙嘉奥、韩伟峰、杨志奇

Balance is More
Edited by Doreen Heng Liu

Audi Urban Future Award "Shenzhen 2030: Balance is More"
Principal Designer: Doreen Heng Liu
Research and Design Team: Doreen Heng Liu, Ismael Martinez Merchan, Miao Liu, Xiaolin Ji , Anni Pan
Academic Advisor: Yuxing Zhang
Design Period: 2012.04 – 2012.10

2012 Audi Urban Future Award Berlin Exhibition
Design Team: Doreen Heng Liu, Jiebin Huang, Anni Pan, Miao Liu, Huang Jinyu, Yiye Lin
Photography: Xiaoci Bai
Multimedia: Richie Gelles (Interview: Playhouse Studio Limited)

Graphic Design
Xiaoyong Lu, Yun Lin

Article Authors and Interviewees
Doreen Heng Liu, Mi You, Yuxing Zhang, Rem Koolhaas, Jun Jiang

Editorial Institution
Shenzhen University–The Greater Bay Area Innovation Design Lab

Editorial Team
Si Liu, Caizi Xiao

Graphics Assistant
Yijuan Wu, Jing Li, Jia'ao Sun, Weifeng Han, Zhiqi Yang